Culture Wars

EASA Series
Published in Association with the European Association of Social-
Anthropologists (EASA)

CULTURE WARS

Context, Models and Anthropologists' Accounts

Edited by

Deborah James, Evie Plaice and Christina Toren

Berghahn Books
New York • Oxford

Published in 2010 by

Berghahn Books

www.berghahnbooks.com

© 2010, 2012 Deborah James, Evie Plaice and Christina Toren
First paperback edition published in 2012

Library of Congress Cataloging-in-Publication Data

Culture wars: context, models and anthropologists' accounts / edited by
Deborah James, Evelyn Plaice and Christina Toren. -- 1st ed.
   p. cm. -- (EASA series ; v. 12)
  Includes bibliographical references and index.
  ISBN 978-1-84545-641-2 (hbk.) -- ISBN 978-0-85745-661-8 (pbk.)
  1. Anthropology--Fieldwork. 2. Anthropology--Research.
3. Anthropology--Methodology. I. James, Deborah, Dr. II. Plaice, Evelyn
Mary. III. Toren, Christina.
  GN34.3.F53 C85 2010
  301.01--dc22

British Library Cataloguing in Publication Data

A catalogue record for this book is available from the British Library

Printed in the United States on acid-free paper

ISBN 978-0-85745-661-8 (paperback)   ISBN 978-0-85745-662-5 (ebook)

To Adam Kuper

Contents

Introduction

Culture, Context and Anthropologists' Accounts

Deborah James and Christina Toren

It is by now well known, almost a commonplace, that the knowledge produced by anthropologists about the lives of others is mediated or refracted through a series of lenses. That this is so does not, however, necessarily vitiate the ethnographic text, which remains a powerful means of analysing what it is to be human in all its multiplicity. The point here is to recognize that, because the analyst is always historically located and always the carrier of an intellectual legacy that is inevitably projected into the text, it follows that we need to understand the social processes that produce us as anthropologists. Knowing that ethnography is bound to be an artefact of the historical processes that made the anthropologist who he or she is does not invalidate an analysis. Rather it allows us to evaluate such knowledge as an outcome of the process through which field observations arise from, and are fed and shaped by, two things. One is the ethnographer's relations with the people whose lives are the object of study, and the other is the lived history that the ethnographer brings to the field and that continues at once to manifest and transform itself in those very relationships and observations.

Over the past thirty years of critical engagement with our discipline, anthropologists have developed new understandings of how social processes generate differentiated subject positions producing mainstream and peripheral views, dominant and subordinate narratives, whose coexistence is sometimes recognized by informants, sometimes unrecognized or rejected. Often enough it happens that the anthropologist as analyst detects apparent anomalies or contradictions or paradoxes between ideas and practices that suggest the necessity of further investigation, for what looks like a paradox from one point of view may be entirely explicable from another. Understanding that social processes are bound to inform the constitution of ideas (and thus their very continuity and transformation over time) entails the realization that culture as an analytical category has little purchase on the world unless the use of the term itself is made the object of investigation. Several of the papers in this volume show what culture-as-category looks like as an object of ethnographic enquiry; that is to say, they examine how the idea of culture is taken up and used as a function of contemporary social processes among people whose different histories produce different understandings of what may be claimed to be 'the same' object. The resulting ethnographies of what might otherwise be dismissed as 'cultural essentialism' delineate its contours in each case, enabling us to understand how a particular idea of culture informs people's lived (and as such transforming) understandings of themselves and the world. In so doing, these contributions incidentally address issues raised by Ralph Grillo (2003) in his excellent discussion of culture as a vexed question requiring continuing systematic investigation.

Ethnographic studies of the processes that produce ideas of and about culture are certainly necessary. A perception of culture as a singular and monolithic thing that is possessed by a specific social group is ubiquitous in public life, paraded every day in the media. The fact that different and sometimes conflicting usages of the term are in play does not obviate this observation. The point is rather that culture is taken for granted as at once the badge of, and the explanation for, difference between groups: between multinational corporations, between ethnicities, between consumers of high culture and mass culture, and so on. Culture is represented as a simple fact of existence, and anthropologists' analyses of social processes that inform the ideas and practices that are taken to come under culture's rubric are often little appreciated outside the discipline. All the more reason for us to develop an engaged anthropology (Hylland Eriksen 2006) that is capable of coming to grips with the popular idea of culture as self-evident, and as explanatory of what humans are and can be.

Once the use of culture as an analytical tool has been thrown into question, it also becomes necessary to question the idea that the interpretation of culture is the anthropologist's primary task. And when it becomes clear that culture is not in any sense a text that is there for the reading, then context – the tool of the cultural analyst as interpreter – becomes equally questionable. The possibility of interpretation in context (or of context) slips out of the analyst's grasp once we recognize that context always remains to be explained, because what counts as context itself shifts as a function of any given person's perspective (for further discussion, see Dilley 1999). Understanding this, the anthropologist takes on the task of finding out through field work, and making sense of, the manifold social processes in which key ideas and practices are at once expressed and constituted somewhat differently by persons whose somewhat different histories produce different perspectives. The resultant ethnography is valid to the degree that it respects and takes into account a multiplicity of perspectives, producing a richly layered analysis of the research questions that emerge out of the analysis of field data as those that might have been said to be obvious at the outset – had one only known.

It is not necessary here to rehearse the details of the intellectual trajectory which led anthropologists, in particular, to adopt a self-aware, critical approach to the knowledge produced by themselves and their colleagues. Nor is this the place to give a detailed account of, or reasons for, anthropologists' failure to broadcast this awareness to the wider world. But it is interesting to look at these two sets of issues again from the perspective of a scholar who has made it a particular matter of concern to explore them (and their mutual implications). Adam Kuper has both analysed anthropological knowledge as a historical product, and striven energetically to bring relevant debates and analyses to public attention, bridging the gap between academics and people in the street. (He is, as was said on the occasion of his receiving the Royal Anthropological Institute's Huxley medal, one of the few anthropologists who can also be said to be a public intellectual.) He has resolutely maintained too that extreme cultural relativist positions are invalid, and that some objectivity and some forms of universalism remain crucial. Some might think this contradictory given his interest in the historical processes that gave rise to anthropological knowledge. But, as we show towards the end of this introduction, this apparent problem can be resolved.

Adam Kuper's writings demonstrate his nuanced awareness of the social processes that produce specific understandings of what counts as knowledge. Not only does he explore how ethnographers' own histories give rise to certain theoretical paradigms, he also examines the philosophical traditions produced out of these same paradigms, showing how self-perpetuating sets of Euro-American ideas – or 'myths' in the Malinowskian sense – achieve continuity over the generations, producing particular ways of thinking about non-Western settings. Take 'society', for example. His interest is in the ways in which people conceptualize society (and their place in it): in how they produce models of what society is and how it works.

In *The Invention of Primitive Society: Transformations of an Illusion* (Kuper 1988) and its later revision *The Reinvention of Primitive Society* (Kuper 2005) he shows how intellectual predispositions gradually developed, in combination with increasingly sophisticated – but never, of course, completely 'objective' – methods of ethnographic fact gathering, to produce such models. Writers such as Tylor and Frazer, for example, were concerned to discover and to systematize how marriage rules and associated totemic beliefs operated among 'primitives'. In so doing, as Kuper shows in his work on these and other members of the nineteenth-century British intellectual elite, these thinkers simultaneously developed a model of how, in contrast, such rules operated among themselves, the 'civilized'. The civilized condition, as he stated in his Huxley lecture, 'is defined as the opposite of an imaginary primitive state, and so it is equally imaginary. To compare civilized and primitive is to compare two imaginary conditions' (Kuper 2008). But it is precisely the form taken by this 'imagination' – this modelling – with which Kuper is preoccupied.

Following a line of exploration inspired by Kuper, the papers collected in this volume aim to show how the social processes that are entailed in anthropologists' ethnographic investigations, their production of knowledge, and their relations with the people whose lives are the object of study, implicate one another. To trace these series of inter-connections and mutual implications is to challenge, and to transcend, a set of analytical dichotomies that have continually returned to haunt the discipline despite having been roundly, and repeatedly, refuted over the years. These include the contrasted pairs mentalist vs. materialist (Silverman 2005: 290, 336); collective vs. individualist (Kuper 1992a); subject vs. object, action vs. thought, fact vs. value (de Coppet 1992: 70); culture vs. biology, structure vs. process, ideal vs. material, mind vs. body (Toren 1999: 1–20). A persuasive account of, and exploration of the fallacious thinking behind, the deployment of such dichotomies is given here by Pina Cabral (this volume).

The contrasted pairs which have most relevance to our topic are those which concern the 'modelling' mentioned above. Again, despite frequent refutation, it remains the case that local or folk models are often presumed to be ideal or cultural whereas analysts' or outsiders' models concern themselves with real – often social – phenomena. Put slightly differently, this corresponds to the assumption that only native voices can offer authentic accounts of culture and hence that ethnographers can only ever be analysts of it; and that the former arises through lived experience whereas the latter is captured through conceptualization and analysis. The papers gathered here problematize all these by showing how the anthropologists' theoretical stances are constituted both in the processes that engage them with their subjects, and in the consequences of these stances (which include anthropologists' interventions – or failures to intervene – in public life). If anthropologists are, themselves, engaged in social processes that generate particular kinds of theoretical discussions; if scholarly interventions about (and modellings of) the lives of informants thus arise as an artefact of particular lived histories; and if informants generate their own models of behaviour, these processes are bound to inform one another and this must mean that such sets of paired but contrasted opposites are analytically untenable.

National Traditions and Marginal Figures

There has, of course, been much written on the different anthropological traditions of Europe, North America and the U.K. (Dracklé, Edgar and Schippers 2004; Barth et al. 2005). Although their mutual interrelations and reciprocal influences have been scrupulously documented, the resulting scholarly traditions often tend to be imagined as having a rather monolithic character. As we pointed out above, context can never be taken for granted as explanatory; for not only does context shift as a function of the observer's perspective, but even if we agree on what the context might be it evidently does not necessarily generate homologous forms of knowledge. Our histories shape how we think and our thinking in turn may have a formative impact on others. Boas, for example, brought to the U.S. an understanding of culture which derived from his early training in Germany, as well as owing something to his Jewish upbringing and experience of emigration. He was for much of his life in contention with the mainstream American ethnological establishment, based at the Smithsonian Institution. But out of this marginal, outsider experience was born an alternative vision of a modern, more cosmopolitan anthropology which was to supplant its predecessor (Kuper 1994b, 2005; Silverman 2005). The Polish émigré Malinowski, likewise, was an outsider who turned his marginality into an advantage, founding a school of anthropology of which the 'professional outsider' and his ability to observe while participating were hallmarks: this school, while quintessentially British, was also sophisticated and transnational in a way that its predecessors were not. Thus, if anthropologists, formed by a specific history with specific social, cultural and national dimensions, migrate into different scholarly environments, this transforms to a greater or lesser degree their scholarly approach – but they may also, by virtue of the new ideas they bring with them, likewise significantly inform and transform that new situation and its scholarly traditions. This, indeed, could be taken as an account of the career of Adam Kuper himself (see Niehaus, this volume).

Several papers in this volume focus upon the processes that produced particular kinds of anthropological knowledge. In addition, all of them contain some discussion of the way anthropology has been applied or 'put to use', producing different historical trajectories. These include the terrible case of Nazi Germany, where certain anthropologists were apologists for and actively worked in the service of Nazi projects which privileged the *ubermensch* and plotted the extermination of other races. Gingrich's paper reminds us, however, that there were dissident anthropologists here too. There are also papers documenting cases, like Canada or South Africa, in which policy issues concerning the fate of ethnic minorities, native majorities, or subordinate, so-called racial, groupings have been a major preoccupation. Finally, there are papers documenting European settings: Greece, whose eventually successful aspirations to membership of the European Union (EU) were accompanied by gradual changes in ideas about culture in the academy (Gefou-Madianou, this volume); and the Balkans, still conceptualized as 'other' within mainstream Europe (Bošković, this volume). In Greece, anthropology variously played a role in celebrating – and sometimes unintentionally stereotyping – 'folk' culture; in serving (but in disputed ways) to uphold national culture at the more 'civilized' end of the spectrum; and later in achieving a more typically detached and cosmopolitan, less nationally oriented, academic profile in the course of striving for admittance to the EU.

The complex trajectories of émigré anthropologists, specifically those in the German tradition who moved to Britain or interacted with members of the British school, is the topic of Gingrich's chapter (this volume). Their experience challenges easy assumptions about anthropologists' roles in endorsing narrowly nationalist projects, and about the neatness of fit between anthropologists' apparent socio-cultural background and their concerns and theoretical preoccupations. Gingrich discusses the extent to which British anthropologists, after a period in which they engaged with their German counterparts, later came to practise a policy of careful 'avoidance', embarrassed about the extent of this earlier involvement. While he points to differences between the practitioners of German *Völkerkunde* (anthropology, lit. '[academic] knowledge about [foreign] peoples') who remained within the German mainstream and supported, sympathized or colluded with the Nazi cause, and the refugees and emigrants who took a different intellectual route because 'they understood that combining good research with civil standards was incompatible with Nazism and racism', he also shows that these differences were not absolute. Indeed, the fact that we now know more about the refugees and emigrants than we do about their – at worst condemned, at best ignored – counterparts who remained within the country, says much about the way in which broader theoretical trajectories are formed. Gingrich shows how, in retrospect, we sympathize with the dissidents and how 'the anthropologists among refugees who managed to find asylum either in the British Empire or in the Americas often established new careers with additional inspiration drawn from their suffering through refuge and exile'. But dichotomous judgements of this kind can over-simplify: even some of those such as Fuerer-Haimendorf who were judged to be 'on the right side' and welcomed by the British establishment because they chose to emigrate from Nazi Germany, appear to have sympathized with the Nazis for a while, and published accordingly, before they reconsidered. In similar vein, some who were welcomed by the British establishment before the war, such as Günter Wagner, chose to join Nazi Germany during the war (and, after it, worked for the apartheid regime in South Africa).

The case of anthropology in South Africa, where Adam Kuper was born and received his early education, is likewise shown by several chapters here to challenge any easy assumptions (Sharp, Barnard, Plaice, this volume). In that country, two settler communities with divergent national and religious origins and opposed political visions of the future – English and Afrikaner – have long been thought of as having developed two distinct traditions in anthropology. Social anthropology, with origins in the British school, endorsed an assimilationist vision for South Africa, while *Volkekunde* (anthropology), in the German/Calvinist tradition, endorsed cultural and racial separatism. Exponents of the former have roundly condemned those of the latter for having legitimated the harsh policies of apartheid.

While this representation of the contrast may be true in its broad outlines, it obscures many subtleties. The *volkekundige* (anthropologist) Werner Eiselen, for example, did derive some of his ideas from his Lutheran upbringing, and did indeed go on to become one of apartheid's key architects. But his early experiences in formulating policy gave him – momentarily – a morally-grounded view, founded upon pragmatism and practice, which in many respects approximated the assimilationism of the liberal, English approach (Sharp, this volume). Without defending the apartheid project, Sharp shows that our original assumptions about Eiselen were based upon his writings and those of his colleagues. As important, however, both in his academic capacity but also as a mandarin masterminding education, was what he did. (As Gudeman points out in his paper, in an analysis that suggests the continuing relevance of Bourdieu's (1977) argument, models and ideologies do not precede practice but arise from it). Sharp examines how, in peripheral settings like South Africa where neo-colonialism was still at issue (in contrast to the metropole where its traces were gradually being effaced in the post-war period and supplanted by new discourses of 'development'), anthropologists' ideas were taken notice of and put into practice – and they were accordingly, eventually, judged more harshly than were scholars like Malinowski in Britain whose theories were only ever assessed against the standards of academe. If Malinowski, claims Sharp, 'had managed to get his foot in the door of state power, as Eiselen did, the questions posed of him now might be far more searching than they are, because he would have had to choose one or other side of his ambiguous stance'.

Like Sharp, Plaice follows Kuper in exploring whether culture and models of culture – including those that anthropologists put into practice in their daily activities as well as in their theoretical contributions – are necessarily always viewed in dichotomous ways. Do scholars and practitioners always opt for an essentialized model of culture, as did apartheid's architects, or do they uniformly subscribe to a hybrid, assimilationist and universalizing one, as did Canada's planners in the early days? Or might these separate tendencies converge more readily than one might have assumed? It is just this universalizing and assimilationist drive of early-twentieth-century Canadian policy makers that has been most railed against by current First Nations peoples, and to which the current government is addressing itself with new separatist policies such as special fishing and logging rights and the recognition of aboriginal rights in claims to land. The results display a certain irony: the small new territory of Nunatsiavut in the north of Labrador is an ethnic enclave along the lines of the old South African Bantustans.

Other papers further explore this theme, revealing – in specific national cases – the complex relationship between anthropologists' endorsements of cultural particularity and their embracing of universalism and generality. In Greece, for example, an initial nationalist imperative to defend a particular culture found expression in a narrowly defined view of anthropology, but this later gave way to more universalist and cosmopolitan ideas of scholarly detachment as the Greek academic establishment sought to find its home within the EU. In a sense, this new approach served in new ways to foster novel forms of national consciousness. Illustrating how conceptualizations of culture shift the meaning of that term under different conditions of use, Gefou-Madianou discusses the delayed introduction of anthropology into the academic realm in Greece in the light of wider national political concerns in that country. She shows how a powerful and ethnocentric tradition of folklore, alongside a tradition of history and archaeology in the service of the national project, initially obstructed the emergence of social sciences in general and of anthropology in particular. When the Greek academy gradually shifted from its initial nationalist commitment to a specific culture toward a stance enabling anthropology to put forward a more cosmopolitan view of culture(s) in general, this appeared to parallel Greece's move towards 'modernity' and its accession to the EU. Even this process, however, was far from unambiguous. However Europeanized Greece tried to become, it maintained its connection with ancient Greek civilization, a connection which lay at the very basis of the country's claims to being part of Europe. 'The same argument that animated the whole project of nation building in the nineteenth and early twentieth centuries, namely the inalienable kinship of modern Greece with its glorious ancient civilization,' claims Gefou-Madianou, 'came to inform the late twentieth-century discourse that propelled the country into the fold of the European Union'.

In all these cases, the ideologies that predominate as artefacts of national histories are constituted in practice and transformed in the self-same process. Analyses of this process in the case of anthropology reveal how a specific academic tradition transforms nationalist ideologies in complex and unpredictable ways.

Anthropologists' Accounts: The Politics of Analysis

In the book *Culture: The Anthropologists' Account* (Kuper 1999b) and in several papers published around the same time, Kuper seeks to explore the social and intellectual heritage which has shaped perhaps the most powerful national anthropological tradition in the world, that of American anthropology. In the final chapter he talks of two opposing positions. One is neo-enlightenment and conservative: it posits the submerging of specific identities into a single national, even international one. The other is anti-enlightenment and radical: it posits the enshrining and respecting of difference. Is the anthropologist forced to choose between these? Does the choice depend on the kind of social order in which anthropologists find themselves? Or might some or most anthropologists be prompted by morality to adopt an *alternative* position to the one being more or less hegemonically adopted by state and society?

The critical social science tradition of the British and American schools – whether liberal or Marxist-oriented – tends to favour the stripping away of the veil rather than endorsing what appear self-evidently to be untruths. Deconstructing essentialized cultural identities, showing them to be 'invented', or demonstrating how their ideologies derive from the social settings that produce them, thus may seem – and has largely been – the obvious response. If, in contrast, anthropologists agree to affirm such identities, they might, in so doing, be thought to be contributing to a thoroughly illiberal project of obfuscation. Yet, since anthropologists increasingly find themselves investigating situations in which their informants are hyper-conscious of their own distinct cultural identities and of what can be gained from asserting these, such affirmation of identities is what they are increasingly called upon to do.

Those who intervene as public intellectuals may be subjected to coruscating comment, particularly if their interventions appear to undermine the political positions of those they analyse. Kuper has been one of these, particularly in his paper 'The Return of the Native' (Kuper 2003), which generated a furious response. His proposition here follows on from an earlier paper in which he took a critical stance toward the postmodern critique of anthropology's exoticizing tendencies (Kuper 1994b). This critique, founded upon the concern to give privileged hearing to muted voices of marginal groups, has resulted in a fundamental doubt about anthropologists' – or anyone's – right to represent 'the native'. It is a short step from this to Kuper's deprecation of the indigenous peoples' movement for replicating such essentialist notions about culture and identity, and for venturing into territory which borders upon the racist (see Niehaus, this volume).

Isn't this problem inherent in the very idea of culture which inevitably brings in train its opposing category – biology or nature? Arriving at this impasse, should anthropologists adopt an uncompromisingly critical stance, as Kuper does, or is it possible to reconcile such a stance with a sympathetic insider's perspective?

Writing about the emergent iconography deployed by the government of post-1994 South Africa, Barnard attempts to do the latter. Here, too, historical processes prove crucial. Barnard shows how, in the new South Africa, indigenous people and the ancient past both become symbolic tools deployed to overturn the recent past and to create a new ideal in which diverse peoples, languages and cultures are merged. The problem of this collective indigenousness is interesting precisely because of its apparent contradictions: it evokes division and competition between divergent groupings each of whom asserts a prior claim, but is here being deployed to create unity. This national unification is a political project of which the author approves in principle but one which as an anthropologist he attempts, in detached analytical fashion, to understand as the artefact of a social process that attempts to integrate the diverse elements in a conflicted society. Since South Africa's original inhabitants, the Khoisan, are now largely extinct or have been politically marginalized, none of the racial/cultural groups presently in contention can claim true 'indigeneity': the concept thus becomes a potentially unifying device whose power resides precisely in its flexibility, which Barnard recognizes. But remembering that culture had historically been a divisive policy tool, he simultaneously shows that we should be on our guard against uncritical endorsement of essentialist claims.

Comparing the South African case with the Canadian one, Plaice's paper extends these concerns. She shows not only how anthropologists' views might be influenced by informants' claims to indigeneity but also, conversely, how anthropologists' theoretical orientations and the resulting models contribute to shaping policy frameworks – and thus, ultimately, to shaping such claims in turn. Her paper ranges across various periods of native policy in the two countries to illustrate the interplay between anthropology as a discipline and the changing status of cultural difference in both of them. This leads her into an exploration of some of the potential contradictions which come into play when anthropologists agree to involve themselves in cultural advocacy.

In a setting closer to Europe, Bošković's analysis shows, in similar vein, how monolithic images of Balkan culture have been built up through a series of reciprocal interactions with mainstream Europe, each of which has progressively deepened the prejudice felt by one side for the other. Images of culture in and of the Balkans have become more rather than less essentialized. Bošković, concerned to explain these models of behaviour and images of national culture, shows how they are constituted in relation to one another. On the one hand, the Balkans are identified by the West as that which it abhors and sees as primitive: they appear as a 'mythic place' where it is thought that utterly different modes of behaviour and custom prevail. People from the Balkans are represented as child-like, intellectually lacking and requiring adult leadership. Conversely, and partly in reaction, Balkan citizens are convinced that their culture is impenetrable to all but themselves. Indigenism, in the Balkans, lends itself to a position of absolute intellectual and moral superiority, and suggests that its protagonists possess unquestioned access to the truth. 'The West', seen as guilty of misrepresenting the 'natives', is dismissed as irrelevant. Bošković neither endorses nor condemns this deeply held conviction – from either side – about the true character of Balkan culture. But he argues that it is crucial to understand it.

All these cases demonstrate that, like any other lived idea, indigeneity is historically constituted and thus transformed by virtue of the same processes in which it is maintained. In the case of arguments about indigeneity, the analytical (and political) point here may be the necessity for anthropology to acknowledge and take into account what is happening in international law. Here, argues Zips, 'indigenous rights discourses are not about primitiveness, cultural purity or exclusive ancestral roots, but about unfolding *in practice* such notions as equality, procedural justice and a universal right of self-determination that the idea of human rights has always promised' (Zips 2006: 28)

Models and (Mis)Representations

To make matters more complex, it is particularly difficult to know what stance should be taken where it is the public response – including that of the media which, depending on one's perspective, seems by turn to arise from the public response and to shape it – which attributes ethnic or cultural logics to particular events when these are in fact better explained by historical, political and/or economic factors that have little to do with culture in the essentializing sense. Writing about modern Britain, two of this volume's chapters address precisely this question: in relation to Asian 'gangs' in Southall (Baumann) and to white working-class youths in Bermondsey (Evans).

These two chapters also provide commentary on the question of insider models and their relationship to outsider or analysts' models (see Kuper 1994b). Baumann and Evans both illustrate a complex interweaving of the different models in play, such that an accurate understanding of the processes that produce particular ideas of culture requires a layered and subtle exploration of their mutual implications. The two papers attempt to undo commonly-held misconceptions, particularly those propagated by the media but also by government bodies such as the school inspection directorate, about the extent to which race and/or culture inform behaviour – especially 'youth' behaviour – in modern Britain. The chapters explore the emergence of essentializing ideas about culture across divergent temporal settings in London, with Baumann's addressing a situation in the early 1990s in the predominantly Asian neighbourhood of Southall, while Evans's paper is set about a decade later among the white working class of Bermondsey.

A 'multi-dimensional misrepresentation' is discussed by Baumann, in which a media-inspired moral panic developed concerning the existence and practices of 'Asian gangs' in and around Southall, West London. He unpicks the processes at play, showing how we should understand these as local transformations and crystallizations of wider, sometimes transnational, conflicts and constellations, despite their representation as culturally and territorially-bounded and set in a specific urban context. Public assumptions tended to merge race and culture, to create an overdetermined explanation of youth gang behaviour. Instead, Baumann shows, 'any culture that "they" or "we" might define as such was interacting with any other culture' to create a complex set of dynamics. However, to understand what is relevant here requires a sorting and resorting of the various accounts, such that local conceptualizations of what is happening require further disentanglement according to an analyst's – Baumann's – perspective. To answer the question of 'whose accounts' one might accurately deploy to understand the situation, it was necessary to recognize that all accounts needed to be available to the ethnographer, and that none ought to be privileged to the exclusion of any other.

Whereas one of the key frameworks used by Baumann as a means to analyse the conflict in Southall is a history of international political alignments (and particularly Britain's colonial involvement with Sikhs in relation to its other Asian former colonial subjects who have ended up living cheek by jowl in crowded urban Britain), Evans's chapter develops another aspect that appears too in Baumann's analysis – that of socio-economic hierarchy. For the Asians of Southall, the relevant status mediating culture was that of caste; in Evans's case, it is through the prism of class that claims about race and cultural difference are viewed. White working-class people, particularly in Bermondsey where she did her fieldwork, are indeed preoccupied with their culture. In a time when discourses of social class have become politically moribund, Evans shows how this assertion of 'white working-class culture' is a response – and an act of resistance – to the influential discourses of multiculturalism that are used to describe and enable black and Asian people's lives in Britain. White working-class people use culture as a means to capture and describe what they feel is distinctive and valuable about their way of life, in the face of the strangeness and threat posed by immigrants. Setting the rising influence of the British National Party in context, Evans reveals the right-wing implications of multiculturalism, showing how – without a viable class politics in New-Labour Britain – white working-class people are forced to trade on their differences and compete against black and Asian people for resources and recognition. Paradoxically this led, in the contemporary moment, to a media representation of the white working class as a 'new ethnic group' with all the connotations of a marginalized people who conceive of themselves as fighting for rights in their native land.

Giving an ethnographically grounded history of the relationship between community formation and local politics in Bermondsey, Evans explains more generally how multiculturalism arose as a resistance movement to racial prejudice in the working class. She shows how the formation of ethnic communities of difference made it difficult to conceptualize a multiracial working class which had shared struggles and common ways of life. Making these developments the background of her analysis of arguments about cultural politics in Britain, Evans shows how different nationalist movements clash over multiculturalism, leading to various conceptualizations of British-ness, all of which eclipse the ongoing relevance of social class distinctions in Britain. This makes it difficult for policy makers to theorize adequately about the question that an exclusive focus on cultural issues obfuscates: what kinds of social structure are we asking immigrants to integrate into and how do those structures work in practice?

Both chapters show how an understanding of the interrelationship between these outsider accounts and those of the actors themselves generates a more subtle analysis than either can do on its own. Both allow space for universalizing models which are used to explain social phenomena, but show how these derive in part from both anthropologists' own and their informants' ethnographic models which are in turn historically constituted as lived practice. There is a strong suggestion here, echoing much of Kuper's work, that one can provide objective and analytical comment even as one seeks to understand the processes in which such comment arises.

Anthropologists' models draw on ethnography and arise out of fieldwork, simultaneously adopting but also distancing themselves from informants' models. In its demonstration of this point, the chapter by Gudeman provides the means to think further about others in the volume. Like Baumann and Evans, but specifically in relation to our understanding of economic behaviour, he explores the relationship between insider and outsider or 'local' and 'derivational' models. He looks, that is, at models in whose terms people comprehend their own behaviour and those at one remove deployed by analysts. The latter, in studies of economy, comprise calculative models of rational choice. But these, although taken for granted by many economists and by the public at large as the sole motivation governing economic action, are misleading. This is because they portray rational choice as the only impulse at work, thus failing to take account of an apparently irreconcilable impulse: that of mutuality, which often corresponds with the 'local' model.

Moreover, even calculative choice does not simply direct action: rather, as the artefact of a historical process, it arises out of and at once informs (and transforms) everyday lived practice. Rational choice, in other words, is both generated by and endorses an everyday 'cultural practice', and hence constitutes a transforming folk (or local) model of ordinary life in modern society. Gudeman goes further, transcending the duality which understands these kinds of models as dichotomies. An analyst's or 'derivational' model, he explains, is in fact a

> 'local', historically situated way of arranging things that is legitimated by stories about its universal presence and completeness. Conversely, local models are unfinished, because they can never fully describe the plenum within which we live, but they are 'universal' or transcendent in the sense of being necessary for experience. Even if the market dynamic with its reverberations, cascading and habit-forming practice is powerful, it requires communality that it would also contradict.

The rational actor, then, is a result of the lived experience of anonymous trade rather than the cause of it.

Engaging Anthropological Knowledge

Certainly anthropologists can find a way out of continually reasserting their subject matter in terms of sets of paired and opposed dichotomies. In the present volume, the escape from binaries is termed dialectical by Gudeman. By contrast, Pina-Cabral, who proposes 'a new engagement with the historicity of anthropological knowledge' as the 'very ground for the possibility of social anthropology', explores a different way of transcending these sets of 'modernist polarizations'. It is possible, he says, to reclaim what is valuable about our anthropological heritage even while rejecting certain of its tenets, by entering our discipline through a 'door in the middle'. Pina-Cabral is especially concerned to provide theoretical space for anthropology as a comparative project informed by ethnography, but if ethnography is to be useful it has to acknowledge and strive after empirical (note, not positivist) validity, even while it consciously rejects the 'modernist sociocentric mould', essentialized ideas of 'group-ness', semiotic theories of representation, simplistic conceptualizations of agents' motivations, and a range of associated ills. His approach, calling for the discipline to recognize that our shared world is an inextricable part of our ethnographies, and that 'earlier acts of communication' are already present in each social setting that an anthropologist investigates, speaks in a similar register to Kuper's when he called for a 'cosmopolitan anthropology' (Kuper 1994b). A cosmopolitan anthropology, advocated by Kuper well in advance of the subsequent voguishness of the idea, is one whose rich and sophisticated ethnographic accounts are generated out of a series of communicative interfaces. Both these 'earlier acts of communication' (Pina-Cabral, this volume), and subsequent interchanges between ethnographers and informants – as was the case, says Kuper, in Gudeman's work with Rivera (Gudeman and Rivera 1990) – give rise to such cosmopolitan frameworks, which in turn ought to feed 'into broader theoretical and comparative projects' and 'engage in debates that address long-running questions about social and cultural processes in general, as ultimately contributing to the larger conversation of the human or social sciences' (Kuper 1994b: 551).

Such an anthropology, which 'cannot be bound in the service of any political programme' (ibid.), could serve to reconcile an empathy for local views of culture or claims to indigeneity with the kind of critical and analytical faculty which would normally be deployed to deconstruct such essentialized identities. Might such an approach to anthropology be deployed to intervene in the sphere of policy, activism and public affairs less obtrusively, less insensitively, than was the case in some earlier examples presented here? Or, conversely, might it actively negate the possibility of such intervention?

It is clear from several of these chapters that scholars applying anthropological theories to real-life social issues have often done so with disastrous consequences. From the German anthropologists working to further the cause of racial and cultural separatism and extinction, through South African scholars working in a broadly similar tradition and to similar ends, blame has been rightly laid at the door of those who have espoused doctrines of cultural particularity in order to further state policies based on such doctrines. Yet Sharp's paper on Eiselen demonstrates that even where one might expect to find such cultural particularism at its most fanatical, unexpected experiments with more universalist approaches, and with assimilation, were taking place. To use archival research in laying bare such exceptions to the stereotype, as Sharp does, might in turn have future public significance. Scholars in the formerly bitterly divided anthropological factions, who have already begun the process of reconciliation, might be thus encouraged further to bridge the gap between them; members of the Volkekunde camp might be further drawn into the fold of a more modern and cosmopolitan, less culturally isolationist, anthropological tradition in South Africa (van der Waal and Ward 2006).

Greek anthropologists, similarly constrained but for different reasons within a cultural essentialist approach, were attempting to move beyond this to embrace a more universalist vision (Gefou-Madianou, this volume). Not that assimilationism, and the universalist ideas on which it was based, were bound to meet with uniformly heartfelt approval. Canadian anthropologists espoused such an ideology in their dealings with First Nation groupings in that country, only to be later rebuffed by those whom they had been attempting to bring into the mainstream. These groupings, most recently, have demanded the recognition of their separate identity and have pursued the awarding of rights based on claims to first-ness. In such a setting, the Labrador Metis, being not 'aboriginal enough', were often debarred from claiming land as part of an aboriginally bona fide group by their own relatives who had successfully negotiated the status of aboriginal belonging for themselves. And when the Metis did finally succeed in establishing a legally recognized right to claim for themselves, there was a general discomfiture among anthropologists that they had 'gone too far' by leaving behind an avowedly indigenous identity (Plaice, this volume).

If, perhaps where there are apparently fewer immediately demanding political issues at stake, anthropologists see their role as less directly interventionist, can such a stance be justified? Some of the papers here suggest that it can. When Barnard assesses the likely effect of indigenous claims in South Africa, he recalls that two contrasting anthropological traditions have co-existed in that country. The 'cultural' claims advanced by the Afrikaner Volkekunde tradition are counterposed to the more socially oriented analyses of its British counterpart. His immersion in the latter gives him a certain detached scepticism about the essentializing claims of the former. Similarly detached is Bošković's analysis. When he discusses a sequence of anthropological controversies as a means to explore how reactive cultural claims made in the Balkans proceed by ever more intense rejection of the European mainstream, his deployment of a critical and sober style of analysis along lines first suggested by Barth (1969) exposes these strongly counterposed mythical identities for what they are. And when Evans explores essentialist images of black and white culture in modern Britain, her analysis yields an understanding of the profoundly politicized character of these identities. In these cases, the authors are explaining the processes that give rise to their informants' models and forms of cultural self-awareness; to analyse and explain these shifting identifications is not to espouse them. Baumann and Gudeman, however, describe ethnographic cases where there is blurring between outsiders' and insiders' models. For Baumann, a fully nuanced analysis must take both into account, weighing each up to ascertain in each instance where the other might supplant, improve or transcend it. Scholarly detachment remains important, but it must acknowledge its own limits. And Gudeman takes this point one step further by showing, in the case of economic behaviour, how these models are inextricably interrelated.

These varied and contrasting cases merit further consideration. When as analysts we attempt to understand the processes that give rise to particular approaches to anthropology, and to anthropologically oriented policy making which bears on particular national cases, we bring ourselves and our particular histories to the analysis. This observation cuts through the relativism vs. universalism debate by virtue of recognizing that everything human evinces the historically constituted processes that make it what it is. We can usefully compare these constituting processes and by these means understand how the particular and the universal are aspects of one another: what differentiates us, as Pina-Cabral concludes (this volume), is a function of what we have in common – our lived history, which we cannot help but project onto the present where it informs the processes that will constitute the conditions of our future lives. Like the alternating faces of the visual illusion that is a Necker cube, the universal and relative at once invoke and obviate each other precisely because the viewer literally cannot, at one and the same time, see both faces as having common dimensions.

This is evident in the present volume, in the cases explored here. It is also evident in Kuper's own work where the universalist perspective he espouses in his response to indigenist arguments is one which proposes limits to relativism, and which implies that if we agree to affirm such identities we will be endorsing obfuscation and untruth. Elsewhere, however, in showing how anthropological knowledge itself is an artefact of historical processes, he might appear to be throwing into question his own commitment to objectivity. Of course, a theoretical disposition towards universalism, and the associated rejection of cultural particularism, is one such anthropological artefact – an observation that allows us to see why it makes little sense to try to separate the universal from the particular and why, by contrast, we favour an analysis of the lived historical processes that give rise to any given intellectual or political stance.

Any theoretical disposition is informed by anthropologists' relations with others, especially those that contribute to their first impressions and early training. It is just such a suggestion that is made in the final chapter in this volume, an account of Kuper's own oeuvre which traces aspects of his approach to his upbringing as a Jewish South African. Niehaus goes beyond the stereotype that posits an affinity between Jews as 'ethnic outsiders' and anthropologists as 'professional strangers'. He takes up a point made by historian Hugh Macmillan (2000) that Jewish scholars working in Central and

South Africa were influenced by their 'experiences of the diaspora, anti-Semitism and of nationalism' to theorize ethnic identities as 'fluid, optional, multiple and selected in the context of specific situations'. It was not, however, only a Jewish background, but also that of a dissident South African brought up during the harshest years of the apartheid regime out of which, in Kuper's case, such an approach emerged. From these combined influences upon an exceptional mind, argues Niehaus, sprung Kuper's 'profound theoretical critique of ethnographic particularism' and eventually his questioning of 'the very notion of culture itself'. Thus Kuper's own history and the ideas to which it gave rise, like all our histories and all our ideas, are enmeshed in and evince aspects of broader social processes that emerge in the politics of nations, and the intellectual development of scholarly disciplines. It is difficult, always, to determine the strands of any given person's lived experience and of course Kuper explored a variety of other questions which arose in the trajectory of his scholarly journey from South through East Africa, via the Netherlands, to Britain, with many stopovers in the U.S. But no doubt we can discern, especially here in his critical approach to culture, some key aspects of the history that shaped Kuper's anthropology.

Conclusion

The example of Adam Kuper himself, like that of others discussed here, prompts us to ask what we as anthropologists need to acknowledge and understand about our own histories. And what, if anything, we might need to repudiate. Can a renewed commitment to a field-work-based tradition of modern anthropology as advocated by Malinowski – one in which it is the anthropologist's commitment to fieldwork that generates theory rather than merely contributing the detail and data upon which such theory is built (Kuper 1992a: 1–4) – be reconciled with a critical awareness of the positionality and specificity of all anthropological perspectives? We think so. Provided that we remain committed to the necessity of knowing and understanding the history of the discipline, and provided we do our field studies in good faith, allowing ourselves to be led by the preoccupations of the people with whom we work, our ethnographies – however much they are bound to illuminate aspects of our own intellectual histories – will at the same time provide valid accounts of what it is to be human. Elsewhere Toren has suggested that we analyse the processes through which the people with whom we work make sense of themselves and the environing world and by these means render analytical their key categories (Toren 2002). We could, of course, by the same means, gain an enlightened understanding of our own. Indeed such analyses are good for comparative purposes for they can reveal how people (ourselves included) come to hold historically constituted ideas to be self-evident: inherent in the nature of things.

This is not an exercise in interpretation, but rather is a matter of showing how, exactly, ideas come to have material force, how (from the perspective of those who live them) they evince themselves in the world in the realities of people's daily lives, and how these realities have differing historical trajectories, differing material implications, even though the terms we use seem to suggest we are dealing with 'the same thing' – terms like 'culture', 'human rights', 'ownership', 'indigeneity', 'exchange', 'kinship' and countless others that anthropologists have argued about since the inception of the discipline.

Because ideas have material force, it follows that the task of ethnography is to make them work analytically in any given case and this requires that we do away with the distinction between what is universal and what is particular. Rather, we have to recognize that the universal and the particular are aspects of one and the same phenomenon: what is universal necessarily manifests itself in particular forms – in particular human beings, for example, whose similarity to one another is a function of how much lived history they have in common and whose difference is a function of the fact that the lived history they have in common diverges to a greater or lesser degree. So, where people make use of the idea of culture, the anthropologist's task is to find out its material significance for those who use it. Ditto for those other terms that demand ethnographic investigation.

The chapters presented here demonstrate some of the complexities of how we make sense of the world. Anthropologists immersing themselves in their fieldwork, and thereby having become aware of some of their background assumptions, begin to apprehend the processes that provide for the emergence of rather different assumptions, different models of the world and human being, even perhaps different ontologies entailing different epistemologies. They also understand how the process of making sense means that people's ideas transform, more or less, as a function of accommodating to the ideas they encounter – whether these be the anthropologist's ideas or any other's. So writing valid ethnography involves recognizing and explaining the social processes that give rise to both our own assumptions and those of our informants, and finding out how they might bear on, or oppose, or obviate, one another.

Chapter 1

Alliances and Avoidance: British Interactions with German-speaking Anthropologists, 1933–1953

Andre Gingrich

Although the investigation of separate national traditions of anthropology is a very fruitful exercise, one to which Kuper has contributed substantially, it represents only one step in the creation of the 'cosmopolitan anthropology' for which he has called.[1] His pioneering work in this field shows – in the case of British and American traditions – how contexts mould academic concerns and how these concerns shape their contexts in turn (Kuper 1973, 1999a, 1999b). Debates in specific national settings, he shows, have been 'generated within, and in relation to, real … dilemmas' which those settings present (Kuper, in Gibb and Mills 2001: 214). But he has also noted the danger that these separate national traditions can become 'inward-looking and isolated' (ibid.) His active encouragement of the development of other schools and efforts to promote dialogue and debate amongst and between these – in part through the formation of the European Association of Social Anthropologists (EASA) – represent important moments in the struggle against such isolationism, and in the creation of new cosmopolitan standards in anthropology.

The extent to which ongoing connections have occurred between these allegedly separate traditions has often, however, been overlooked. German Völkerkunde, for example, is sometimes thought to have been so tailored to the maintenance of Nazi ideology and practice during the Third Reich that it bore very little resemblance to its intellectual counterparts in the rest of Europe or in the U.K. The present chapter attempts to set the record straight. It documents the extensive interactions which British and German-speaking anthropologists had with each other, and shows how all the major trends of international anthropology had specific German equivalents: historical diffusionism, functionalism and structuralism. The German case thus challenges facile assumptions about the neatness of fit between anthropologists' socio-cultural background and their concerns and theoretical preoccupations.

Anthropology in Germany: The Background

Germany's history between the ('second') Reich's foundation in 1871 and the First World War has been aptly described by some authors as part of the country's belated entry process into modernity (Böhme 1972; Eder 1985; Dumont 1994). In 1848, the bourgeois and liberal revolutions in various German countries and principalities had failed to achieve democratic liberties and a unified German state for the promotion of the domestic market economy. It was almost a quarter of a century later that Prussia, as the strongest among the remaining principalities, thus implemented Germany's unification through military and administrative means 'from above'. After 1871, those forces that had come to power inside the newly founded German empire also began to act as the junior newcomer in the European and colonial fields of growing imperial rivalry. In increasingly successful ways, the natural sciences and humanities were promoted at the service of these ambitions and aspirations at home and abroad.

Völkerkunde emerged as the established professional German term, around the turn of the twentieth century, for what became known as social anthropology in the British realm.[2] Literally meaning '(academic) knowledge about (foreign) peoples', urban museums were the field's first institutional sites during the second half of the nineteenth century (Penny 2002; Penny and Bunzl 2003). During the first decades of the twentieth century, the Berlin Museum für Völkerkunde (Museum of Anthropology) was the largest museum of its kind in the world, based on collections from German colonies (until 1918) in Africa and Melanesia, but also from the Americas and elsewhere.

Germany's defeat in 1918 and the loss of her colonies accelerated ongoing changes inside academic life. Folklore studies or *Volkskunde* – that is, knowledge about the (domestic, German) people – was made into a specialized academic field of its own, while Völkerkunde could no longer pursue its priority for collecting ethnographic objects in the colonies and elsewhere. By the 1920s, its institutional centres of gravity eventually shifted to university departments, similar to earlier developments in Britain, France and the United States. In the course of these shifts, Völkerkunde largely became separated from *Anthropologie* (physical anthropology), although many researchers and teachers were still trained in both, and many museum departments and learned academic societies continued to cover both under one name. This continued to characterize the institutional academic landscape until Hitler came to power in 1933.

The present chapter discusses British interactions with anthropologists from the German language zone in the two decades after 1933 – that is, before, during and after the Second World War. I want to identify major trends and to illustrate them through a few significant examples. With a specific interest in the different groups of German-speaking anthropologists with whom their British colleagues interacted, I shall try to outline what is known from previous and current research, and to formulate a few hypotheses and suggestions for the future.

During the Nazi period, the partial institutional and organizational differentiation between physical and social anthropology that had been achieved before 1933 was now reversed to some extent. In several important instances, it was replaced by a new racist Nazi priority for close cooperation between both fields under the rubric of 'racial studies'. Recent assessments of Völkerkunde in the period right after the Nazis had come to power (Hauschild 1995; Streck 2000; Gingrich 2005) have clarified the widespread support for Naziism of most institutional representatives of Völkerkunde in Germany. It has been pointed out that the transition had been a fairly smooth one, because many professional anthropologists either had already sympathized with Naziism before it came to power, or because after the Nazi takeover many others adjusted to the fact. Given the elitist organization of German academia in general, and of Völkerkunde in particular, the number of Jewish and democratic opponents to Naziism with formal positions inside Völkerkunde had been relatively low from the outset. Most of them were persecuted, forced into emigration, or murdered either before or after the war began. By 1935/6, institutional academic Völkerkunde was already as firmly controlled by the Nazis as most other fields in the humanities in Germany. With Austria's occupation in March 1938, the same type of violent process swept through the second largest Völkerkunde institute in the German language zone (Gingrich 2006a). With the exception of that institute's later subordination under Naziism, Völkerkunde was therefore fully integrated into the Nazi Reich long before the war began.

It would be naive, however, to assume that the full integration of an academic field into Naziism went hand in hand with a monolithic inner structure of that field. On the basis of explicit academic allegiance to state and party in theory and practice, Naziism accepted the coexistence of various research directions within all kinds of fields and even promoted them out of its own social Darwinian premises and priorities. Moreover, historians have pointed out that while Naziism itself presented dictatorial internal coherence on all levels, in reality it always combined in bizarre ways with quite the opposite, namely with fierce and frequently chaotic internal competition (see Byer 1999). This, then, was the institutional and ideological context to be kept in mind when discussing anthropology under Hitler: Völkerkunde had several different research directions, whose representatives were mostly eager to demonstrate their support for Naziism, and who competed for official recognition within the Third Reich against each other, and within a context of

Nazi funding sources and offices competing, in turn, among themselves (ibid.)

In this context, many German social anthropologists also attempted to enhance their academic and intellectual affinity with the Nazis' 'racial studies' and to particular Nazi versions of physical anthropology. In their own terms, proponents of Völkerkunde were relatively successful in proving their usefulness either through their interests in 'applied anthropology', or by means of their 'theoretical' proximity to Nazi ideology, or both. Key examples of 'applied' anthropology under the Nazis include the activities of Otto Reche and Karl Anton Pluegel. Reche held the chair at Leipzig and was responsible for official racial identification reviews. The results of these reviews determined the extent to which individuals were said to belong to an inferior race, which could, in turn, imply a decision about life and death (Geisenhainer 2003). Another case in point is Karl Anton Pluegel, who held a key position in the Nazis' Kracow Institut für Deutsche Ostarbeit during the German occupation of Poland and contributed to the planning and establishment of the Jewish ghetto (Michel 2000). In ideological terms, Wilhelm E. Mühlmann represents the most prominent case of German anthropological efforts toward reorientating the whole field in line with Nazi priorities while at the same time contributing to the Nazi worldview by anthropological means (Michel 1991). Compared with what is known about other fields (Hausmann 2001), I estimate that, through the allocation of grants and institutional positions, Völkerkunde became part of an upper echelon of subjects within the humanities and social sciences which were clearly promoted under Hitler – together, that is, with fields such as psychology, German studies, Celtic studies, folklore studies (*Volkskunde*), Indo-Aryan studies, or archaeological prehistory.

If this outlines some of the more general background in the period prior to and during the war, before going on to discuss British interactions with German anthropologists during the 1933–1953 period we must highlight a few contextual aspects that were more specific to the prewar years. After Hitler came to power, his government was eager to demonstrate and to improve his 'new Germany's' respectability and its external image. There were ideological as much as strategic reasons why Great Britain represented a key arena for these prewar Nazi propaganda efforts. In turn, these Nazi propaganda efforts consisted of regular demonstrations within Britain aimed at demonstrating that normal, good research was taking place in Hitler's Germany. This should help to introduce what otherwise might come as an unpleasant surprise.

The Prewar Years, 1933–1939: Alliances, Mostly

The years before the Second World War display a dense network of alliances and interactions between Great Britain and Germany. This is true for many fields of economic, social and cultural life in general, and for much of academia, including most fields that related, in one way or another, to the colonies. In these contexts, British–German anthropological interactions played a not insignificant role. Germany lost its colonies in Africa and parts of the Western Pacific in 1918. Less than fifteen years later, when Hitler came to power in Berlin in January 1933, most German colonial linguistic and ethnographic expertise persisted, ready to be reinvigorated but without its 'own' colonial fields of practice. German colonial academic expertise thus seemed to be available, and, to an extent, it was. Besides, as an institutionalized language, German continued to be the major international academic lingua franca that it had been since the nineteenth century. Long-term factors, colonial German practical expertise and Germany's academic status all help to explain the extent of continuing cooperation between British and German anthropologists until 1939. In a way, it seems that British academia dealt, from a distance, with Hitler's rise to power in a similar manner to the way in which many German academics dealt with it in their much more immediate contexts: the pursuit of 'business as usual' was a widely prevailing attitude.

These and other long-term factors were advanced, and peaked, together with a well-known third element: British 'appeasement' as personified, of course, by Neville Chamberlain. So, an uncomfortable fact has to be acknowledged: from Hitler's rise to power in January 1933 until the outbreak of the Second World War in September 1939, six and a half years passed that were shaped by relatively intense interactions and alliances in anthropology. These were pursued by a number of major British academic institutions and their anthropologists, and by the official anthropological representatives of a Germany already ruled by Nazi dictatorship. Those years of relatively intense alliances were in fact somewhat longer than the war period itself. Because of the war, and because of everything that became known about Nazi crimes against humanity before and during its course, those pre-1940 academic alliances became something of an embarrassment later, often passing into oblivion after 1945. The years of prevailing British–German alliances in anthropology, however, were not monolithic and unambiguous. They had their internal resistances, their ups and downs, their rivalries and contests.

One of the main British institutional platforms for British–German alliances in anthropology before September 1939 was the International Institute of African Languages and Cultures in London (today's IAI). The debate about its changing roles and functions in colonial history (Kuklick 1991; Kuper 1996: 99–101; Mischek 2002: 46–56) seems to have clarified that the London African Institute was not the exclusive, single-purpose tool of British colonial interests, as some authors have tended to portray it. Rather, it was an international, or 'global-colonial', centre, and in this sense it also functioned as a clearing house and a research forum.

In this context, German, and German-speaking, experts on Africa held senior institutional positions in the institute right up until 1939. Most prominent in the hierarchy was the German linguist Diedrich Westermann, one of the institute's two directors and coeditor of its journal, *Africa*. Since the late nineteenth century, German research in and about Africa had been held in fairly high esteem in Britain, and this continued in several practical ways until the war broke out. Westermann had been a Protestant missionary in Africa for almost two decades and he never became a member of the Nazi party. His skills and competence as a linguist are beyond doubt. Yet from 1933 onward, he also acted as one of the Nazis' top academic representatives and as advisor for their rising colonial ambitions in Africa (Mosen 1991; Byer 1999: 305). These ambitions eventually turned out to be seriously practical: while tacit cooperation with the Portuguese Salazar regime in Africa was continued during the war, German expertise in and about Africa also contributed to open Nazi support for Boer academic and political ambitions in southern Africa, and to Hitler's logistical back-up for Mussolini in eastern Africa. These ambitions intensified during the first phase of the Second World War (before the Stalingrad battle), i.e. together with the fall of Paris and with Rommel's northern African campaign.[3] German interests in the African Institute before 1939 thus were not harmless. Moreover, Westermann's role as codirector and coeditor at the African Institute until 1939 was not a unique case: several Völkerkunde experts on Africa from Germany and Austria also served on various executive councils and governing bodies. Among them were not only those who supported Naziism, it should be said, but also those from the Vienna theological diffusionist school, such as Wilhelm Schmidt and Paul Schebesta, who were then ousted after Austria's annexation in 1938 (Mischek 2002).

So, to an extent, contributions from the German language zone to the London African Institute did reflect some modest variety within Völkerkunde. On the level of academic training and publications, several among those who were about to become most prominent representatives of German Völkerkunde under Nazi rule received funding and training through the African Institute, or published in its journal. Two important examples are Hermann Baumann and Günter Wagner.

Baumann was a leading representative of what we may call the German school of secular diffusionism, to be distinguished from the Vienna school of Catholic theological diffusionists. Two generations before Baumann, the early phases of that same school of secular diffusionism had been the formative environment for Franz Boas during his Berlin years, and he took some of that with him to the United States (Bunzl 1996; Jacknis 1996; Cole 1999: 83–105). By the mid 1930s, Baumann had gained a name as an expert on Angola, and in fact was one of the few German secular diffusionists with a serious field work record in Africa. Simultaneously, he belonged to the inner circle of early Nazi party members in the field of Völkerkunde. In 1934, Baumann published an article in the African Institute's journal, in which he presented some of his ethnographic field material from Angola in his diffusionist perspective. He combined this with a fierce attack on his contemporary in African studies in Germany, Leo Frobenius at Frankfurt. He argued that Frobenius had separated the notion of 'culture' from the notion of 'race' in an unacceptable manner (Baumann 1934). The mere publication of this article in a prominent London-based academic journal decisively promoted Baumann's opaque career within the 'Reich' (Braun 1995), and accelerated the fall of the Frobenius phenomenological school into official disgrace (Heinrichs 1998; Schuster 2006). It is thus hard to deny that in some crucial instances, the almost seven years of alliances between British and German anthropology had clear effects. They gave international academic legitimacy to the rise of racist German views in anthropology, and they helped to further marginalize the views of those who did not explicitly share those racist ideologies. After all, Frobenius's main follower, Adolf Jensen, would soon be among those in anthropology who were marginalized and persecuted by the Nazis (Gingrich 2005: 108, 116; Schuster 2006).

British institutional interactions thus provided some opportunity to upgrade the dominant trend of secular diffusionism in German Völkerkunde. British anthropology's primary interest, however, was devoted to the more recent trend of German functionalism. Richard Thurnwald continued to be its leading and internationally best-known figure – well known as a person and, in Britain, appreciated with some reservations as an author.[4] Inside Germany, many junior scholars regarded Thurnwald's brand of functionalism with its social Darwinist tendencies as an example to be followed, and as an alternative to diffusionism's historical speculations (Gingrich 2005: 118), a development that was observed with some sympathy in Britain. In fact, it seems a viable hypothesis to me that German functionalism was viewed from the British side first and foremost as a potential junior ally and partner, and only to some extent as a minor rival. The training of Günter Wagner, who was on his way to becoming a well-known expert on the Kavirondo in Kenya, is a case in point. For his Ph.D. studies, his teacher in Hamburg had sent him to do field work in the U.S. south-east under the guidance of Franz Boas, and his doctoral dissertation with Boas, a grammatical sketch of Yuchi, was published in Volume 3 of the *Handbook of American Indian Languages*. Wagner, however, was not satisfied with Boasian diffusionism. Eventually, Malinowski was persuaded to accept Wagner as his student. Wagner's biographer Udo Mischek has shown in splendid detail (2002: 62–80) how Malinowski guided Wagner's early post-doctoral field work in Kenya, and even visited him there, and how Wagner gained additional support from the African Institute, while gradually moving into the circles around Evans-Pritchard, where he also interacted with Siegfried Nadel. From the records it seems that Wagner would have preferred to stay in England. Although not an active supporter of Naziism until then, he still felt obliged to return to Germany when the war broke out (ibid.: 78–83).

The case of another young star of German functionalism was that of Fürer-Haimendorf in Vienna, who decades later would serve as a president of the Royal Anthropological Institute. In 1939, just before the outbreak of the war,

Fürer-Haimendorf chose to move in exactly the opposite direction to that of Wagner. For a long time, Fürer-Haimendorf's story has been interpreted in too simplified a manner, something facilitated by his autobiography (Fürer-Haimendorf 1990). In fact, he had been an early member of the Nazi party in Austria, before it was declared illegal there in 1934 (Linimair 1994). After Austria's annexation in March 1938, Fürer-Haimendorf tried to keep his options open for a while, perhaps speculating about a possible success for Chamberlain's appeasement politics. His ties by marriage to the British Bernardo family, and his enthusiastic support for Malinowskian field work methods, led him to publish his early bestseller, *The Naked Nagas*, in both countries, the book being simultaneously released in Britain and Nazi Germany in 1939. At the Vienna Institute, he served as the Nazi party's key contact person, publishing a number of articles with explicit Nazi terminology, while he prepared everything for his move to British India (Gingrich 2006b; Schäffler 2006). It is still unclear to what extent this short period of explicit collaboration with the Nazis was just a pretext to get out smoothly, and how much of it was still marked by his previous pro-Nazi sympathies. At any rate, Fürer-Haimendorf, whom I personally knew, never explicitly denied his early Nazi affiliations – and, after all, he chose to defect. Many of his colleagues would also have had that choice, but did not pursue it.

The War Years, 1939–1945: Comprehensive Avoidance and Refugees

As soon as the war broke out, the whole context of British interactions with German anthropologists completely changed, in profound and enduring ways. What had been a dominating pattern became not only marginal but, from autumn 1939, also illegal – inside Britain as much as inside the Reich – after which there was avoidance of any official contact with the other side. Parallel to this closure of further academic relations with institutional German Völkerkunde abroad, thorough screening processes of German refugees within Britain took place. Several anthropologists were among them. Eventually, more liberal and lively forms of academic cooperation emerged with many of these anthropologists who had fled from Naziism or who had been forced to emigrate.

To an extent, British interactions with anthropologists who had emigrated from the German language zone had already been a significant part of prewar developments. Some of them had been creative and constructive, others less so. In the realm of the British integration of emigrants, refugees and defectors among German-speaking anthropologists, the case of Siegfried Nadel is best known. In view of the growing anti-Semitic atmosphere there, Nadel left Vienna long before the rise of Naziism, after completing his musical training, and his anthropological formation took place in Britain (Salat 1983). Some later cases are similar to his, in so far as Eric Wolf, for instance, also came to

England and then to the U.S. in 1938 as a Jewish refugee from Vienna, long before he could begin his studies in anthropology after the war (Silverman 2007).

These cases differ from those refugees who had already completed their anthropological training in Germany. They included Leonhard Adam, who managed to establish a new career in anthropology in Melbourne after escaping from a long and bitter struggle inside German Völkerkunde. Another example is ethnomusicologist Erich Hornbostel, who lived in exile in London, the author of a classic reference book that is still quoted today (Riese 1995). A last example here is Paul Kirchhoff, who belonged to the small but significant wing of an early Marxist anthropology in Germany between the two wars, and published articles on South American native kinship systems (Kirchhoff 1931), which Marshall Sahlins later rediscovered under the term 'conical clan' (Sahlins 1968). As Michael Young's junior colleague Geoffrey Gray has shown, the Jewish communist anthropologist Kirchhoff was not granted asylum in Britain and Australia for political reasons during the early 1930s, and barely managed to find refuge in Ireland (1932), where he received encouraging letters from Malinowski. He later moved to France (1934), the U.S. (1935/36) and finally Mexico, from where he later established close cooperation with Julian Steward (Gray 2006). Some anthropologists among the refugees thus did gain asylum and a basis for new careers in the British Empire, while some others who had managed to escape did not.

It seems significant that examining anthropologists' refugee stories from those years soon leads to a number of well-known names, with connotations that may continue to interest us. This is not merely so because most of us tend to sympathize with these biographies, rather than with those of the collaborators, but also because the anthropologists among refugees who managed to find asylum either in the British Empire or in the Americas often established new careers with additional inspiration drawn from their suffering through refuge and exile. Both of these factors, our sympathy and their success, are certainly relevant for understanding how, in contrast with the collaborators and others inside the 'Reich', many among them became much better known in the English-speaking academic world that shaped global debates after 1945. In addition, we may identify a third factor to explain the remarkable influence and the good names among the emigrants and refugees from the German language zone, in our field's history: phrased in simplified terms, these were mostly critical and sharp minds and thus they understood that combining good research with civil standards was incompatible with Naziism and racism. In one way or another, most of them pursued academic research as pathways to either liberal or progressive visions of modernity. Meanwhile, the dictatorial and murderous version of modernity peaked in Germany.

Within and at the margins of these main trends during the war, a few developments behind the scenes may need further clarification. For instance,

Evans-Pritchard and Meyer Fortes fought quite hard with British censorship to get Günter Wagner's contribution published in their classic 1940 volume, *African Political Systems* (Wagner 1940). They could not possibly have known that at exactly the same time that they were engaging themselves in furthering his academic standing inside the U.K., Wagner had already found employment with Joseph Goebbels's propaganda ministry. One of his tasks was the censorship of anthropological book publications, while other tasks included colonial planning for what the Nazis already called German East Africa, and, in that context, the early planning of the Jews' deportation to Madagascar (Mischek 2002: 84–93).

At about the same time, Fürer-Haimendorf was debriefed by the British authorities in India about the University of Vienna, and then went on to carry out his next field work campaigns among various tribal groups in India during the war for the British administration. Simultaneously, the Nazis were made to believe that he was still a heroic prisoner of war, and they published excerpts of *The Naked Nagas* as late as 1944 as a mass booklet for entertaining the Wehrmacht (Campregher and Mihola 2006; Schäffler 2006). The booklet was given a title, borrowed from one of the author's chapters, which in 1944 surely conveyed gruesome additional significance: *Der weiße Kopfjäger* ('The White Headhunter').

The Postwar Years, 1945–1953: Embarrassment and Continuing Avoidance

The postwar period is perhaps the least interesting one in my discussion, and little research has been done in this regard. For these reasons, I shall merely comment on what seem to be the two most typical dimensions after 1945: embarrassed gestures and continuing avoidance.

I think that 'embarrassed gestures' is the best term for understanding the contributions of prominent anthropologists – among them Alfred Kroeber and Robert Lowie from the U.S. and A.P. Elkin from Australia – to Richard Thurnwald's celebratory volume for his eightieth birthday in 1950 (Thurnwald 1950). Thurnwald clearly had emerged as the most famous and influential anthropologist from the German language zone during the first half of the twentieth century. Yet the fact that his record during the Nazi years was anything but clean was already known by then (Gingrich 2005: 106, 121–23, 130). Similarly, it is not easy to grasp what led a number of British anthropologists to provide written testimonies in support of Günter Wagner's official de-Nazification in 1948, among them Evans-Pritchard, Meyer Fortes, Daryll Forde and Siegfried Nadel (Mischek 2002: 132). They testified that they had known him as a good professional anthropologist before the war, which was fair enough. Still, in view of what is known today it seems to me that these testimonies by prominent British anthropologists, two of whom came from Jewish families with continental backgrounds, were too hasty.

Shortly after that, Wagner could promote his career by moving to South Africa. However, he died soon after taking up employment with the new National Party government (Hammond-Tooke 1997).[5]

Apart from such embarrassed testimonies for a few prominent – and more or less implicated – German anthropologists such as Thurnwald and Wagner, the general British attitude after 1945 towards German Völkerkunde nevertheless continued to be one of avoidance. To an extent, this was perhaps a consequence of retrospective insights about how far the alliances had gone before the war, and how advisable it might be to remain careful in the present at least. In other ways, however, professional avoidance was also based on the well-informed British insight that German Völkerkunde was no longer of any wider interest, now that its most creative and exciting representatives either lived in the British Empire and in the Americas, or, in fact, were dead. Former supporters of the Nazi party – such as Baumann (Munich), Plischke (Göttingen), Krickeberg (Berlin), Heydrich (Cologne), Hirschberg (Vienna) and Mühlmann (Heidelberg) – continued, after their de-Nazification procedures, to play prominent roles in the local academic landscapes of Völkerkunde in West Germany and Austria. Understandably enough, to my mind at least, silent avoidance continued, therefore, until late into the 1960s and 1970s.

Conclusion

In the end, this short overview of British–German interactions in anthropology between 1933 and 1953 may provide an additional perspective upon German Völkerkunde in the Nazi period. Adopting a British perspective has helped to identify the main proponents and directions within German Völkerkunde, and how they related to their international counterparts and rivals.

The example of Hermann Baumann's 1934 article in *Africa* showed how German Völkerkunde under Hitler promoted the nationalist and more racist variant of a secular diffusionism, while ousting theological diffusionism and marginalizing Frankfurt's phenomenology. Two generations after Boas had left Berlin, this German variant of secular diffusionism still shared some intellectual components with its counterpart, the non-racist diffusionism of Boas and his students. It was relativist and historicist, and it combined a territorial 'area' or 'circles' orientation with (very different kinds of) physical anthropology.

Through the cases of Thurnwald, Fürer-Haimendorf and Wagner, it was possible to identify British interests in German functionalism, which flourished under the Nazis. German functionalism had a strong social Darwinian component, which was largely absent in British anthropology, and it maintained a stronger recognition of historical dimensions. Nevertheless, both variants shared a number of similar features, among them a priority for systemic and structural analysis of societies in the present which facilitated a pragmatic usage for applied purposes.

We now may add that in Leipzig's Völkerkunde, the Nazi party member Fritz Krause also entertained a local variant of early structuralism (Geisenhainer 2003). Krause interacted with linguistic schools of thought at his local university that were strongly influenced by early linguistic structuralism (Rosenberg 2001). He had been among the authors of an early letter of allegiance to Adolf Hitler, jointly signed by physical and social anthropologists to emphasize their importance for the regime (Gingrich 2005).[6]

The refugees and defectors among German-speaking social anthropologists comprised a much wider range of theoretical orientations. They included theological and secular diffusionism, functionalism, Marxism, phenomenology, ethnohistory and quite a variety of other maverick orientations. In fact, this pluralist variety of orientations among the refugees marks a noteworthy contrast against the more rigid blocks of those three theoretical and methodological orientations inside Germany which were promoted and upgraded by the regime. These three orientations were not the entirely speculative, old-fashioned political fantasies that one might expect. They certainly were thoroughly tailored in ways that fitted hegemonic Nazi requirements. Yet the somewhat surprising if not counter-intuitive result of this investigation indicates that those three orientations of Völkerkunde which did receive support from the Nazi regime were specific German versions of their international counterparts: diffusionist relativism, functionalism and early structuralism.

A perspective upon British interactions with German-speaking anthropologists before, during and after the Nazi period thus helps us not only to reconsider some often neglected episodes of our discipline's history. Beyond that, this endeavour may also shed some additional light on the monstrous experience of Naziism itself. There could be some wider significance in the existence of all the major trends of international anthropology in their particular German variants in that era – of historical diffusionism, of functionalism and of structuralism. In fact, this indicates that Naziism was not only a primitive, reactionary form of nationalist revitalization through industrial means. By assessing Völkerkunde as a miniature example from the humanities, our findings seem to confirm what a number of historians and historians of science have already pointed out for other and more important fields (Cornwell 2003; Proctor 1999), by identifying the competitive levels of some medical and technological research under the Nazis. In relation to scientific research in general (and medicine in particular) during the 1930s and 1940s, Nazi Germany was at the cutting edge in many areas. The Third Reich never would have come close to being a serious military challenge to its opponents, without such accompanying efforts in science and research (Griffin 2007). As a sequel to Germany's belated detour into modernity, Naziism was also a murderous and dictatorial German effort to gain the lead within a competitive modernity.

Notes

1. Several of the themes discussed here were first examined in my seminars on anthropology under Naziism, held at the University of Vienna (2002–2007). I thank my students in those seminars. This chapter is based on a contribution to the workshop, 'Culture, Context and Controversy', held in honour of Adam Kuper at the EASA 2006 Bristol conference, and on an earlier presentation (2004) at the LSE anthropology department. I thank Deborah James, Evie Plaice, Christina Toren, Jonathan Parry, Martha Mundy and many others who provided valuable suggestions and comments on both of these occasions. I also wish to appreciate an illuminating dialogue with Michael Silverstein (University of Chicago) about the history of linguistic structuralism in Leipzig and Germany. Through his work in the history of anthropology (Kuper 1996, 1999a), Adam Kuper has provided intellectual inspiration, but also personal encouragement. Both factors have supported my contributions to the opening lectures at the Max Planck Institute in Halle, Germany, in 2002. From those lectures emerged the book *One Discipline, Four Ways* (Barth et al. 2005). If not quoted otherwise, the argument in the present chapter further elaborates several points I first raised in that book. Julene Knox (London) has provided generous assistance in editing the final version of this chapter, for which I am more than grateful. In addition, I wish to acknowledge that support for carrying out some of this research came from the Austrian Science Fund's Wittgenstein Award 2000.

2. The term Anthropologie originally embraced several disciplines: Völkerkunde, Folklore studies (Volkskunde), Archaeology, Prehistory and Physical Anthropology.

3. As of September 1939, the War's first phase of Germany's military expansion into many parts of continental Europe included the German occupation of Poland and France, the Wehrmacht's invasion of the Soviet Union and also, Rommel's military campaign in North Africa. The Stalingrad battle became the Second World War's turning point in February 1943.

4. Due to the current state of research, most of the references and examples presented in this chapter rely on sources and publications in German. The same themes still require a thorough investigation of relevant British sources.

5. It is well known by now that Wagner's short involvement with the emerging apartheid regime represented merely one episode within a much more intense and enduring engagement between German Völkerkunde before, during and after the war on the one side, and the Afrikaner variant of Volkekunde in South Africa on the other. John Sharp (1980) has added to these insights the crucial point that the chief architect of apartheid policies, Hendrik Verwoerd, received his main inspiration about the separate existence of differing cultures from Richard Thurnwald's most influential pupil, Wilhelm E. Mühlmann. Mühlmann perhaps was the most active and intelligent among all Nazi activists in German Völkerkunde. During the postwar decades, he continued to act as a central figure in West German Völkerkunde, until student protests after 1968 forced him into early retirement (Michel 1991, 2000).

6. After 1945, Fritz Krause continued to occasionally publish in East Germany (Krause 1952). His case is thus also noteworthy as an example of postwar continuities in both parts of Germany. Among those who had collaborated with Naziism, most of the more well-known representatives of Völkerkunde continued their careers in West Germany. A few, however, like Fritz Krause and Bernhard Struck, tried to do so under the communist regime in the German Democratic Republic.

Chapter 2

Serving the *Volk*? Afrikaner Anthropology Revisited

John Sharp

At the height of the apartheid period, the Afrikaner nationalist anthropologists (or volkekundiges, as they called themselves) perfected a theory of the irreducibility of ethnic belonging. They argued that South Africa was divided into a series of primordial *Volke* (Peoples, s. *Volk*), which differed from each other in respect of their cultures and identities. There were certain differences of emphasis among the volkekundiges on this score, with some arguing that a Volk's culture could change (as a result of internal innovation or external influence) while its essential identity remained constant, and others insisting that the inevitable continuity in a Volk's identity meant that the extent of culture change possible was severely limited. These ambiguities reflected the role of Volkekunde in this period, when apartheid had become thoroughly institutionalized. The discipline's purpose had become to provide a common-sense understanding of South Africa that shut down, rather than stimulated, questions from students at the Afrikaans universities, as well as from the general (white) public. In an attempt in the 1980s and 1990s to reveal the ugly reality of Volkekunde, my colleagues and I (for instance, Sharp 1980, 1981; Gordon 1988, 1989, 1991; Schmidt 1996; Hammond-Tooke 1997; Kiernan 1997) came to the conclusion that its practitioners had set out simply to justify the existing system of apartheid and that, in Gordon's memorable phrase, they were 'serving the (Afrikaner) Volk with Volkekunde' (1991: 79–97).

This interpretation was undoubtedly an accurate depiction of Volkekunde's role in the 1960s and 1970s, but it relied very heavily on our reading of the texts that the Afrikaner nationalist anthropologists had produced in this period. Those of us who embarked on this early critique of Volkekunde, before the apartheid state had fallen, were limited to these sources – the textbooks, articles and published lectures produced by the nationalist anthropologists at the height of the National Party regime's power.

Two decades and more after I fired the first salvo in the critique of Volkekunde, I find myself at the University of Pretoria (the home of the leading exponents of the discipline during the apartheid era). This position gives me access to the university's internal archive relating to the early years of its Volkekunde Department, and I have found new evidence to show that its leading figures did not necessarily start the apartheid era with the arrogant confidence in the unassailable truth of the counter-enlightenment, cultural-essentialist vision of South Africa's inhabitants that they and their followers displayed twenty years later. On the contrary, as I will show below, the first volkekundiges at the University of Pretoria were willing to experiment with more enlightened ideas about culture as well, and to seek a way of reconciling the notion of a universal civilization, to which all in South Africa should aspire and conform, with the particularist idea about culture as the authentic property of an ethnic group or nation.

In this chapter I review some of the material I have found in the internal archive of the University of Pretoria (hereafter UP).[1] I do so because this material clarifies what Volkekunde and its adherents stood for, at least in the discipline's early years at UP. It also raises questions about how, and why, the volkekundiges made the fatal descent from relative flexibility in the 1940s to rigid orthodoxy in the 1960s and after, and these questions, in turn, suggest interesting links to wider issues in the enduring debate about 'culture' (especially Kuper 1999b). I should say at the outset that nothing I have found makes me any better disposed to the ideas and activities of my new predecessors than I was a quarter of a century ago, but I have – I think – been able to focus my criticism of them more accurately.

The material in the UP archive relates not so much to what the Afrikaner nationalist anthropologists wrote, since they wrote very little by way of academic texts in the late 1940s and 1950s. It is, rather, about what they did in the early years of National Party rule in South Africa in their capacity as anthropologists.

The Rise of the *Kolege ya Bana ba Afrika*

The main thing the first professors of Volkekunde did after they joined UP was to mount strenuous efforts to involve their new institution in the provision of tertiary education for black South Africans in the northern part of the (then) Union of South Africa. UP, they argued, should take the lead in fostering the establishment of a 'Native University College' in Pretoria, to rival the already-existing University College of Fort Hare in the Eastern Cape. They insisted that UP should take an active part in the management of such an institution, in overseeing its academic standards, and in providing the lecturing capacity necessary to get the institution up and running. Werner

Eiselen was appointed as the first professor of Volkekunde in 1947, on the strength of the decade he had spent – from 1926 to 1936 – teaching anthropology at Stellenbosch University in the Western Cape. He was extremely keen to involve UP in this project, and his attempts to induce the university to endorse and follow his ideas in this regard constituted the centrepiece of his brief, two-year stay at UP.[2] His successor, P.J. Coertze, appointed in 1950, displayed similar enthusiasm. The university entrusted the continuation of the effort to him, as the resident anthropologist, and he too produced several reports in the early 1950s urging that UP, as the most important Afrikaans centre of learning in the north of the country, had a duty to play a leading role in the provision of university education for black inhabitants of the region.[3]

Evidence of the effort they put into this project in no way contradicts the fact that they were fervent supporters of the principle of apartheid, as I show below. But this evidence sits uneasily with the notion that they supported apartheid because they believed that black people were incapable of rising to the level of Western civilization. Some of my fellow critics at the end of the twentieth century argued that the volkekundiges' espousal at the height of apartheid of rigid ideas about primordial Volke and their ostensible attachment to their own cultures was proof that they had never abandoned the racist premise that 'civilization' was quite beyond the grasp of black South Africans (Alexander 1983; Dubow 1987, 1994). But if Eiselen and Coertze had been convinced that black people could not benefit from higher education, or did not need it because they were destined to remain a subordinate stratum of the population, their labours on behalf of the proposed University College would have been entirely nonsensical. Indeed the reports they wrote to UP in support of the project show that they did not hold these views. These reports made many references to the need to cater for 'gifted Natives', and to the inevitable, and entirely understandable, growth in the demand for university education on the part of a segment of the population that was becoming rapidly urbanized and increasingly involved in a modern, industrial economy.

Eiselen was highly critical of the fact that not enough had been done to these ends under the segregationist regime that prevailed before 1948, and was well aware of the shortcomings in this respect because he had spent the decade prior to his UP appointment as Chief Inspector of Native Education in the Transvaal. In this capacity he had undertaken the unusual step of giving vent to his frustration at the slow pace of progress in the provision of schools and well-trained teachers in his official report of 1941 (Kros 1996: 212–3). Moreover the records I consulted reveal Eiselen uttering very similar views – in fluent Sepedi – in a speech he made in 1946, at the opening of a small, private college that had been established to help fill the gap in university education for black people in the Transvaal.[4] Eiselen was speaking on this occasion not only as Chief Inspector of Native Education but also in a private capacity as a founder member of this college – the *Kolege ya Bana ba Afrika*

(College of the Children of Africa). This small institution – which was able to enrol no more than twelve students in its first year of operation – was the vehicle Eiselen chose in making his plea for UP to become involved in establishing a University College, and the Kolege ya Bana may, indeed, have played a significant part in his decision to quit the civil service and return to the academic world in 1947.

Both Eiselen and Coertze believed, of course, that while Africans could and should be educated to the same levels as whites, they should not get exactly the same training at the same institutions. This is where their willingness to extend Western civilization to all in South Africa came up against their commitment to a particularist view of culture. They made this point repeatedly in their reports to the UP Senate and Council. The curricula of the courses offered at the University College should be different from those of UP courses. UP should guarantee that the degrees provided by the college were of a high standard, but these degrees should go by names different from the ones awarded by UP. And UP's assistance to the University College should be only temporary (a stipulation they regarded as a major, and progressive, move beyond the principle of 'perpertual trusteeship' that had been articulated by Smuts and his followers during the segregation era).

Eiselen's and Coertze's reports to the university provided detailed reasons for the above recommendations. Their main arguments were couched in terms by no means dissimilar to those Malinowski had used in the public lectures he gave on 'Native Education' in South Africa in the 1930s (Malinowski 1936). Western education, Malinowski had said, would certainly add to the lives of black South Africans, but would also take something away by 'estranging a number of individuals from the traditions still controlling the rest of the tribe'. It is worth recalling the conclusion to his analysis of the topic.

> African education has to proceed on two fronts. The Native has to receive schooling that will prepare him for his contact and cooperation with the European section of the population. He has to be taught subjects and skills that will secure him the best possible economic and social situation. At the same time this schooling should be carried out in a manner that will produce the minimum of disintegration and still keep him in harmony with his own group. (ibid.: 494)

Compare this to Eiselen's attempt to persuade the UP Senate about 'the intention behind the proposed creation of an additional university institution for Natives' a decade later.

> The Universities of the Witwatersrand and Cape Town, which presently admit white and black students on an equal footing, provide an entirely foreign education from which all South African orientation is lacking. In the nature of things such institutions cannot give rise to genuine education for Natives that will serve their true needs. The right goal must surely be to train gifted Natives in such a way that they will help their own communities to develop a higher level of productivity and civilization.[5]

It is clear that, in these cited passages, both Malinowski and Eiselen were trying to find some middle ground between the 'civilizing mission' – the idea that Africans had to be instructed in the virtues of Western civilization (and obliged to abandon those aspects of traditional culture that were repugnant in the light of 'universal' standards) – and the view that African cultures were uniquely appropriate for Africans. It is, by now, common cause that Malinowski's 'culture contact' analysis in the 1930s was highly irresponsible, not least when he attempted to persuade the British colonial, and also the South African, authorities of its practical value. The worst one can say is that the argument put forward by Eiselen (and Coertze) was no more ill considered than his, and they had his considerable authority in the discipline behind their use of it. But whereas Malinowski was rescued from the consequences of his folly by the colonial refusal to take his 'practical anthropology' seriously (Kuklick 1991: 183–241), Eiselen and Coertze advanced the same argument at a crucial point when the UP authorities, and indeed the new South African government, were willing to take advice from academic experts, including anthropologists.

Eiselen left his job as Chief Inspector for the Volkekunde Professorship at UP in August 1947. The UP archive makes clear that part of the reason for this was his frustration over the lack of progress in African education under the Smuts government, and his belief that the Kolege ya Bana ba Afrika provided a spontaneous avenue by which a real advance could be made.[6] Hence the rapidity with which he placed this small college on the university's agenda – barely a month after he took up his position he persuaded his Faculty, and the UP Senate and Council, to endorse his proposal that the Kolege ya Bana should become the platform from which to create a future 'Bantu University College', and to appoint him to head an ad hoc committee to consider ways and means to the end of placing the Kolege under UP's 'protection'.[7] His faculty reminded him forcefully that whatever plan he put forward would have to be 'strictly in accordance with the principle of apartheid'.[8] But since this stern admonition was issued in December 1947, several months before the National Party unexpectedly won the election that brought it to power in South Africa for the next half century, it was not to a clear-cut policy of the state that the faculty was referring, but rather to a principle that was shared by many members of the university. In fact, given the timing, Eiselen was required to work out, on the hoof, what the 'principle of apartheid' should actually mean in practice in respect of the proposed relationship between the Kolege ya Bana and the university.

The main recommendation he made in his report to Senate of August 1948 was as favourable to the Kolege and its students as he could make it, since he proposed that a clause in UP's founding statute (Act 30 of 1930) should be used as the basis of the relationship, even though the clause in question read as follows.

If the Council of any University College, now existing or subsequently to be established, has, with the approval of the Minister [of Education], made arrangements with the University whereby such College may become affiliated with the University, the Governor-General may, by proclamation in the Gazette, declare such College to be so affiliated, and thereupon students of such College may be admitted to any examination and degree of the University on conditions prescribed by the statutes.[9]

Eiselen was prepared, in other words, to see the Kolege ya Bana formally incorporated into UP on these terms, and to take care of the 'principle of apartheid' by internal, administrative means. All the evidence suggests that he came to this bold proposal because he was genuinely keen on promoting the Kolege, and because he was personally acquainted with many of the people associated with it. His friends at the Kolege ya Bana were varied. They included the Reverend J.H. van Wyk, the leader of the group from the Dutch Reformed Mission Church that had taken the initiative to start the Kolege in 1946 (Van Wyk enrolled as a postgraduate student under Eiselen's supervision in 1949).[10] And they also included Dr William Nkomo, a prominent African medical practitioner in Pretoria, who gave evidence to the Eiselen Commission on Native Education on behalf of the Kolege ya Bana in 1950. Nkomo was an intriguing figure, in that he had been one of the founder members of the ANC Youth League in 1942, and had been known in those circles as a radical Trotskyite (Walshe 1987: 357). Yet he and Eiselen found at least some common ground over the Kolege ya Bana, although it is also true that other prominent figures in the black elite on the Witwatersrand expressed severe criticism of an institution devoted to racially separate education. For example, R.V. Selope Thema, editor of *Bantu World* and another ANC stalwart, wrote several highly critical editorials on the subject in the late 1940s.[11]

The picture emerging from this episode is a far cry from the conventional depiction of Eiselen as one of the main architects of apartheid in practice, and in particular of the vastly inferior system of Bantu Education that was implemented in the 1950s and continues to blight South Africa to the present. The alternative to this stereotype has much to recommend it, particularly if one sees Eiselen's role as Chair of the Commission of Inquiry into Native Education (1949–1951) as a continuation of, rather than a radical departure from, the part he played in relation to the Kolege ya Bana. Cynthia Kros's careful thesis (Kros 1996) on the origins of Bantu Education argues that there was a yawning gulf between Eiselen's intention to create an elaborate system of 'separate but equal' education for black pupils in South Africa, and the system that actually resulted from Verwoerd's strategy, as Minister for Native Affairs, of appropriating Eiselen's rhetoric but marrying it to a determined maintenance of white domination. In other words, as Kros suggests, it was Verwoerd rather than Eiselen who determined that Africans should not be educated 'above their station', and set the sorry practices of Bantu Education in motion (ibid.: 397–404).

The material in the UP archive persuades me that Kros's interpretation is very likely to be correct. Kros did not have access to the material about Eiselen's efforts on behalf of the Kolege ya Bana, but it clearly supports the main outline of her thesis. To the extent that this is true, however, the material also points to one of Eiselen's (and Coertze's) main failings, particularly in their capacity as anthropologists. In order to highlight this failing, I must complete the story of the Kolege ya Bana in the late 1940s and 1950s.

The Demise of the Kolege ya Bana ba Afrika

Eiselen received the invitation to chair the new National Party government's Commission of Inquiry into Native Education just before he submitted his recommendations on the Kolege ya Bana to the UP Senate.[12] In both instances the authorities concerned sought his advice on educational matters on the strength of his spell as Chief Inspector and his standing as an anthropologist. Faced with the reality of their unexpected election victory, National Party leaders were willing to take advice on how to translate the principle of apartheid into practice. Eiselen stayed on as professor of *Volkekunde* while running the Commission of Inquiry for most of 1949, but was obliged to resign from the university when he was also appointed to the important civil-service position of Secretary to the Union Department of Native Affairs in October of that year.[13] UP sent his report on the Kolege ya Bana to the Minister of Education, along with a request for generous financial support to facilitate the incorporation,[14] but the Minister's response was slow in coming, and Eiselen was unable to take any further part in the discussions surrounding the proper relationship between UP and the Kolege.

By mid 1950, UP's Vice-Chancellor informed the Minister that he felt obliged to refer the matter back to Senate, because the latter's original decision in favour of Eiselen's proposal was now two years old.[15] In Eiselen's absence, Senate passed the issue to his successor for guidance. Coertze prepared several reports on the matter between August 1950 and mid 1951.[16] In each instance he rehearsed Eiselen's high-minded observations about UP's 'duty' to assist in creating a new University College for black students, and endorsed his practical proposals regarding equal standards, and different curricula and degrees. But he was reluctant to support the manner of forging a relationship between the two institutions that Eiselen had recommended.

> Senate does not recommend that the *Kolege ya Bana* should be incorporated forthwith into the University of Pretoria under present legislation, because this would mean that Bantu students of the *Kolege* will become members of Convocation of the University, with all the rights and privileges associated with this, and because Senate is of the opinion that this would be totally irreconcilable with the principle of separate development of the different racial groups in this country.[17]

This inflexible position was curious, given that the rest of Coertze's report made it very clear that he wanted to sustain, rather than end, the prospect of a close relationship between UP and the Kolege in the interests of high educational standards. Moreover, his rejection of the notion of incorporation was not a climbdown in the face of already established policy, because the Education Minister's indecision on the matter was an indication that no definite policy existed at this early stage. Coertze attempted to anticipate what future policy might be, and clearly wanted the Minister of Education to grant the Kolege formal recognition as an independent institution so that UP might become its trustee, and 'protector', without having to incorporate it.

But his attempt to give guidance in this instance backfired, because UP's Senate took his exposition of the implications of 'separate development' at face value. After his final report was accepted, the question of the university taking direct responsibility for establishing a University College for black South Africans disappeared from the agendas of UP's Senate and Council, and the university turned its attention, instead, to giving the Departments of Education and Native Affairs advice and assistance regarding the devising of a completely separate system of higher education for black people.[18]

While all this planning was going on, the Kolege ya Bana and its students were relegated, as one might expect, to a position of increasing obscurity. Removed from the city-centre premises it had been loaned by Pretoria City Council, the Kolege ended up in a dozen prefabricated huts on a vacant site near the present-day (black) township of Mamelodi, well outside the city. UP lecturers who wished to offer their services to teach there continued to be granted leave to do so. But there were limited funds to remunerate these lecturers or to provide bursaries to attract students. Coertze continued to be involved with the Kolege in a personal capacity, but it became clear to him, in the course of the 1950s, that the educational partnership with UP on which he and Eiselen had pinned such high hopes had no place at all in the apartheid state's emerging dispensation. The Kolege finally closed its doors in 1958, the year before the apartheid government passed the notorious Extension of Universities Act, which closed the hitherto 'open' universities to black students and forced them to attend the new, strictly segregated University Colleges which were far removed from the possibility of any partnerships with existing (white) institutions, and subject to stringent state control. After setting up University College of the North, at Turfloop in the far northern Transvaal, the Kolege ya Bana's students were offered the possibility of transferring to this new institution (Mawasha 2006: 68).

Although they had been directly associated with the Kolege ya Bana, and knew many of the people involved in it personally, neither Eiselen nor Coertze made any discernible comment, in public, on its demise. This was a failing they displayed over and over again in the coming years. They played down the fate of the Kolege ya Bana because their attention had turned to the establishing of a whole system of separate university education for black South Africans. And they overlooked the manifest shortcomings of the resulting institutions, such as the University College of the North (and all the other Bantustan universities), because their utopian gaze had turned to even bigger and more important projects.

Eiselen and Coertze were by no means the rabid racists they are often made out to have been. As Kros (1996: 324–95) argues, Eiselen made plans, before and during his time as Secretary for Native Affairs, to right what he saw as the wrongs of Native Education during the segregation era (prior to 1948). These included the shortage of funds, schools and teachers, as well as the smug belief (as he saw it) on the part of white liberals that by admitting a small number of black students to the 'open' universities (such as Cape Town) they were making a signficant impact on the plight of the masses. Yet he sat quiet while his plans were dismembered in the course of political infighting within the government department of which he was Secretary, and while his Minister, Verwoerd, told the world that Bantu Education was intended to keep black South Africans under permanent white domination.

Eiselen and Coertze were members of the coterie of intellectuals whom Lazar (1993) called apartheid's 'visionaries'. These visionaries congregated in the South African Bureau for Racial Affairs from the late 1940s to the end of the 1950s (Coertze, indeed, became UP's official representative to this organization's conferences throughout the decade). But in the late 1950s and early 1960s Verwoerd rooted them out of this organization and humiliated them. He did so on the grounds that their idealistic vision of apartheid as a means to create a society combining racial separation with racial equality was an embarrasment to his altogether more pragmatic strategy of sustaining the tried and tested methods of white domination (ibid.: 386).

In an interesting contribution to the earlier critique of Volkekunde, Kuper (1999a) suggested that Eiselen became privately disillusioned by the obvious gap between his ideal and the actual practice of apartheid towards the end of his period as Secretary for Native Affairs (just at the point when Verwoerd confronted the visionaries). But as Kros noted, even if this were so, Eiselen maintained his public faith in the system as it was being implemented until the end of his life in the early 1970s. P.J. Coertze and his son – who succeeded him to the chair of Volkekunde at UP – maintained this public faith even longer. Their students tell me, however, that they had private doubts, and it should have been obvious to them from their field research in the Bantustans that the actual programme of 'separate development' offered its victims nothing by way of real advancement. Indeed the Coertzes kept their peace until the 1980s, when they finally broke with the National Party and its most powerful, behind-the-scenes secret society, the *Broederbond* (lit. 'Brotherhood'). But far from taking this opportunity to bear witness to all the many Kolege ya Bana-type disasters they had encountered along the way, they joined the even more right-wing Conservative Party, which still contrived to promise that the utopia of 'true' apartheid – total segregation with real equality – was just around the corner. Under their leadership, Volkekunde became a fully-fledged millenarian movement, and their junior colleagues who did not renounce the faith entirely were rendered mute, merely waiting for the cargo to arrive and save them.

'Culture' as Delusion

It seems to me now that the dogmatic theories of primordial Volke and immutable cultures that were the hallmark of Volkekunde at the height of the apartheid era were worked out in the course of the practical encounters in which the Afrikaner nationalist anthropologists were involved in the late 1940s and 1950s. The preceding sections of this chapter have presented some of these encounters, and drawn attention to the setbacks, and possible disillusionment, these anthropologists experienced in the course of them. The material in the UP archive suggests that the volkekundiges did not begin the apartheid period with a detailed and tighly-constructed ideology that was intended simply to justify the unfolding system of apartheid. This instance may therefore be taken as an illustration of Gudeman's argument (this volume) that the formulation of an ideology often occurs in the course of practice, rather than as a prelude to it.

Nor did Eiselen and Coertze begin as the lackeys of an already-existing system. The Kolege ya Bana episode suggests that they started by helping to define an ideal from which the system in practice came to depart radically. This means, on the one hand, that they have to be held accountable for their long silence about this departure, and that their failure lies as much in what they refrained from saying as in what they and their followers eventually came to say. On the other hand, however, it also means that they have to be held accountable for their original ideal, given that they arrived at it by a process of rational consideration rather than as a result of irrational prejudice.

This takes one back to Malinowski and his irresponsible views about Native Education with which Eiselen and Coertze agreed. Malinowski's saving grace was that he was at least wildly inconsistent in his pronouncements about the course of 'culture contact' in South Africa, arguing both that Africans had to have their own system of education and that segregation, in this and other fields, was impossible to sustain. If he had got his foot in the door of state power, as Eiselen did, the questions posed of him now might be far more searching than they are, because he would have had to choose one or other side of his ambiguous stance.

In much of his 'culture contact' writing on (South) Africa, Malinowski (1945) presented himself as a mediator between the opposing sides of the fierce debate he encountered during his visit to the country. It is as if he went out of his way, in the interests of selling the practical value of his discipline, to reassure both the proponents and the opponents of the 'civilizing mission' that he understood their respective concerns and would show them a reasonable compromise. Hence, in the field of education, his argument that Africans should undergo a measure of Western education, but that this should be tweaked so that it would not alienate the individuals fortunate enough to receive it from the 'traditions still controlling the rest of the tribe'. Quite how this was to be done neither he nor, indeed, the volkekundiges were ever able to explain coherently.

But, on the other hand, there were occasions when he realized that questions about whether or not to expose Africans to Western 'civilization', or about how to achieve a suitable balance in this exposure, were simply the wrong ones to ask. There is a remarkable footnote in the lecture on 'Native Education and Culture Contact' (possibly added after the lecture was given) in which Malinowski challenged the South African Native Affairs Commission of 1932. Noting that the Commission's report insisted that 'the native economic question is how best the Native population can be led onward step by step in an orderly march to civilization', he responded trenchantly, 'I beg to differ. The native economic question is how the Native can live on an insufficiency of land, on artificially cut wages, and without any capital whatever which he can devote to the development of his land and the purchase of his working tools'. Moreover, he went on, 'you cannot educate anyone to live on two ounces of bread per day if he needs sixteen' (Malinowski 1936: 494).

It would be unfair to suggest that Eiselen and Coertze were totally blind to considerations such as these, or that they were trapped from the outset within the straightjacket of the culture contact debate. But it would be true to say that they were able to look beyond this framework only when they were being critical of the pre-1948 government's shortcomings, or of what they regarded as the liberal, pro-'civilizing mission', establishment or, indeed, of their fellow white South Africans. In these contexts, as their UP reports show, they could recognize that the questions at stake were not whether Africans should be 'controlled' by 'tribal traditions' or the dictates of Western civilization, but were, rather, about the deliberate underfunding of black education, the unreasonable prejudices of white South Africans, and the liberal propensity to favour a small elite at the expense of the masses.

But once they entered the corridors of power they discovered that they could not pose these questions of or to the National Party politicians. They hoped, at the outset, to lead these politicians by means of their 'wise' counsel, but ended up serving them and becoming more and more trapped in the 'culture contact' language because it was the only one to which the politicians would listen. And they discovered, of course, that there was no 'reasonable' middle ground between the extremes of the culture contact debate. Their ideal of 'separation and equality', the anthropological dimension of which they modelled – in large part – on Malinowski's muddled prescriptions, was yanked from under their feet in the course of the 1950s, as the Kolege ya Bana episode shows, and they were left with the flat assertions of cultural particularism that their texts displayed at the height of the apartheid era.

Kuper started his controversial review of American culture theory by making reference to the protracted debate about 'culture' in his native South

Africa, and the role of the practitioners of Volkekunde in that debate (Kuper 1999b: xii–xv). He had two reasons for making this reference. One was to explain his sceptical approach to the whole notion of 'culture' when it is conceived as an independent variable, determining (or at any rate, strongly shaping) the manner in which people think and behave. The other was to give insight into his disquiet at the 'culture wars' in American academe in the last decades of the twentieth century – the endless argument between those championing the virtues of a universal, high civilization to which all should aspire and conform, and those engaging in an often uncritical celebration of cultural difference and diversity (ibid.: 226–47).

I think the details of the sad episode of the Kolege ya Bana ba Afrika add to the link that Kuper saw between past and present 'culture wars'. These details reinforce his insistence that it is necessary to get outside these debates in order to grasp their futility. Earlier criticism of Volkekunde concentrated on the objectionable aspects of its narrow vision of a South Africa fractured into a series of culture-bearing ethnic groups. But part of this critique was an unstated rehearsal of some of the tenets of the 'civilizing mission'. The unspoken question underpinning this critique was why the volkekundiges would not recognize that there was a universal culture to which all South Africans could, and should, conform. The 'civilizing mission' can, however, easily be as dictatorial, and as condescending, as its particularist opponent, as Kuper's reflections on the American 'culture wars' (ibid.) remind us. Would black South Africans necessarily have been better served in the middle of the last century had the proponents of universal 'civilization', including the stern censors of 'objectionable' African custom, actually won the day?

The tale of the UP volkekundiges and the Kolege ya Bana serves to highlight one further aspect of current debate. Kuper argued that the American culture wars are, in many ways, futile because they turn on a premise the antagonists actually share: the idea that culture is more than an abstraction to be 'described, interpreted and even perhaps explained', that it is 'a source of explanation in itself' (ibid.: xi). The volkekundiges may have shifted their stance within the South African culture wars over the period between the 1940s and the 1960s, but they stuck very firmly to this particular premise throughout the apartheid period. In the circumstances they faced, this premise brought them to an unparalleled disaster.

If anthropologists wish to wield sensible influence in a world presently obsessed with 'culture', one might conclude from the example of Eiselen that their biggest single contribution may be to show that 'tribes' are not controlled by 'traditions'.

Notes

1. All translations from Afrikaans in the text below are mine.
2. University of Pretoria Archives (UPA), B3: UP Minutes, Vol. 6. Minutes of the Meeting of Council, 13 September 1948. R2948 (Report of the Committee regarding a University Institution for Natives under the protection of the University of Pretoria [Chairman: Professor W.M. Eiselen]).
3. UPA, B3: UP Minutes, Vol. 8. Minutes of the Meeting of Council, 25 August 1948. R7448 (Tentative proposals to Senate for consideration by the Committee regarding the Kolege ya Bana ba Afrika); B3: UP Minutes, Vol 8. Minutes of the Meeting of Senate, 14 September 1950. S7509 (Report of the Committee regarding the founding of a Bantu University and the future of the Kolege ya Bana ba Afrika [Chairman: Professor P.J. Coertze]); B3: UP Minutes, Vol. 9. Minutes of the Meeting of Council, 27 August 1951. R7830 (A Bantu University under the Trusteeship of the University of Pretoria).
4. National Archives of South Africa, TAB Pamphlet P274 6375. Kolege ya Bana ba Afrika: University College for Non-Whites – Yes or No? (Pamphlet issued by the Temporary Committee) Johannesburg, 1946.
5. See note 2.
6. UPA: Personnel Files (Restricted): Professor W.M. Eiselen (1947–9). Dr W.M. Eiselen to the Rector, UP, 17 August 1946; Dr W.M. Eiselen to the Registrar, UP, 10 April 1947.
7. UPA: B3 UP Minutes, Vol. 6. Minutes of the Meeting of the Board of the Faculty of Humanities, 15 September 1947; Minutes of the Meeting of the Board of the Faculty of Commerce and Public Administration, 17 September 1947; Minutes of the Meeting of Council, 3 November 1947.
8. UPA, B3: UP Minutes, Vol. 6. Minutes of an Extraordinary Meeting of the Board of the Faculty of Commerce and Public Administration, 3 December 1947.
9. Statutes of the Union of South Africa. University of Pretoria (Private) Act (Act 30 of 1930). Cape Town: Government Printer.
10. Author's interview with *Eerwaarde* (the Reverend) J.H. van Wyk, Pretoria, 3 August 2006.
11. J.H. van Wyk (see note 10) recalled these editorials clearly, and ruefully, after more than fifty years, so one may assume that their criticism of the Kolege ya Bana, to which he was devoted, was pointed.
12. UPA, Personnel Files (Restricted): Professor W.M. Eiselen (1947–9). Secretary, Union Department of Education to the Registrar, UP, 4 September 1948.
13. UPA, Personnel Files (Restricted): Professor W.M. Eiselen (1947–9). Professor W.M. Eiselen to the Rector, UP, 14 October 1949.
14. UPA, Academic Administration Microfiche Files (AAMF), Roll 135 (*Samewerking met Kolleges* [Cooperation with Colleges]). Registrar, UP, to the Secretary, Union Department of Education, 11 October 1948.
15. UPA, AAMF, Roll 135. Rector, UP, to the Secretary, Union Department of Education, 28 June 1950.
16. See note 3.
17. UPA, B3: UP Minutes, Vol. 9. Minutes of a Meeting of Council, 27 August 1951. R7830 (A Bantu University under the Trusteeship of the University of Pretoria), 27 August 1951.
18. UPA, B3: UP Minutes, Vol. 12. Minutes of a Meeting of Council, 14 October 1957. R751 (Memorandum of Evidence regarding the Implementation of the Policy of Separate University Education); UPA, AAMF, Roll 135. Secretary, Commission to consider the Draft Legislation on Separate University Education, to the Registrar, UP, 18 October 1957; UPA, B3: UP Minutes, Vol 12. Minutes of a Meeting of Council, 21 November 1957 (Draft Legislation on Separate University Education for Whites and Non-Whites: Evidence submitted by a Sub-Committee of Council); UPA, AAMF, Roll 135. Secretary, Commission to consider the Draft Legislation on Separate University Education, to the Registrar, UP, 2 April 1958.

Chapter 3

'Making Indians': Debating Indigeneity in Canada and South Africa

Evie Plaice

For a rather slim document, the Canadian Indian Act is extraordinarily contentious. Considering that it governs the everyday lives of a small but vital sector of the Canadian population, perhaps this should come as no surprise. But for those who are not First Nations Canadians, the Act and its unerring impact on all manner of daily choices and decisions goes largely unnoticed. Just how forceful the impact of the Indian Act has been on Canadian First Nations, and just how divisive, became abundantly clear when Bill C–31 was introduced in 1986. This long anticipated piece of legislation reinstated generations of Canadian aboriginal women and their children who had lost their aboriginal status when they married non-aboriginal men. Its implementation involved sorting through many thousands of documents tracing individual women's lives in order to ascertain their right to Indian status, a process aptly described by a Mi'kmaq colleague and former Indian Affairs employee as 'making Indians.'

The Indian Act has in fact been 'making Indians' since its inception in 1876. Bill C–31 is just a particularly stark example of this. In the following discussion, I use Canadian and South African case studies of land restitution to illustrate how anthropology has aided and abetted the process of making policy to manage difference in what Gerald Sider describes as 'more or less ... a patch-job over the contradictions between race and nation' (Sider 2006: 4). More to the point, the practice of anthropology itself has been influenced by its involvement in the policies of identity management. Anthropology is in large part a comparative discipline and, as this volume shows, comparison works as well for the practice of the discipline itself as for its subject matter.

In their introduction to this volume, Deborah James and Christina Toren draw a distinction between the universalizing and the diversifying tendencies in anthropology, a distinction that can be discerned in the parallel but opposing trajectories taken by anthropological practice in South Africa and in Canada. Both the distinctions and the involvement become clearer in comparison: South Africa's rejection of apartheid has caused its social scientists to privilege universalist values and focus on policies geared to the greater public good, while in light of the 'rights revolution' (Ignatieff 2000) Canadian academics have privileged difference and are apt to champion minority rights. The theme of this chapter, then, is the interplay between anthropology as a discipline and the status of difference in two contrasting contexts – South Africa and Canada – and is also in part a response to Adam Kuper's 'The Return of the Native (2003).

When Kuper wrote 'The Return of the Native', his attack was aimed at the advocacy movement in anthropology for revitalizing in the term 'indigenous' the defunct and pejorative category of the 'primitive.' For Sider, however, much more appears to be at stake. Anthropology's involvement with the task of nation-building has 'left anthropology with an analytical legacy that is a continuing intellectual disaster for us, for whatever public that now remains interested, and especially for the peoples we seek to study and to serve' (Sider 2006: 2). These two commentaries tackle the issue of indigeneity in markedly different but complementary ways, and I draw upon them here to elucidate my discussion of anthropological practice in South Africa and Canada.

Anthropology and Policy

During the late 1990s, South African anthropologists underwent a period of introspection about the nature of their disciplinary practice: its motivations, its meanings and its history (Hammond-Tooke 1997; McAllister 1997). Such a process would have been equally pertinent for Canadian anthropology. The influence of the social sciences and especially anthropology on the shaping of twentieth century South Africa is all too apparent. Several key Afrikaner ethnologists were in various ways supporters of the nationalist movement that gave rise to the National Party, and their thinking about difference helped shape the system of apartheid (see Sharp, this volume). The connections may be somewhat less contentious in Canada, but they are equally invidious. Working within the constraints of the Indian Act, Canadian social scientists have researched treaties and land claims and assisted social and welfare organizations serving aboriginal communities. Before the Second World War, ideas about ethnic diversity were not that different in the two countries. The Ethnological Section of the South African Department of Native Affairs was set up to administer 'the Bantu races.' Black South Africans were confined to economically unviable 'Bantustans,' while the requirement to pay 'hut taxes' ensured a steady flow of male workers to the gold mines and their hostels around Johannesburg. In Canada the Indian Act arose out of a need to 'manage' aboriginal populations, either by keeping them separate or attempting to assimilate them into mainstream Canadian society, and led to treaties, reserves, relocations and residential schooling. This 'management' of Canadian aboriginal peoples over the past century has since been critiqued as at best 'misplaced benevolence' (Furniss 1992) and at worst 'cultural genocide' (Chrisjohn 1997). Apartheid, of course, turned South Africa into a pariah state. The academics, scholars and intellectuals whose ideas lay behind these policies believed in what they were doing and felt it their duty to engage in policy making and political advocacy. Some became profoundly disturbed by the eventual outcomes of their ideas and, of course, there were always hidden agendas.

South African anthropologist, David Hammond-Tooke, discusses the role played by the government Ethnological Section and suggests that, for the most part, anthropological research was too ponderous and slow to support the demands of apartheid policy-makers (1997: 117).[1] However, certain key concepts current in anthropology at the time did have influence. Between 1930 and 1969, the Ethnological Section was run by N.J. Van Warmelo, a German-trained Afrikaner linguist specializing in Nguni languages. A Boasian in his attention to vernacular texts and micro-history, Van Warmelo's *Preliminary Survey of the Bantu Tribes of South Africa* (1935) became a seminal text for both anthropologists and the South African government. Though Van Warmelo himself was not an active nationalist, his detailed survey was later used to establish the Bantustans of the apartheid regime. The nationalist component was added by Van Warmelo's colleague Werner Eiselen, who founded the country's first Department of Ethnology at the University of Stellenbosch in 1926, and Eiselen's student P.J. Coertze, who introduced ethnology to the University of Pretoria. Coertze developed the idea of politically and economically independent Volk (People) units in his introductory textbook (Coertze 1959), which Hammond-Tooke describes as almost identical to Boas's *General Anthropology* (1938).[2] Coertze's textbook formed the basis for all ethnology taught in Afrikaans universities during the apartheid era, including the 'historically black universities' set up under apartheid to cater for non-white students.

In their government directed pamphlet, Coertze and his colleagues presented two potential solutions to the 'Native problem in South Africa': equality through assimilation, or differentiation and segregation. In post-Second-World-War, nationalist South Africa, it was the idea of apartheid that took root. The Afrikaner National Party was elected into office in 1948 as a direct rebuke to British imperialism, and especially to Smut's support for Britain in the war. Integral to the idea of nationalist-inspired separation was the philosophy of 'ethnos,' or distinct and enduring cultures, and although these ideas were also debated among American and European social scientists of the time, they were pushed to extremes in South Africa.[3] Nationalist ideologues developed rationales for implementing apartheid that had the dual effect of enhancing

Afrikaner ethnic identity through affirmative action at the same time as allowing for the social separation and economic exploitation of the black population. Schoeman, another of Eiselen's students, strongly advocated that 'blacks, especially women and children, should be isolated as far as possible in reserves so that Western influences could be controlled' (Gordon 1988: 541). Eiselen himself thought that the 'Race Question' was as much a white problem as it was black, and argued for government policy to be geared towards 'developing a "higher Bantu culture and not producing Black Europeans."' In fact, according to Gordon, Eiselen felt that 'assimilation was encouraged precisely because officials and other whites denigrated indigenous culture' (ibid.)

Eiselen's comments were evidently aimed at the largely liberal English-speaking social anthropologists who, as a counterbalance to the growing vigour of nationalist apartheid, argued for assimilation rather than separation. These included Winifred Hoernlé, Philip Mayer, Ellen Hellman, Monica and Godfrey Wilson, J.D. and Eileen Krige, and Hilda and Leo Kuper, many of whom had attended seminars given by the key social anthropologists of the time, including Radcliffe-Brown and Malinowski, and who helped form departments of social anthropology at the English-speaking universities of Cape Town, Natal, Rhodes (in Grahamstown) and the Witwatersrand (in Johannesburg) (see Barnard, this volume, for a more detailed discussion). Despite counter-arguments and resistance on the part of many social scientists, however, the National Party was able to sustain its apartheid regime for more than forty years. It is hardly surprising that the response of my Natal colleagues to the demise of apartheid during the 1990s should be an ardent belief in social justice derived from democratic and universalist principles. The anthropological response to apartheid was almost ostrich-like in South Africa. As the apartheid state became established – following Nazi lines and installing Afrikaner nationalists with links to the Dutch Reformed Church and the Broederbond (lit. 'Brotherhood')[4] in key positions of government, business and education – so the English-speaking intellectual and academic community sought to distance themselves. The discipline of anthropology was riven into the two distinct traditions of British social anthropology and Afrikaner volkekundiges (ethnologists/anthropologists). Theoretical positions and intellectual ideas became inseparable from political allegiances. If not active proponents of apartheid, the ethnologists were at least sympathetic to the National Party government. They explored difference, focused their research on the customs and traits that made groups distinct, and indulged in affirmative action – supporting research at Afrikaans universities and eventually establishing the historically black universities with a full complement of pro-National Party Afrikaner academics. The social anthropologists, on the other hand, focused increasingly on social structure, migration and change. The theoretical and ideological paradigm of political economy when it arrived on the academic scene during the 1970s, gave vital intellectual credence to their liberal socialism in the inevitable shadow cast over the discipline by colonialism and apartheid.

The sea change in academia has come stealthily in the wake of political transformations. In 2000, the two societies that had grown out of the Volkekunde tradition and social anthropology joined forces and set aside moral and political principles that previously neither had wanted to surrender. The ANC government even has an Anthropological Service whose task is almost identical to the one Van Warmelo carried out thirty years ago under the National Party government.[5] The new South Africa, it seems, is redolent with hard-earned cultural identities that no one wants to give up. Like the many established literary writers in the country, South African anthropologists are confronting the complexities of the new social and cultural orders in their 'Rainbow Nation,' including difference. Kiernan describes the situation that anthropologists faced under apartheid as being a 'David and Goliath' affair, and lucidly outlines the limitations that political choices foist upon anthropological research as the pre-eminent form of social criticism to the neglect of analysing human cultural creativity (1997: 65–6). This gives a rather different spin to the choices thus far explored: that while cultural advocacy remains a matter of supporting the powerless and the voiceless, it should not be at the cost of change, transformation and creativity.

In Canada on the other hand, and despite decades of what Paine (1971, 1977) and his colleagues described as 'tutelage', the overwhelming thrust of government policy has been assimilationist. Concurrent with government policy that aimed to keep aboriginal people on reserves removed from white settlement and development in the south, assimilation was thought to be the only humane and practical way to save remnant indigenous populations. The Indian Act has been fundamentally flawed from the outset by the need to address these contradictory goals, effectively placing Native people in a 'goldfish bowl,' where they are simultaneously in full view of Canadian society yet unable to participate (Dyck 1991). The epitome of this impossible dilemma must surely be the system of residential schooling which removed Native children from their families, denied them the right to speak their own languages or practice their own cultures, and trained them in domestic and labouring skills so menial that they were effectively precluded from entering larger Canadian society. And yet, assimilationist policies were not only seen as moral but also reflected the theoretical orientations of many Canadian policy makers and social scientists of the time (Buchanan 2006). Diamond Jenness, for instance, was Dominion Anthropologist in 1947 when he proposed the termination of the Indian Act, and much of his writing advocates assimilation (Kulchyski 1993). This accords well with the influential beliefs and practices of Duncan Campbell Scott, who was in charge of the Department of Indian Affairs from 1913 until his retirement in 1932. Scott's ideas about his Native charges are eloquently exposed in his poetry, and were initially inspired by his experiences as a commissioner for Treaty 9, signed in 1905, between native peoples in northern Ontario and Edward VII of Britain (Dragland 1994). Indian administration prior to Scott's time had been guided by concerns to open up the country for development – with or without the compliance and acquiescence of its aboriginal peoples. Given these circumstances, Scott's desire to assimilate could at least be seen as a marginally more humane guiding principle in administration (Cullingham 1995: Titley 1986).

The turning point for Canada came in 1969, when Trudeau's proposal to dismantle the Indian Act galvanized the First Nations into organized response. Very much part of both the policy making process and the ensuing debate was the Hawthorn Report of 1966 and 1967. Professor of Anthropology at the University of British Columbia, Harry Hawthorn, and his colleague Marc-Adelade Tremblay, Professor of Anthropology at Laval, were commissioned by the government to conduct a survey explicitly to help in the formation of new Indian policy.[6] Yet *A Survey of the Contemporary Indians of Canada* (Hawthorn 1966–1967) was all but ignored by the writers of the 1969 White Paper which proposed to abolish the Indian Act. The writers of the Hawthorn Report acknowledged that most aboriginal rights emanate from the Indian Act and, far from advocating its dissolution, recommend that it be enhanced by a programme of 'Citizen Plus' which would guarantee continued special rights for Canada's indigenous peoples. Hawthorn and his colleagues argued that the role of the Department of Indian Affairs should be one of advocacy through lobbying government on behalf of Native interests. In short, the Canadian shift away from policies of assimilation, towards multiculturalism and increased advocacy for First Nations demands, began some time before the 1960s in anthropological circles, and should have found a powerful voice in governmental policy making through the Hawthorn Report. The Report instead formed the basis of the First Nations' rejection of government policy, and Canadian anthropologists have become increasingly involved in aboriginal advocacy ever since. First Nations claims to land, resources and self-governance have been strengthened by legal precedents recognizing and furthering aboriginal title, and by the social science research into land use, occupation and way of life which supports this. Throughout the 1990s, dramatic exposés of the effects of residential schooling on aboriginal families and communities added to the general discomfiture over the abject failure of past policies.

In Canada, then, assimilation has been roundly rejected in favour of a kind of constitutionalized affirmative action for First Nations people whereas in South Africa democracy is interpreted as supporting a universalist principle and is used to enhance majority rule against any kind of claim to special status that ethnic identity might bestow. One might be tempted to say that each country has come to its present understanding by parallel paths moving in opposite directions, and that each is likely to suffer very similar learning curves as a consequence. However ardently fought-for, the granting of reserve-based self-government for Canada's First Nations begins to look eerily like the imposition of Bantustans by the National Party government of apartheid South Africa, where John Amagoalik's call for 'the right to self-government, a right to govern yourselves with your own institutions' (quoted in Asch 1997: 214) almost perfectly paraphrases the ideological justification of apartheid: 'The Boer Nation is not so selfish and short-sighted by nature that it cannot give to the black race rights to autonomous development in his own separate area' (Schoeman, quoted in Gordon 1988: 541).

Whether reserves or Bantustans, self-defined or externally imposed, this kind of separation is surely untenable because it is so vulnerable to inequality. Canadian First Nation reserves are every bit as poverty stricken as South Africa's Bantustans, and largely for the same reasons: that neither is economically viable. Duncan Campbell Scott may have been the perpetrator of what has been described as some of the worst Indian policy in Canadian history (Cullingham 1995), yet his ideas on coerced assimilation were shared by most of his liberal Canadian contemporaries. Late twentieth-century reaction has been to enhance aboriginal identity. Sally Weaver once drew attention to the conundrum posed by the Citizen Plus status proposed in the Hawthorn Report by observing that Canadian politics were always likely to reflect the underlying liberal-democratic and universalizing values of Canadian society, and that in order to retain special status aboriginal peoples 'will have to counteract this force by fully rationalizing their own position with each change in the political climate' (Weaver 1983: xii). The connection between anthropology and apartheid again becomes apparent: while anthropological theory moved in a very different intellectual direction to the one taken by the apartheid ideologues, the ideas in both countries and in both contexts have a disturbingly common basis in their attempts to classify human groups as enduring cultural categories *and* administer them as such. As South Africa is now finding out, once established, ethnic and cultural identities are hard to resolve, especially since so much injustice and suffering has gone into defining and defending them. Indeed, is it possible to address the wrongs of past policies without recourse to the same imposed categories that gave rise to inequality in the first place? In using the example of a 'self-styled delegation of South African Boers' attempting to claim threatened minority status at the inaugural meeting of the Forum of Indigenous Peoples, Kuper's answer (Kuper 2003) is straightforward: rights claimed on the basis of ethnic difference are hard to justify in any circumstances. Canada's Citizen Plus status might also prove his point since it has enabled the Indian Act to continue to ghettoize much of the country's aboriginal population.

Rights and Ethnic Identity

My first example reinforces Kuper's point by illustrating the immense difficulty of identifying the appropriate sector of a population to be the recipients of rights based upon ethnic identity. The actual process of defining sheds light on the nature of cultural identities. Both in the case of the Boers and in my experiences in Labrador, assessing who has a legitimate claim to these kinds of rights has a lot to do with the context in which the definition emerges. It often seems that who *qualifies* varies according to *who* qualifies.

In short, the process by which these categories become legitimated is very much part of the definition. I arrived in Labrador for my first stint of fieldwork during a period of intense ethnopolitical activity among Labradorians, triggered in response to Trudeau's aboriginal agenda. As early as 1949, however, the province's first premier had scuttled any claims to ethnic difference for Labrador's aboriginal population by insisting that his new province contained only Canadians. The Indian Act thus had no jurisdiction in the province. Instead, a series of Native Agreements between the federal and provincial governments covered costs that would otherwise have been paid by the federal Department of Indian Affairs. Whole communities rather than individuals were designated 'Native', a tidy solution to administrative problems that left the messy business of identifying who was 'Native', who was 'Aboriginal' and who was 'Indigenous' to the various Native organizations that emerged during the 1970s. The problem reached its apogee during the 1980s as more and more rights were confirmed and concessions made to Labrador's Native populations (Plaice 1990, 1996). But there had always been a protracted debate around membership in these organizations. The Innu Nation has remained exclusive, covering the First Nation communities of Sheshatshit and Utshimassits (now Natuashish). The Labrador Inuit Association (LIA) on the other hand has always included the descendants of over two hundred years of Scottish, English and Inuit miscegenation, known locally as Settlers. The LIA's justification to its parent organization, the Inuit Tapirisat of Canada, was that Settlers and Inuit were inextricably bound by family ties, way of life, and shared political and economic goals (Brice-Bennett 1977).

In choosing to define its constituency through way of life rather than bloodlines, the LIA had to rely heavily on historical and geographical factors. The 'Labrador way of life' is a coastal adaptation shared by both Inuit and Settlers that delineates the territory the LIA can claim through extensive and enduring land use and occupancy. However, the way of life is essentially seasonal, fluid and mobile, qualities that were exacerbated by the arrival of Goose Bay Air Base in 1941 when droves of Inuit and Settlers moved to central Labrador for work. The LIA's attempts to manage the vagaries of economic migration by limiting membership to those whose affiliation with the coastal communities predates 1941 left many outside its mandate. Once the LIA began to receive health and educational benefits, the divisions became acrimonious, splitting communities and even dividing families where it is not uncommon for siblings to be excluded on the basis of the season and hence the location in which they were born. In 1986, the Labrador Metis Association was formed to accommodate those excluded from the LIA, but it was a decade behind in its ability to attract support: neither bureaucrats nor academics have shown much interest in an ethnically 'Metis' organization that is pitted against longstanding and 'bona fide' aboriginal organizations such as the LIA and the Innu Nation (Kennedy 1987, 1988).

The case of the Settlers raises questions about the criteria for inclusion in groups that are motivated by ethnic or cultural minority status. While the LIA avoided the use of bloodlines and therefore race as a criterion, the essential problem of exclusion and inclusion did not go away. In fact, the LIA had to resort to using bloodlines increasingly as their status as an aboriginal organization stabilized. There is a particular poignancy here: adaptation to challenges and circumstance shaped the Labrador way of life for both Inuit and Settlers, yet it is adaptation that now selectively discredits claims of aboriginality or indigeneity in Labrador. What makes the Labrador Inuit and Settlers unique is also what renders them slightly less than legitimate: as ethnic populations they are neither discrete nor primordial. The definitions of Settler, Metis and Inuit are, of course, largely political constructs. They have been shaped over the decades by the strictures of the Indian Act which, in 1939, was changed to include Inuit under its definition of 'Indian'.

Minorities and the Public Good

The scales of justice seem to have swung in the opposite direction in the new South Africa, where there is a clear reluctance to allow minority groups to pervert what is now seen as the 'public good.' My second example illustrates precisely this. Cato Manor, one of the first cases to be brought before the newly formed Land Commission Court of South Africa, was the first legal test of the notion of 'public good' (Plaice 1998). Part of the Greater Durban Metropolitan Area (eThekwini), a fast-growing urban zone of at least 3 million and the country's premier port on the Indian Ocean, Cato Manor consists of some 4,500 acres of vacant land surrounded by white suburbs on the city's outskirts. Like District Six in Cape Town and Sophiatown in Johannesburg, Cato Manor was cleared under apartheid during the 1960s. It had been the farm of George Cato, Durban's first mayor when Natal was declared a British colony in 1843, but increasingly accommodated Indian indentured labourers brought over by the British to work in the sugar plantations and who later became market gardeners for the city's growing population. By the time it was incorporated into the Greater Durban Metropolitan Area in the 1930s, Cato Manor had become a thriving 'shackland' community with most of the land owned by Indians and sublet to Africans (Maylam and Edwards 1996: 416). Various Group Areas Acts progressively controlled land ownership until 1958, when Cato Manor was designated white and the land was expropriated. The estimated 120,000 African and 48,000 Indian inhabitants were relocated to townships at a considerable distance from the city, but Cato Manor itself had become too contentious to attract the intended white development. It remained vacant until the House of Delegates[7] began building low-cost housing for their constituents in the 1980s. However, a massive invasion of black squatters in 1992 put a stop to any further development.

The development of Cato Manor offered a rare opportunity to redress apartheid imbalances in urban housing. Cato Manor Development Association (CMDA) was formed in 1992, coordinating thirty organizations including the ANC, residents' and squatters' groups, and Durban City Council, and aiming to provide low-cost, largely black housing. However, despite financial support from the South African Reconstruction and Development Programme and the European Union, development in Cato Manor was stalled because of the contentious nature of land ownership in the area. In 1995, CMDA applied to the Land Claims Court to enforce Section 34 of the 1994 Restitution of Land Rights Act.[8] Their case was that the greater public good was served by allowing the comprehensive development project to go ahead unimpeded by claims from individuals that had been dispossessed during the clearances. Largely comprising social scientists that had fought apartheid, the executive had gone to court to bring about a quick and just resolution of the wrangling for the benefit of the greatest number of people, and in the witness stand they painted a glowing picture of the utopia they hoped to build in Cato Manor. Six weeks of contentious court hearings soon apprised them of the tenacity of former tenants' aspirations of return, however, and their utopian views were slowly pulled apart by the testimony of the claimants and their lawyers. The claimants argued that there was little to separate the current attempts at social engineering from the original clearances under apartheid except, perhaps, in that it was blacks rather than whites that were to benefit. Nevertheless it was a second dispossession and, given the slow and cumbersome developments to date, equally unlikely to have a utopian outcome – a claim with which even the development's key beneficiaries concurred – since violence had become endemic in the squatter community. The feeling was that Durban City Council, the original perpetrators of the clearances as well as an active member of CMDA, 'had blood on their hands' from these two socially engineered clearances of Cato Manor and, as 90-year-old Mr Seebran succinctly put it, 'they should get out of Cato Manor now, and stay out' (Plaice 1998).

Despite the obvious plight of Cato Manor's claimants, CMDA had the overwhelming support of most social activists, many of whom were academics from the local university. Most academic writing about Cato Manor's past sympathized with the black majority who had been unable to own land within the city of Durban. Not only was this a matter of 'public good' then, but also a matter of championing those most oppressed. In some ways, the claimants represent a more nuanced instance of the kind of claim that the Boers had attempted to make at the Indigenous Peoples Forum – except of course the Afrikaners had come by their own choice while the Indians had arrived as indentured labourers under the British Raj. My concern here is how, as anthropologists and advocates, we go about selecting the causes we champion. In South Africa, the long, painful and to some extent guilt-inducing journey out of apartheid has inevitably been one of the persuading factors in making these choices. Allegiances are slow to die, and for much of the previous five decades, the 'enemy' had been clearly identifiable as the ethnically biased Afrikaner National Party of the apartheid government. Those in need of championing were the oppressed black majority, and all others were somehow lost sight of in the battle. Old Mr Seebran may well have been an extortionist landlord. But he had also been an ardent supporter of the ANC and a committed activist against apartheid. The area is still ringed by some of Durban's most impressive Hindu temples, built by Tamil- and Telugu-speaking labourers with artefacts and skills brought with them from India when they settled in Cato Manor. These are now included in regular tour itineraries, especially during *Holi, Diwali, Kavadi* and the colourful local firewalking ceremonies, flocked to by many local Indian families, holy men and mystics as well as an increasing number of academics and sightseers. Cato Manor has an unmistakeably Indian past, and it is likely to have a very chequered – and hopefully also a very cosmopolitan – future.

Conclusion

In 'The Return of the Native,' Kuper points out that the term 'indigeneity' has become conflated with small-scale, nomadic, largely hunting and gathering societies that were once categorized as 'primitive' in contrast to notions of civilization. It is a ploy he identifies with Eiselen, the 'architect of apartheid,' who 'rejected the conventional racial determinism of white South Africa [and instead] substituted anthropological ideas of cultural determinism and cultural evolution that served just as well to justify policies of segregation. People designated as natives were denied civil rights within South Africa because they were supposed to be completely different culturally from so-called civilized peoples' (2002b: 2).[9] And, Kuper suggests, this also underpins the 'Kalahari Debate' in which Richard Lee's assumption that the San are a pristine hunter-gatherer society is challenged by Edwin Wilmsen's argument that they are the product of colonial history, local politics and regional economics (Lee 1979; Lee and Solway 1990; Wilmsen 1989; Wilmsen and Denbow 1990). It is, nevertheless, usually the small-scale nomadic and dispersed societies that have been marginalized by colonialism and who are, potentially, in need of advocacy. A clause in the constitution of the American Anthropology Association calls for anthropologists to support the endeavours of all indigenous peoples, regardless of the merits of these endeavours. This begs the question of whether this is the case merely because they are indigenous or because such cases are a matter of 'culture', something about which anthropologists are wont to specialize? In similar vein, Canadian anthropologists are reacting against the most flawed strictures of the Indian Act in which their advocacy becomes an apology for the bad assimilationist policy of the past, over which there is still considerable shared guilt. Like the tendency for social scientists and especially anthropologists in South Africa to side with the demands of the majority regardless of those trampled by such demands, Canadian social scientists want to be seen to be actively in support of minorities, especially where these are also cultural minorities who can be categorized as indigenous. The past entanglements from which anthropology in both countries is emerging can best be summarized in Sider's assessment, that anthropologists have mistaken as legitimate those categories which are in fact the political tools of nation building. Given that the discussion is of 'culture' rather than 'indigeneity,' Kuper's warning is very similar:

> the more one considers the best modern work on culture by anthropologists, the more advisable it must appear to avoid the hyper-referential word altogether, and to talk more precisely of knowledge, or belief, or art, or technology, or tradition, or even of ideology ... There are fundamental epistemological problems, and these cannot be solved by tiptoeing around the notion of culture, or by refining definitions. The difficulties become most acute when ... culture shifts from something to be described, interpreted, even perhaps explained, and is treated instead as a source of explanation in itself ... Political and economic forces cannot be wished away, or assimilated to systems of knowledge and belief. And that, I will suggest, is the ultimate stumbling block in the way of cultural theory, certainly given its current pretensions. (Kuper 1999b: x–xi)

Courts in Canada and in South Africa seem to prefer historians to anthropologists as expert witnesses. Perhaps as much as anything else, this should give us pause to reconsider what it is that anthropology can bring to the task of advocacy and to the selection of causes.

Notes

An earlier version of this chapter was published in R. Darnell and J. Harrison (eds), *Historicizing Canadian Anthropology*, Vancouver: University of British Columbia Press. I gratefully acknowledge the permission of University of British Columbia Press to use this version here.

1. Weaver (1981) made the same comment about Canadian policy making.
2. Except for his contentious treatment of the concept of culture (Hammond-Tooke 1997: 129).
3. Sharp (1981) gives the most sensitive non-partisan discussion of this theory as it was applied in South Africa.
4. A white male secret society, in the nature of freemasonry, with strong Dutch Reformed Church links and substantial influence in both government and business in South Africa during apartheid.
5. Still staffed, ironically, not by the social anthropologists of the anti-apartheid struggle but by Volkekunde-trained ethnologists.
6. Lester B. Pearson was still in power at the time. He retired and was succeeded by Trudeau in 1968.
7. Institution which enabled Indian representation in South Africa's apartheid tricameral government.
8. Section 34 of the Act allows for the dismissal of land restoration if, 'a) it is in the public interest that the rights in question should not be restored to any claimant; and b) the public or any substantial part thereof will suffer substantial prejudice unless (such) an order is made'.
9. This quote is drawn from an earlier version of Kuper's paper, later given at the Max Planck Institute for Social Anthropology, Halle, Germany, June 2002 and eventually published as Kuper (2003).

Chapter 4

Culture in the Periphery: Anthropology in the Shadow of Greek Civilization

Dimitra Gefou-Madianou

'Culture wars' have raged in anthropology for more than a century.[1] Definitions of the concept have been advanced and fiercely contested. In one of the strands of this debate, proponents of a single culture–civilization nexus have confronted those who propose the existence of a multiplicity of cultures. Situated in the context of evolutionary theory this concept assumed a universal hierarchy of progress: as civilizations evolved through time, humanity became increasingly more sophisticated and logical, more 'cultured' in the Latin sense; in other words, the theory went, people accrued more civilization. For specific historical and political reasons, this notion of culture has prevailed until today, although not unchallenged, in the confines of universally hegemonic Western discourses (like the case discussed here).

Anthropology, at a very early stage, questioned the validity of such evolutionist assertions and repudiated their obvious political implications. Franz Boas's suggestion, early in the twentieth century, that cultures should be thought of in the plural and approached within their own contexts, dealt a severe blow to hierarchical concepts of civilizations based on technological or other forms of progress. Cultures, for Boas, came to refer to historically determined ways of life, expressed through artefacts, institutions and ways of behaviour that are culturally acquired through learning and socialization: a process through which new characteristics are appropriated in an 'open' and creative manner. Boas's approach to cultures was not, however, adopted by later anthropologists (Stocking 1968; Rapport and Overing 2000).

Bringing a useful critical perspective to bear upon these culture wars, Kuper's characteristically eloquent historical and contextual account traces many of the preoccupations of the American tradition of cultural anthropology to three European traditions: French, German and British (Kuper 1999b, see also 1994b). He suggests that in order 'to understand culture, we must first deconstruct it', separate its elements so as to 'explore the changing configurations in which language, knowledge, techniques, political ideologies, rituals, commodities, and so on are related to each other' (Kuper 1999b: 245). Maintaining that culture cannot be explained in its own terms, he suggests it should be approached in terms of what people are doing with it in everyday practice (ibid.: 246–7). Most of us attribute to the concept a variety of traits and meanings depending on the theoretical approach we espouse which in turn depends upon the politics we serve (Baumann 1996; Rapport and Overing 2000).

This chapter will follow Kuper in approaching culture not as a taken-for-granted analytical tool, but as an ethnographic term and/or category. In this manner, it will seek to examine how 'culture' has been used in the context of anthropology's development within the Greek academy, and how it shifts its meaning(s) under different historical and political context(s) in which – and by which – the term is shaped.

Culture Coming to the Periphery: Whose Term is *Politismos?*

With the debate over culture still open in the centres of anthropological thought in Europe and North America, in countries like Greece, whose role in the development and entrenchment of anthropology has been historically more circumscribed, an added dimension of the issues discussed above should be taken into consideration. This will reveal that it is not only the meaning and usefulness of the concept of culture that are debated, but the status and content of anthropology as a discipline. In this peripheral European milieu, the debate over culture involves additional dimensions which, on top of their academic nature, exhibit socio-economic and political aspects intimately related to local historical and socio-political traditions embedded in deep and often divisive national histories. Among other things, these aspects are intimately associated with the delayed introduction of anthropology into Greek universities (Gefou-Madianou 1993), the manner in which this entrance was planned within the wider framework of national politics, the way it developed in the last two decades, and the logic governing its dialogue with other powerful disciplines in academia and Greek society at large. What is very clear is that both social anthropology as a discipline and 'culture' in the anthropological sense of the term were absent from Greek academia until the late 1980s.

As I have argued elsewhere, the delayed introduction of anthropology into Greek universities is directly associated with the prolonged process of state formation in modern Greece, and with the strong tradition of ethnocentrism which underpinned it (Gefou-Madianou 1993, 2000, 2003a). The predominance of a century-long ethnocentric tradition of folklore, whose echo is somehow still reverberating, and of a positivistic historiography and archaeology[2] in the service of the national project led, on the one hand, towards a narrow, introverted and ethnocentric definition of culture; and, on the other, obstructed the timely development of social sciences in general, and of anthropology in particular. Indeed, this ideology was further aggravated by the fact that Greek discourses about culture were formulated not only locally, but also in dialogue with European and more global discourses wherein Greek state formation was directly linked with ancient Greek culture and civilization (Danforth 1984; Herzfeld 1987). This obstruction worked both at the level of ideology and at that of a deeply rooted collective consciousness.

The main reason for this state of affairs is that all social sciences, and anthropology in particular, are informed almost programmatically by a critical intellectual and ideological stance toward the logic and practices entailed in all national – or for some nationalistic – projects. The hegemonic discourse of the Greek nation-state could only promote a scientific knowledge which would be useful, objective and 'nationally correct'; in other words, a science in the service of nation building. This nation was imagined as a monocultural linear descendant of the great ancient Greek civilization and culture, namely *politismos*.[3] It was this understanding of culture that was at the very centre of the self-conceptualization of the state itself and of society.

This picture is aptly expressed in the semantic ambiguity with which the term politismos has been loaded in Greece. I would argue that the meaning of culture in Greek entails not only the familiar ambiguity between culture and civilization, discussed above, but also an epistemological debate within Greek academia. On the one hand, the concept of politismos has for a long time been identified with classical archaeology and ancient monuments, that is the love of ancestors and antiquities, or *archaeolagneia*. On the other hand, a great number of folklorists, drawing from the German romantic idea of culture (*kultura*), have for a long time tried to link ancient Greek politismos with modern Greek folk culture, and through this with national identity at the level of language, material culture and the arts. In fact, this ideology was largely imported to Greece from European centres of classical studies where it was cultivated.[4]

This state of affairs continued for a long time until after the Second World War for a number of reasons, each connected with a specific historical conjunction. We had to wait until the end of the 1967–1974 military dictatorship or even the mid and in some cases the late 1980s in order to see the establishment of the first social science university departments and sections in general, and of social anthropology in particular. The introduction of new academic disciplines, including anthropology, was part of the 1982 New Reformatory Law for Higher Education Institutions, which changed the scene radically both at the level of ideology and also institutionally.[5] It is in this context of democratization and modernization that the aforementioned institutional development should be considered. Definitely, such processes towards modernization in the political, social and institutional life of the country have had a history that went back long before the 1970s. Clearly, though, in the above mentioned period they took on renewed urgency and were impregnated with a new set of meanings for another reason as well: the country's accession to the European Union (EU) in 1981. From having been conceptualized as the cradle of European civilization, what Herzfeld (1987) called 'a living ancestor' of Europe, Greece now tried to become an equal partner and member state in the context of the EU. It was during this period that a major shift regarding the concept of culture did occur, both in Greek society as a whole and in Greek academia, a movement from a withdrawn and inward-looking ethnocentric stance to a more open and cosmopolitan one. And while this certainly benefited the development of Greek social anthropology, it also had some negative implications as well. As it turned out, the situation was more complex than it had seemed to be.

More precisely, in contradistinction to the success of the relative democratization project, that of modernization came up against a number of difficulties not unrelated to the country's modern history. With the benefit of hindsight, the impulse to modernize produced rather mixed political and economic results and Greece remained largely a peripheral European country vis-à-vis the Western brokers of power in the EU. At the level of ideology and institutional policies, the concept of culture embedded in the modernization project – despite its seemingly open character – remained discursively confined within the positivistic arguments which had informed the grand narrative of Greek nation building. However Europeanized Greece tried to become, it hesitated to cut all ties that supposedly connected the country with ancient Greek politismos (civilization). In a sense, this insistence was at the very basis of the country's claims to be European. Moreover, it should be stressed that Europe, too, utilized Greek cultural symbols (like the Acropolis) for the construction of its own identity, as observed in the process of 'building' the EU. Similarly, Greece has appropriated, and often used locally, Western or European cultural constructs in its depiction of itself as the birthplace of Western civilization (Just 1995; Shore 2000). The same argument that animated the whole project of nation building in the nineteenth and early twentieth centuries, namely the inalienable kinship of modern Greece with its glorious ancient civilization, came to inform the late twentieth-century discourse that propelled the country into the fold of the EU.

This understanding makes itself accurately felt even at the level of everyday rhetoric. Culture and civilization are denoted in Greek by the same word, politismos, one refering to the other in an almost mechanical manner, and consequently any form of plurality imparted to the concept of culture is nullified and voided. It was only in 1998 that a newly published and highly acclaimed dictionary of the Greek language parted company with all other dictionaries in adding an entry for the term culture (kultura) itself, thus distinguishing between culture and civilization (Babiniotis 1998). Nevertheless, the new dictionary entry did not solve the problem, since for some intellectuals kultura is not a Greek word but a mere adoption of a foreign term: the concept was not created by and within the Greek language, it has not struck roots in it, and consequently has not produced any derivatives, a fact that makes its use in Greek very limited. Some social scientists including anthropologists still prefer to use the term politismos though they have to explain each time in which sense they use it – civilization or culture(s).

Given all this, anthropology in Greek academia found itself in a peculiar situation. On the one hand, the Europeanization and modernization of the country, however weighed down by its previously mentioned insistence on monocultural existence and attendant positivistic baggage, did introduce anthropology and other social sciences into Greek academia. In this manner, one might reasonably expect such disciplines to find soon their niche and develop their own discursively specific language (Gefou-Madianou 2000). But this was not an unproblematic process.

As was expected, the two newly established anthropology departments, at Panteion University, Athens, and at the University of the Aegean, Mitilíni (on the island of Lésvos), unfolded their wares and opened their doors to other disciplines and society at large, publicizing their very own peculiar trait: the study of human cultural diversity, that is the study of cultures in the plural. The bulk of ethnographic research, Ph.D. dissertations, and published anthropological work in the Greek language during the last two decades, both by Greek anthropologists and – in translation – the works of their European and American colleagues, are remarkable. They study human diversity and focus on cross-cultural comparison within and outside the country.

However, these positive developments were soon obstructed by forces within and outside Greece. At the very time that Greek universities were opening their doors to new critical disciplines such as social anthropology, and were attracting Western-trained scientists to return home and introduce and develop these new subjects, it was becoming more difficult to introduce or strengthen such subjects in Western European universities. This was a result of the audit culture that had been introduced into Western European institutions (Strathern 2000; Gefou-Madianou 2000, 2003a) and was soon introduced by the EU into Greek universities. This was done by means of the Community Support Frameworks funds managed by the Greek Ministry of National Education and Religion and in particular by the funds allocated for the Operational Programme for Education and Initial Professional Training (Gefou-Madianou 2000). This practice, and its attendant ideology, guided the state-dependent Greek universities towards a more applied approach to both research and curriculum development ultimately aimed at meeting the needs of the market. Ironically, then, the European intellectual tradition that had been introduced to Greece by Western-trained anthropologists (among others) who had staffed the newly established departments, turned against itself. The expectation of many academics for modernization in accordance with Western European standards failed. At the same time, the European orientation of Greece and, to an extent, its position as a fund-receiving country of the Southern European periphery, made the newly acquired cosmopolitan gaze of anthropology more vulnerable to the shift in emphasis towards a more market-driven approach to social services and public institutions (Gefou-Madianou 2000: 260–63). This was further underlined – as we shall see below – by the establishment of new departments in Greek universities in the service of this new applied orientation: departments which became the main recipients of EU funding.

At this point, 'culture' appeared to be a commonly used term by anthropologists, other academics, education administrators, policy makers and the market. All these people, or categories of people, including those belonging to the old and more established academic traditions, laid claims on culture in order to attract EU funds and to entrench their institutional position. Even before being officially introduced as a term in the Greek vocabulary, before acquiring a pluralistic and cosmopolitan character, and before being critically discussed, culture was thus appropriated by the technocrats and the market.

Anthropology, then, was faced with yet another problem concerning 'culture', which was far from merely methodological. Many of the above mentioned categories of people used the term 'culture' (politismos) as a taken-for-granted analytical term, defining it in their own way to suit their interests. The question this raised was: whose term is politismos? Who would be powerful enough to appropriate its meaning or, at least, to determine its usages in both the academia and society at large? For anthropologists, though, the question was of a different nature: in using culture as analytical term they were faced with the difficulty of explaining culture as an ethnographic term. At this point, what had become clear to them was that 'culture' warranted even more investigation as an ethnographic category in the Greek context.

Anthropology, Culture and the Powerful: Historical Certainties and Anthropological Dilemmas

To make the above picture more clear some ethnographic examples from within academia will be described. Given the wider context that has just been outlined above, it is evident that anthropology's introduction in the mid and late 1980s presented the new academic discipline with a number of tasks. First, Greek anthropologists had to translate and adapt to a local idiom the discursive framework of contemporary anthropology, with all its theoretical discoveries, controversies and quibbles. To this end, the development of a Greek anthropological discourse was their first priority. Second, they had to make this material, as well as the wealth of ethnographic case studies it involved, relevant to university students, themselves a product of a national education system with a long history of positivistic and 'hellenocentric' training. Third, they had to debate anthropological notions and methods with colleagues from different social science departments, many of whom had little knowledge of anthropology itself. And fourth, they had to 'sell' anthropology to an ever watchful and institutionally powerful Ministry of National Education and Religious Affairs, as well as to Greek society at large.

In the collective memory of the first generation of Greek academic anthropologists it is recalled that the first salvo, however friendly, came from within academia. The late introduction of social sciences into Greek academia notwithstanding, a closer look at the academic landscape suggests that disciplines such as history, archaeology, folklore and philology had been well entrenched in Greek universities for more than a century, with history, archaeology and folklore in particular being among the earliest chairs to be established in the first national universities in Athens and Thessaloniki.[6] With the exception of the interwar period when sociology was introduced as a university course (at the University of Athens), folklore dominated the academic scene until the 1970s and early 1980s (see Gefou-Madianou 1993: 164; 2000: 258). Even today, despite wider socio-political changes as well as changes in the legal framework concerning higher education, these departments have remained strong and some of them faithful to their time-honoured positivistic orientation, which saw politismos as both civilization and culture. In this context, wherever anthropology was taught up until the early 1980s as a distinct course, it belonged mainly to the folklore sections of departments of history and archaeology. Except where anthropology has emerged in the form of an independent academic department, this still remains the case.

Today, two main anthropological departments exist in the country, which offer undergraduate, postgraduate and Ph.D. programmes of studies: the Department of Social Anthropology and History at the University of the Aegean, Mitilíni, on Lésvos, and the Department of Social Anthropology at Panteion University, Athens. Anthropology is also taught as an undergraduate major in the Department of History, Archaeology and Social Anthropology at the University of Thessaly, Volos, while social anthropology courses are also taught in various departments and sections[7] in many other (both well-established and more recently introduced) universities around the country.[8]

In all cases, then, anthropologists in academia have found themselves engaged in a continuous dialogue and often in antagonism with other social scientists concerning the content of anthropology as well as its epistemological status. Especially in the more recently established departments and in those where more than one discipline is taught, there has been much competition over the space that each one of them occupies. In many of these departments the study of 'culture' (politismos) in the form of 'cultural technology', 'commercial exchange', 'cultural communication', 'multiculturalism and educational policy', 'cultural goods', 'cultural heritage', or 'Greek politismos', was stated to be one of their main objectives.

Not surprisingly, then, much discussion, debate and even rivalry – within as well as among different departments and universities – centred on the term politismos. The following incident demonstrates aspects of this issue quite clearly. It refers to the appointment process of an Associate Professorship in Social Anthropology in a department of Balkan, Slavic and Oriental studies in northern Greece, where I was invited to participate as a member of the review and electoral committee a few years ago. Discussing the applicant's critical – but anthropologically standard – reading of issues related to Greek identity, the review committee report emphasized the positive role that anthropology could play in such a department in contesting assumed cultural differences with neighbouring Balkan countries. To this a professor of history from a northern Greek university, and a member of the electoral committee, responded irritably and heatedly, arguing that this attitude was wrong. Among other things, recorded in the minutes of the meeting, he emphatically stated that:

> The mission of this department is to promote Greek language and Greek politismos in the Balkans and all its neighbouring countries with the purpose of developing commercial exchanges and cultural ties, and also promoting Greek values. [And turning to the members of the review committee he continued:] You should know there are historical truths about borders, which were engraved by Greek politismos. These truths govern our relations with all our northern, eastern and even southern neighbours. Historians have worked really hard to establish and preserve these certainties. We do not need anthropology to question our politismos or contest any borders.[9]

The anthropology candidate, impeccably trained abroad and more than sufficiently qualified for the job, eventually took the position. Any optimism that may seem justified on account of the successful appointment of an anthropologist to this position should, however, be qualified. The wider context of this appointment was its situation in a department operating from two cities, Thessaloniki and Florina, which are geographically situated close to the northern borders of Greece. Traditionally, the 'Other' in Greece has for a long time been personified by our neighbours to the north (the Slavs), and to the east (the Turks). Greek anthropologists have made it a point to introduce the discipline into such departments, wishing to ease past tensions and to further cooperation between neighbouring Balkan countries. What is shown by the case of the history professor, whose views were probably influenced by the political climate of the 1990s as we shall see below, is that instead of opening the borders to neighbouring cultures, there is a strong tendency with deep institutional roots to safeguard Greek politismos and the assumed 'Greekness' of borderlands.

Unfortunately, such events are not isolated (see Just 1995; Herzfeld 2003). In many cases, they concern not only appointments of specific anthropology candidates but the establishment of new departments as well. At the new University of Thessaly in central Greece, an incident arose some time ago concerning the naming of the Department of History, Archaeology and Folklore, which a few years later changed its title to the Department of History, Archaeology and Social Anthropology. The change – from Folklore to Social Anthropology – in the title of the department, was hotly debated by the university Senate for months, and was in the national press for weeks. Indicative of the tension was an article in a widely circulated newspaper by a well-known professor of literature and theatrical studies in favour of the term folklore for its assumed services in connecting modern Greece with its ancient civilization (politismos). For the respected academic, anthropology was a novel, untested discipline, with an unknown history and a very critical stance. 'It would be better if anthropology was incorporated into folklore, as was successfully done before', he claimed.

Anthropology, then, was perceived by some to be a threatening new addition to the company of the more established and 'powerful' social sciences with their comforting hegemonic discourses. This was so for two reasons: first, because of its critical stance, its anti-positivistic orientation and its reflexive attitude concerning all sorts of historical certainties and nationally presumed timeless continuities (Gefou-Madianou 2003a). Second, because of the emphasis on culture as one of its central conceptual tools, it prized open a hitherto closed area over which these disciplines had long ago claimed property rights. So culture-cum-civilization, far from becoming the conceptual weapon that would enable the newcomer to have amicable discussions with its longer-standing counterparts in academia, became an inhibiting factor that put anthropology on a defensive footing, epistemologically as well as institutionally.

Following the ethnographic presentation of relevant incidents that were initiated above, a further episode could be mentioned here, this time much more recent and much more directly associated with central educational policies and their financing with national and European funds. At Panteion University, the Department of Communication and Mass Media applied to the university Senate to change its title to the Department of Communication, Media and Culture. There was a lot of discussion in Senate concerning issues of possible overlap of research interests and 'areas of study' between departments. The logic behind the proposal, which was finally endorsed by Senate, was that a great part of its academic work concerned the management of culture and cultural recourses. It also aimed to obtain EU funding through the Operational Programmes for Higher Education, which would not support programmes of studies unless they had an applied, technological and communicational orientation towards culture.

The managerial attitude manifest here is not a novelty in Greek academia and reflects wider trends, which are ideologically and financially supported by the state and the EU. During the last decade, several university departments scattered across the country have followed this road, changing their titles or acquiring new ones, and in this manner adopting an orientation which would fit certain prescriptions clearly specified by EU funding policies – for example, the departments of Cultural Management, Cultural Technology and Communication, and Cultural Heritage at the universities of the Aegean, Peloponnese, Macedonia and others. In this manner they are promoting an applied sense of culture, which rests on the materiality of ancient monuments, Greek folklore and state-sponsored events and exhibitions, but also on mass-media technological processes, which often digitalize tradition on CDs and DVDs for the market. The amount of funds diverted towards such applied projects, which do not take into account the existence or even the concept of academic disciplines, is particularly high.

It could be reasonably suggested then that, first, funds for research in the social sciences are severely limited and they come mainly from the EU's Operational Programmes. Second, these funds are allocated among departments and research institutes by the all-powerful Ministry of National Education and Religious Affairs. Third, this bureaucratic mechanism, almost programmatically predisposed towards an applied and technologically oriented conceptualization of research, favours either traditionally well-established and already economically and otherwise powerful academic departments with their previously described positivistic approach towards Greek *politismos*, or those among the newly established departments of cultural management. From the point of view of the Ministry, even the state itself, such policies are deemed both useful and marketable: if anything else, apart from the Ministry of Education, in post-Olympic Games Greece, *politismos* (civilization-cum-culture) sells well for the Ministry of Culture, the Ministry of Tourism, and the Ministry of Research and Technology. Put differently: if a century ago knowledge had to be useful and nation friendly, today it has to be useful and economy friendly (Gefou-Madianou 2000: 263).

In all cases, anthropological research is severely restricted and put in an antagonistic position vis-à-vis research in other social sciences. This creates unnecessary rivalries, which harm academic knowledge and hamper interdisciplinary cooperation between anthropology and other, better entrenched, academic disciplines. Ironically, even after the introduction of anthropology into Greek academia, researching 'culture(s)' continues to be a highly contested area.

From Monoculture to Multiculturalism

However, it would be unfair to put the blame for tensions and misunderstandings between anthropologists and non-anthropologists on the shoulders of the state and on academics alone. The positivistic trends described above, the love affair with ancient Greek civilization, the attractions of Europe and modernization, the constraints of EU education and other policies, and the temptations which European funds breed, are characteristic traits of Greek society as a whole. Decades of nationalist and religiously inflected education and socialization, if not the entire century and a half of the modern Greek state, have cultivated a picture of a monocultural society with one religion and one language. In such an environment, as has hopefully become clear from the above, anthropologists could only fuel controversy with their critique of culture and its assumed link to Greek politismos (civilization). But, I submit, it is through the same concept of culture, in the plural this time, that anthropologists will make the breakthrough. If anything, the changing (but not always optimistic) picture of Greek society gives one some grounds for such confidence.

Although steeped in the glory of its ancient, and rather too distant, past, the hitherto inward-looking, Balkan-locked, Greek society seems to have gradually embarked upon the road of transforming itself from being the 'Western part of the East' (Skopetea 1988, 1992) into a European member state. Oversimplifying a very complex and still unfolding process, we could emphasize four signposts along the way. First, the European Union accession of Greece in the early 1980s offered the country a feeling of political – and hence social – security after decades of war, civil strife (1944–1949) and military dictatorship (1936–1941, 1967–1974). Second, the entry of Greece into the eurozone in 2001 has offered Greeks a sense of security in terms of economic planning and rationalization, despite soaring costs of living and attendant difficulties concerning necessary structural adjustments. At the symbolic level, to have the same currency as the rest of 'Western' Europe makes many Greeks feel like 'real' Europeans.[10] Third, according to Eurostat, during the last decades the educational level of Greeks has been raised considerably, their knowledge of other European languages has increased, and the general standard of living has come closer to that of the rest of Europe. Fourth, and most important, the cultural outlook of Greece has changed dramatically through migration. The latest developments in the EU concerning migration show that Greece has become a magnet for migrants from the Balkans, former socialist East European countries, Africa and Asia. Greece may never have had any colonies, but now subjects of former European colonies settle in the country in ever increasing numbers. To these people – from the Balkans, Middle East, many parts of Africa, Central and South-east Asia, and the Far East, whose number exceeds in crude estimation 1,500,000 (that is one tenth of the Greek population) – we should also add the growing number of EU citizens settling in the country for business or other purposes.

For all these reasons, and in relation to the expressed wish of Eastern European and Balkan countries as well as Turkey to become members of the EU, Greece has emerged as the centre of the Balkans with regards to language, education, commerce, employment and so on, and aspires to play a bigger role in the entire region of south-east Europe and the eastern Mediterranean. In this context, Greeks are witnessing a dialogue of cultures, a variety of practices intertwined in a post-Balkan Europeanized background with not a few Middle Eastern undertones, and, as a consequence, the slow but genuine demise of old 'historical certainties'.

However, the positive socio-political climate of the 1980s has changed. A renewed positivistic and ethnocentric discourse developed, aggravated by the turmoil in the Balkans in the 1990s. During this period, southeastern Europe and the Balkans went through wars and upheavals, in which national borders changed; old totalitarian regimes collapsed (Albania); new nations were established (the Former Yugoslav Republic of Macedonia, FYROM), while others broke to pieces (Former Yugoslavia). All this confusion and disarray had an impact on Greece as well: Greek armed forces were sent to Bosnia (as part of the United Nations); Greece tried to play the role of mediator in the quarrels between the Bosnians, the Serbs and the Croats; it was (and still is) engaged in a long-term dispute with the Former Yugoslav Republic of Macedonia about the name 'Macedonia'; moreover, an incident in the Aegean islands of Imia was considered by many as a threat to the country's eastern borders with Turkey. The Greek media reported these developments as events in which foreign powers played an important role, an interpretation adopted by many Greeks as well; they also presented the situation as even more chaotic than it was, foreseeing an imminent war. In this climate, Greece once again felt threatened and insecure. Segments of the population, including political authorities, returned to a well-known and 'soothing' ethnocentric discourse, which no longer allowed for a dialogue of cultures. Conversely, chauvinistic, racist and xenophobic attitudes were invigorated in Greek society, especially within the Greek Orthodox Church and among conservative parties (Stewart 1998). This climate was also reflected in academia, as the above-mentioned account of the history professor's remarks illustrates.

This negative attitude had an impact on migrant populations living in Greece, especially on those originating from Balkan countries, such as Albanians (who comprise more than half of the total migrant population). Despite the fact that the various cultures embodied by these diverse migrant groups were conversing vibrantly with Greek culture(s) at more than one level and in various ways, it was assumed by many Greeks that their own culture was 'superior' to all 'other' migrant cultures (Gefou-Madianou 2006).

However, everyday life has in many respects imposed its own logic. Migrant groups have become more and more visible in Greek society; their cultural practices have turned out to be an integral part of Greek urban and rural landscapes; so much so that it has become impossible to imagine contemporary Greece without them. In many cases, migrants have mixed creatively with the local population and they have contributed in important ways to the economy of the country despite the insecurity caused by their unclear legal position. Their socio-economic presence is not only reflected in work places, but is also underlined by their cultural presence and their own 'ethnic' ways of living.[11] This presence has lent an air of exoticism and cosmopolitanism to Greek society with all the positive and negative connotations that these terms entail.

Certainly, this is not the whole picture. Much of the rigidity described earlier is still present, especially in the bureaucratic measures applied both to migrant and local populations.[12] In the context of public sector budgetary constraints, the job market for anthropologists is difficult. A university degree is still considered by most Greeks as a necessary prerequisite for upward social mobility and as a ticket to financial success. But such success, as we all know, is hardly guaranteed. So, for many young students and their families an anthropology degree does not translate into job security. Notwithstanding the many opportunities that the inflow of migrants has created for anthropologists to find employment in the wider public (and also private) sectors dealing with migration-related issues and services,[13] the restrictions of the market are real and difficult to overcome.

It is in this multiethnic society, therefore, that Greek anthropologists, academics and an ever-increasing number of graduate students, are called to live and work; a society no longer considered monocultural but still perceived in ambivalent terms in respects of its plurality and openness towards other cultures. It is in this context, it seems to me, that Greek anthropology can play an essential role. Culture, in its pluralistic sense, emerges once more as the paradigmatic field of study for anthropology, not as a taken-for-granted analytical tool but as an ethnographic approach. The ethnographic studies and Ph.D. dissertations that have been published during the last decade reveal some anticipation for the reinstatement of the term culture(s) in both Greek academia and society. They have contributed in many ways to showing what people in everyday life convey by this term, how they use it and what they do with it (Topali 2005; Gefou-Madianou 2003b).

In this respect, it appears to me that today – despite objective difficulties, despite the insistence of the Ministry of Education that more students enter the university system but without increased funding, despite the legal and other hurdles anthropologists face in the job market – anthropology should remain a critical science and a hermeneutic tradition relishing the wealth and variety of cultures. It is perhaps an opportunity for Greek anthropologists to work ethnographically both 'on and with cultures', unsaddled from their civilizational burdens and nationalist presumptions; this should remain its discursive topos par excellence.

Moreover, the necessity for Greek anthropology to open up its horizons in the wider world outside Greece should also be mentioned. For the first time in the history of the discipline in the country we have a growing number of locally-trained anthropology graduate students doing fieldwork abroad: in the Balkans (Albania, Bulgaria), Eastern Europe, Southeast Asia, China, North Africa and the Middle East. It is as if our students trace the routes of migration towards Greece, the trajectories of multiculturalism that bring together the 'others' and the 'selves' in an effort to institute a discourse of openness and understanding in academia and, conceivably, in society at large. One may wonder, then, if the first steps towards the disentanglement of the concept of culture from that of civilization have been taken.

Conclusion: Is Culture Still Useful to Work With?

In this respect, the question whether it is still useful for anthropologists to work with culture, or – following Adam Kuper – they should do away with it, acquires further urgency in the Greek context, where even more dimensions are involved, and which entail careful and diligent scrutiny. The problem of 'culture' might lie not in the word itself, but in its academic and political use and abuse (Rapport and Overing 2000: 101).

Kuper's attack on culture was based on his experience with the apartheid regime of late 1950s South Africa (1999b: xii). The concept of culture – in this context closer to the notion of race – was used by the regime in order to enforce racial segregation in the country until quite recently. The case of Greece is certainly different, though Kuper's main 'moral objection' remains. In Greece, culture, that is politismos, was not exactly used to 'draw attention away from what we have in common instead of encouraging us to communicate across national, ethnic, and religious boundaries' (ibid.: 247). Conversely, politismos was employed to unite all the autochthonous, indigenous inhabitants of what was considered to be Hellenic land during the revolution against the Ottomans into one ethnos (Hellenic), one nation with a single language (Hellenic/Greek) and one religion (Orthodox Christianity). This was the aim of the modern Greek nation-building project in the nineteenth and early twentieth centuries.[14] Despite the passing of time, this historical experience still colours everyday life and self-perceptions in modern Greece and sometimes abroad. Greeks quite often remind the rest of the world that nowadays Greece is the heir of an ancient global heritage, on which the construction of Western civilization is based. This image has also been reinforced by globally constructed, European discourses. Moreover, in recent years, and especially after Greece's accession to the European Union, many other 'indigenous' groups are claiming their 'cultural' identity (Pomaks, Vlachs, Arvanites, Muslims, Sarakatsani, Gypsies and others) in terms of their linguistic, religious, ethnic, or cultural distinctiveness. Everybody has or claims to have culture, politismos, and/or kultura. 'Culture is on everyone's lips' as Sahlins has rightly observed (Sahlins 1994: 378).

This insistence on the notion of Greek politismos (culture) at all levels (ethnic, national, institutional, personal) should concern Greek anthropologists. They should neither ignore the term nor repudiate it altogether. Having recently come of age, anthropology in Greece should create its own niche, epistemologically as well as professionally, that would allow it to intervene in academia as well as in Greek society at large. One of its main objectives should be the creation of a conceptual space, within which it would analyse (and tolerate) the introverted attitude of Greek academia and society at large, pushing for a more open and cosmopolitan one. There are two essential prerequisites for coping successfully with this endeavour: first, the systematic scrutiny of the term 'culture' and of the specific conditions which have or have not encouraged its (rather one-sided) formulation in Greece; and second, dialogue with all those well-entrenched and more recent disciplines 'dealing' with 'culture(s)'. On both fronts, anthropology's ethnographic approach to culture(s), in the direction hinted at in the previous pages, will continue to be its great strength.

Thus, although I appreciate the logic of Kuper's position when he advises anthropologists 'to avoid the hyper-referential word [culture] altogether, and to talk more precisely of knowledge, or belief, or art, or technology, or tradition, or even ideology' (Kuper 1999b: x), I would be hesitant to take his advice in the case of Greece. Instead, we may use the plurality, openness and creativity – innate characteristics of culture in the Boasian tradition – to gain an insight into the ambiguity and fluidity that characterize the workings and transformations of Greek society. This would allow anthropologists to obtain further insights into both Greek society and the analytical possibilities of an elusive and 'fluidized' concept of culture. Anthropologists should continue to be engaged with the concept of culture(s) in order to resituate it, thus taking advantage of its ability to destabilize and contest all those hegemonic discourses that support cultural domination of any kind.

Notes

1. An earlier version of this chapter was presented at the 9th EASA conference in Bristol, September 2006, in a workshop entitled 'Culture, Context and Controversy', proposed as a celebration of the work of Adam Kuper. I have benefited from the discussion that took place on this occasion and I would also like to thank the convenors, Deborah James, Evie Plaice and Christina Toren, for inviting me to the workshop, their careful and critical reading of the chapter, and also for their comments. I would also like to express my gratitude to my colleagues and friends Rania Astrinaki, Athena Athanasiou, Alexandra Bakalaki, Eva Kalpourtzi, Gerasimos Makris, Effie Voutira and Elenana Yialouri for their insightful comments.

2. This is not to say that social anthropology was the only discipline to criticize this positivistic discourse. There have been critical responses coming from other disciplines as well. Important discourses have developed inside and outside the country, which refuted these ethnocentric and positivistic attitudes: for a critical review of Greek folklore, see Kyriakidou-Nestoros (1978); for relevant publications regarding archaeology, see Bernal (1987), Hamilakis and Yalouri (1996), Kalpaxis (1997), Kotsakis (1998), Meskell (1998) and Yaluri (2001); for anti-positivistic and critical works by historians, see Skopetea (1988), Liakos (2001) and Dertilis (2005).

3. For a detailed discussion of the concepts of culture and civilization, see Gefou-Madianou (1999b).

4. Greek folklorists, archaeologists and classicists were in close contact with these European – mostly German, but also English and French – institutions and were collaborating with their European colleagues during the nineteenth and twentieth centuries (cf. Herzfeld 1987).

5. The new academic disciplines that were introduced by the 1982 Reformatory Law for Higher Education Institutions were social history, sociology, geography and social anthropology, which now would no longer be taught as courses within the old schools, but as established disciplines in their own separate sections and departments. For anthropology this meant that Greece could for the first time produce locally-trained anthropologists (Gefou-Madianou 2000: 258).

6. The strong chairs of folklore studies were established in the first public universities of the country, the National University of Athens (in the School of Classics) as early as 1890, the

University of Thessaloniki (in the Department of History and Archaeology, Section of Folklore) after its establishment in 1926, and the University of Ioannina, Epirus (in the Department of History and Archaeology, Section of Folklore), again after its establishment in 1964.

7. Social anthropology courses are being taught today in the following universities: Athens, Panteion, Thessaloniki, Macedonia, Ioannina, Thrace, Patras, Peloponnese, Crete, and the University of the Aegean.

8. The first general universities (with a broad spectrum of schools and disciplines) to be launched were the National and Kapodestrian University of Athens (1837), established after the creation of the Greek nation-state, followed by the Aristotelian University of Thessaloniki (1926), more than a decade after the area's addition to Greek national territory. Together with the National Metsovion Technical University of Athens (founded in 1936), they have remained the major and most influential institutions in the country. The next group of higher education institutions was introduced in the 1920s following the First World War: the Graduate School for Economic Studies in Athens (1920), the Graduate School of Agricultural Studies in Athens (also in 1920), and Panteion School of Social and Political Sciences in Athens, which was founded after the 1922 Asia Minor Catastrophe. Panteion was officially founded in 1927, and was the first higher education institution for social and political sciences in the country. More than two decades later, after the Second World War and the civil war that followed, the Graduate School of Industrial Studies was established in Athens (1947) and later transferred to Piraeus. This was followed in the 1960s by a number of new higher education institutions.

9. Of course, this stance should not be seen as a generalized attitude of historians or academics in general. The specific professor of history represented only one aspect of the issue; there are different histories and historians in Greece and hopefully also in the particular department to which the professor belonged, despite the fact that he seemed to have influenced (and taken on his side) a lot of people in the electoral body that day. See also note 2.

10. A complicated bureaucratic procedure, currency exchange before travelling abroad had acquired an iconic status over the years, revealingly expressed by exclamations of 'I am travelling to Europe' when visiting London, Paris or even nearby Rome.

11. This is better exhibited in their shops, cafes and restaurants in the centre of the cities, which have become an attraction for increasing numbers of Greeks too, who have assiduously adopted these newly introduced styles of entertainment and consumption.

12. Migrants in particular face considerable problems with visas and work licences, the 'papers' as they call them. In reality, a large percentage of them have no social security and an ambiguous legal status.

13. These services include research centres for migration issues, special offices and agencies operating in town halls to deal with migrants' problems, and also educational and cultural facilities either incorporated in the Greek educational system or operating separately, like the Filipino nursery and elementary schools of Athens.

14. This, of course, suppressed all non-Greek-speaking populations: Vlachs, Arvanites, Pomaks, Turkish-speaking Greek subjects, and others, as well as those (such as Catholics, Jews, Muslims) who were not Orthodox Christians; see Gefou-Madianou (1999a).

Chapter 5

Culture: the Indigenous Account

Alan Barnard

This chapter bears on culture, the indigenous peoples' movement, and apartheid, making comparisons between the latter two in light of anthropological definitions of 'culture'. I shall suggest that the idea of culture and the idea of indigenousness or indigeneity share certain peculiar attributes, notably their problematic nature as anthropological categories and their appropriation by people claiming indigenous cultural status. This is a problem both for anthropology at a theoretical level and for the engagement of the discipline with those of our subjects who make that claim.

My focus here is on these issues in light of anthropology in southern Africa, and especially South Africa. Southern Africa has been subject not only to conflicting political environments, but also conflicting anthropological traditions through much of its history. These traditions, though, have never existed in isolation, but in contact, in juxtaposition and even at times intertwined. For example, Afrikaans-language and American anthropology share similar roots, and similar concerns with culture. Anthropological notions of culture have been appropriated by both the old and the new South Africa. In southern Africa, the idea of indigenousness is deployed for political gain both by small indigenous groups and by nation-states, irrespective of any anthropological theory that might be brought to bear on the subject.

Culture and Indigenousness

The central concern of most schools of anthropology is culture. Yet culture is by no means a straightforward concept. Indeed, it is a contradiction. On the one hand, it is something to do with nurturing, helping to reach maturity. On the other hand, it is an artefact, a thing of the past that determines identity.

And it determines identity not by virtue of one's own actions, but by virtue of those of one's grandparents.

The meaning of culture is also dependent on context, and it changes in time. It was easy to attack 'culture' when the word was used as a synonym for 'race': in the old South Africa a twisted notion of 'culture' became an excuse for a repugnant social system. It is less easy to denigrate culture when that term is employed by disadvantaged people who call themselves indigenous and seek to replicate the values, if not the actions, of their grandparents. People call themselves indigenous for lack of any other obvious label, often as something signifying an essence in their historical lifestyle as 'a people' (collectively) that they want to remember or to protect for their children. Many such people cling to the concept of culture as a means of referencing their identities as different from some wider society. Culture is important then for both the elites of the old South Africa, and for the disadvantaged minorities of the new.

Culture shares with indigenousness similar essences. Both are artefacts of the past, invoked to justify actions in the present. Both determine identities. Apartheid was not unlike either in these senses: its proponents claimed that it reflected the natural order of things. That order of things was of the past: different peoples finding themselves together on South African soil, a few decades ago, or a few centuries ago. Although the word culture is avoided, even the liberal tradition in local historiography defined itself, in the 1960s, precisely in such a way. In the words of *The Oxford History of South Africa*, 'the central theme of South African history is interaction between peoples of diverse origins, languages, technologies, ideologies, and social systems, meeting on South African soil' (Wilson and Thompson 1969: v).

Even if we consider only the essays in this volume, it is apparent that there are many notions of culture within anthropology too:

- Culture in opposition to human nature
- Culture as what all humans share, that is, in opposition to animals (or at least to most animals)
- Culture as symbolic culture, that which distinguishes modern from pre-modern human beings
- Culture in the sense of culture area, as in regional structural comparison
- Culture as a smaller unit: nation or ethnic group
- Culture as subculture
- Culture within the individual

Few anthropologists do not subscribe to at least one of these, and quite diverse theoreticians can subscribe to the same one, or indeed to several. The first three remain important at a high theoretical level, but have little to do with the ethnographic or with cultures in the plural. They may safely be ignored here. Culture in the sense of culture area is different. This is important in some of Adam Kuper's work (e.g., Kuper 1982), although in this the locus of culture still remains above the level of 'a culture'. That latter notion, 'a culture', in other words culture as a countable unit, is what his later work rightly seeks to avoid.

Of all of these notions of culture, it is culture as a nation or ethnic group which is probably the least real. Yet that one is the most common in several traditions in anthropology, and in particular the prewar German anthropology that lay at the root of both the American tradition and the Afrikaans-language tradition in South Africa. A number of chapters in the present volume make similar points (see especially the chapters by Gingrich, Sharp, and Plaice; see also Sharp 2006). This notion is also the one most often picked up today by indigenous groups, as well as nationalists, to represent themselves. In other words, the spectrum of definitions of culture runs from those broadly agreed within anthropology (like culture as opposed to nature) to the more controversial equation of culture with ethnicity. Culture divides humanity from the animals, but at the same time culture divides each branch of humanity one from another, and especially perhaps, 'indigenous' humanity from the rest.

If culture is the core concept of most of anthropology, indigenous peoples are the culture-bearing units that anthropologists tend to find of most interest. It is not just that different peoples are literally indigenous to particular places, but that there is some similarity between hunter-gatherers, isolated and nomadic herding groups, and perhaps small-scale cultivators that differentiates them from larger population groups. If all the world's multiplicity of indigenous peoples have something in common, it is their relation to their respective wider societies. It is not any cultural essence, nor even necessarily whether or not they arrived in a particular place before other groups. (Otherwise, for example, the Himba of Namibia would have trouble claiming indigenous status.)

When culture is appropriated by the larger community, indigenousness can be as well. President Festus Mogae of Botswana had long expressed a view that all citizens of Botswana should be regarded as 'indigenous', and the Botswana Press Agency reported in 2007 that:

> All citizens of Botswana are therefore indigenous to the country with the exception of some naturalised citizens. No tribe or ethnic group is in this regard considered more indigenous than the others in the country and Government rejects outright, attempts by certain quarters to impose on the country, a definition of indigenous people that suits only the narrow and ill-informed agendas and interests of certain advocacy groups.[1]

That statement was in fact timed to coincide with the report on Botswana's surprise decision to support a revised draft of the United Nations Declaration on the Rights of Indigenous Peoples, passed by the General Assembly on 13 September 2007. The notion that any citizen can be indigenous undermines special claims to indigenousness, and renders 'indigenous peoples' no different from any other. It also blurs the distinction between national and other cultures, and allows the nation as a whole, or indeed the state, to claim common ownership of its 'culture'.

Indigenousness and Collective Representations

Several things are conflated in the collective mind of the new South African state. This came out especially with South Africa's launching of its new motto and coat of arms in 2000, where the situation was rather different from that in Botswana. President Thabo Mbeki invoked the idea of indigenous people (in the form of the /Xam, a culturally distinct Khoisan people), the ancient past (with the representation of Khoisan as South Africa's first people and their conflation with 'early man'), and the overthrow of the recent past (apartheid), all in the spirit of a new ideal of diverse peoples, languages and cultures, coming together. All this caused some controversy and confusion in the collective mind of the South African public, but the imagery has interesting implications for anthropology.

President Mbeki launched the motto and coat of arms in a speech given in the small town of Kwaggafontein on Freedom Day, 27 April 2000. The words of his speech strongly implied the great contradictions of indigenousness:

> The motto of our new Coat of Arms, written in the Khoisan language of the /Xam people, means: diverse people unite or people who are different join together.
> We have chosen an ancient language of our people. This language is now extinct as no one lives who speaks it as his or her mother tongue.
> This emphasizes the tragedy of the millions of human beings who, through the ages, have perished and even ceased to exist as peoples, because of peoples [*sic*] inhumanity to others.
> It also says that we, ourselves, can never be fully human if any people is wiped off the face of the earth, because each one of us is a particle of the complete whole.
> By inscribing these words on our Coat of Arms – !ke e: /xarra //ke – we make a commitment to value life, to respect all languages and cultures and to oppose racism, sexism, chauvinism and genocide.
> Thus do we pledge to respect the obligation which human evolution has imposed on us – to honour the fact that in this country that we have inherited together is to be found one of the birthplaces of humanity itself. (Mbeki 2000)

What is going on here is no less than the creation of a 'culture' of national unity in the guise of collective national indigenousness (see also Barnard 2003, 2004). Politically, I am very much in favour of this new spirit, but at the same time it is appropriate that as an anthropologist I try to understand this as a social construction, either conscious or otherwise, that functions as an integrating influence on otherwise diverse elements of that society. The problem of this collective indigenousness is interesting precisely because of its seeming contradictions: the apparent equation of South African with Khoisan, Khoisan with /Xam (one Khoisan people), /Xam with peoples ancient and extinct and with oppression by others, and all this with the birthplace of humanity in general. Elsewhere in his speech he remarks that the figure depicted in the coat of arms (two San clasping hands) is 'both African and universal', and that further: 'It represents the permanent yet evolving identity of the South African people as it shapes itself through time and space' (ibid.) The verbal image of 'permanent yet evolving' is a profound one, and applicable not only to identities but to cultures or any amorphous social phenomena. Indeed it seems to me that those words represent the idea of collective identities or cultures rather better than does what is literally depicted.

Indigenousness, Apartheid and Cultural Tradition

The idea of indigenous culture, as opposed to any other culture, implies temporal sequence, and it implies that 'indigenous' is sequentially first. According to Sidsel Saugestad (2001: 43) 'first come' is one of several characteristics of the definition of indigenous. The other characteristics she identifies are non-dominance, cultural difference, and self-ascription. These other three are all encoded in the choice of colour designations in the old South Africa, which in turn were played out through a definition of South African indigenousness which was quite different from Mbeki's. When I was at the University of Cape Town in the early 1970s, archaeologists there used to point out to their students that blacks crossed the Limpopo into present-day South Africa long before whites settled at the Cape, although the government-influenced schoolbooks the students had grown up on had it the other way around. In a real sense, the schoolbooks were asserting that the whites were just as indigenous as the blacks. Contesting this, the archaeology lecturers were asserting the blacks' prior presence, and hence making a moral point in opposition to apartheid's hierarchy of 'races'. In fact, there is no doubt that whites got to the Western Cape before blacks got to that part of South Africa, if by 'blacks' we mean Iron Age Bantu-speaking agro-pastoralists. Khoisan do not generally consider themselves 'black', but conceptually 'red' in opposition to both 'black' and 'white'. Even today, some of those in the Northern Cape say they are 'yellow people', in order to distinguish themselves from their urban 'brown' kinsfolk and lay claim to a 'yellow' or 'red' indigenous identity.

It is an interesting comment on national culture that South Africa has eleven official languages and chose to put every colour of the rainbow into their new national flag. Botswana, on the other hand, has two official languages and represents black people with a black stripe and white people by two thin white stripes, while Namibia has just one official language, English, and a single, red, stripe for people of all colours and cultures. So who is indigenous to the Western Cape? Probably those called 'brown', as descendants of the 'red' people or Bushmen and Khoekhoe. What about a 'yellow' person whose ancestors migrated north after the Dutch arrived in 1652? Should he or she be granted a smallholding on the side of Table Mountain? Or should any such smallholdings be reserved only for present-day 'indigenous' Capetonians? Of course, rhetoric such as this is nonsense. But it is precisely the sort of nonsense which would follow by applying the doctrine of indigenousness or indigeneity, meaning firstness, to this situation.

A homeland of Bushmanland was indeed established, in 1964, not in South Africa itself but in Namibia, or what was then South West Africa. Bushmanland had in fact been the brainchild of an anthropologist (or volkekundige), P.J. Schoeman, author of a travelogue-ethnography called *Jagters van die Woestynland* (Schoeman 1951) or *Hunters of the Desert Land* (1957). Schoeman's story is interesting, because it highlights some little-known connections between apartheid, indigenousness and mainstream British anthropology. Schoeman's book tells of the detrimental effects of the migration of Bantu-speakers into Bushman or San territories in northern Namibia, and the difficulty San in the 1940s were having in maintaining their hunter-gatherer lifestyle. From 1940 to 1953, he chaired a Commission for the Preservation of the Bushmen, which sought to overturn these effects (Gordon 1992: 160–67). Schoeman is said to have kept two framed references on the mantelpiece in his study, one from Werner Eiselen (the anthropologist commonly believed to be the 'architect of apartheid'; see Sharp, this volume), and the other from the author of 'A Scientific Theory of Culture' (in Malinowski 1944). The latter, Malinowski's reference, is dated February 1935 and supports Schoeman's application to serve as government ethnologist in South Africa. Malinowski notes that Schoeman had studied with him in London for two terms and that he had 'formed a very high opinion of [Schoeman's] scientific character and ability'. He adds that Schoeman 'was able to assimilate some of the fundamental principles of modern anthropology very rapidly' (quoted in Gordon n.d.: 2–3).

Schoeman had done his early field work in Swaziland in 1934, and he was to have a run-in with another Malinowski student and Swazi ethnographer, Hilda Beemer Kuper – Adam Kuper's father's brother's wife. Hilda started fieldwork in 1935 and took exception to a paper published by Schoeman in that year. She showed it to the King, Sobhuza II, who sided with her. That is probably why Schoeman turned to the San, and Hilda Kuper became premiere ethnographer of the Swazi (see Cocks 2000). Hilda completed her second book on the Swazi in 1946, and it was published in 1947, the year before the National Party took power. She begins this book, *The Uniform of Colour*, with the words: 'For nearly one hundred years the Swazi of the Territory have been in direct continuous contact with the technologically superior, politically more complex and socially more individualistic culture of the Europeans' (H. Kuper 1947: 1). Later in the book she speaks of cultural differences between social classes in Western Europe and notes that in South Africa similar differences are 'accentuated by difference of colour, culture, and active tradition' (ibid.: 26). She adds that European goods 'become part of the culture of the people', while the 'myth of race superiority is maintained largely through the political and economic organizations of the Territory' (ibid.: 36). She contrasts the 'cultural features' brought by missionaries, such as monogamy, with 'the traditional culture against which these influences operate' (ibid.: 107). She summarizes with these words:

> The constituent elements of modern Swazi culture cannot be mechanically allotted to the traditional and European mother cultures. While it is true that certain items, more especially material goods, could be listed as belonging initially to one or to the other, the process of culture contact involves psychological and social adjustments, for culture is articulated by human beings, who adopt certain items and reject others. The human carriers are, however, propelled by social trends of which they are not necessarily aware. (ibid.: 153)

More succinctly, Winifred Hoernlé speaks in the foreword to *The Uniform of Colour* of Swaziland as 'one society with two cultures struggling to adjust themselves to one another'; the 'White culture' is dominant, Hoernlé says, because 'force of every kind is at its disposal' (Hoernlé 1947: viii).

That pre-apartheid distinction between culture and society reflects the influence of Radcliffe-Brown as well as the quite different approach of Malinowski. While the wording is Malinowskian, the sentiment suggests the spiritual presence of both Malinowski and Radcliffe-Brown. In his address on 'Social Structure', originally published in 1940, Radcliffe-Brown wrote:

> The study of composite societies, the description and analysis of the processes of change in them, is a complex and difficult task. The attempt to simplify it by considering the process as being one in which two or more 'cultures' interact, which is the method suggested by Malinowski ..., is simply a way of avoiding the reality. For what is happening in South Africa, for example, is not the interaction of British culture, Afrikaner (or Boer) culture, Hottentot culture, various Bantu cultures and Indian culture, but the interaction of individuals and groups within an established social structure which is itself in process of change. What is happening in a Transkeian tribe, for example, can only be described by recognizing that the tribe has been incorporated into a wide political and economic structural system. (Radcliffe-Brown 1952: 202)

Radcliffe-Brown (e.g., ibid.: 3–5, 190) rejected the idea of culture as a 'concrete reality' and called it 'but an abstraction, and as it is commonly used a vague abstraction'. But he did not reject the idea of what he called 'cultural traditions' or 'the cultural process'. The cultural process involves 'the transmission of learnt ways of thinking, feeling and acting' (ibid.: 5), and is made up of traditions including, in his examples, language, gender roles, and occupational training. In other words, the problem is in the conception of culture as a whole, not in the specifics of cultural traditions operating within a wider society. For Radcliffe-Brown, cultural tradition is what distinguishes human social life from the social life of other species. Admittedly, he could have avoided the mention of 'culture' altogether by referring simply to 'traditions' as opposed to 'cultural traditions', but he did not. 'Culture' was of course already a well-established concept, and to remove the word might not have solved the problem.

The difference between 'culture' and 'cultural tradition' is that the former implies an unchanging essence, while the latter accepts both continuity and change. In 1910, a group of well-known, mainly German, writers produced a strange book called *Die Welt in hundert Jahre* ('The World in a Hundred Years'), with chapters on war, women, music, art, medicine, sport, and so on in an imagined world a hundred years later. The chapter that interests me here is the one on the colonies in a hundred years. The author predicts that in the year 2010, German colonists in Africa will be living one or two thousand metres above the land (or higher in the tropics), in a fleet of hovering zeppelins. On the ground, black servants, presumably culturally undifferentiated, will provide the necessary labour to support their lofty lifestyle. The author of that chapter was the notorious traveller-journalist of East Africa, Karl Peters (1910), and he was writing just five years after the savage attempt by his compatriots in German South-West Africa to wipe out the Herero. Possibly as many as 80 per cent of all Herero men, women and children were killed in a few short months in 1904 and 1905. Peters predicts, in effect, apartheid but no culture.

In reality of course, some Herero did survive and still survive as a proud people with a clear identity. Their double-descent system, the distinction between patrilineally-inherited sacred cattle and matrilineally-inherited ordinary cattle, and so on, continue to this day and have for several decades been noted in anthropological writings (see, e.g., Gibson 1956). Ironically, even their style of dress for adult women still resembles late nineteenth-century German fashion. And if Herero retain such cultural traditions, the branch of the Herero-speaking peoples known as Himba are still characterized by many people as 'indigenous' in the narrowest sense. Their social organization and beliefs are pretty much identical to classic Herero. The difference between the groups, if I may simplify, is that while Herero have entered the mainstream of Namibian life, most Himba have not. They live in a particularly harsh and remote area, and they wear leather loincloths and copper bangles instead of full, flowery dresses. They are the subject of television programmes emphasizing their exotic lifestyle, of picture books, and of popular and anthropological accounts alike (see, e.g., Crandall 2000). The trajectories of cultural tradition have differed between Himba and Herero, but in each case there is continuity of the kind implied by Radcliffe-Brown.

Peters' description of life in 2010 was just five years after the Herero holocaust. It was also just five years before the end of German rule. The colony was captured for the allies by a South African force led by Jan Smuts in 1915. And just five or six years later, Smuts, as prime minister of the Union of South Africa and as chancellor of the University of Cape Town, would become instrumental in the establishment there of social anthropology, under Radcliffe-Brown (see Kuper 1999a: 145–8). Peters never anticipated that an 'indigenous' Himba 'culture' would outlive German rule, much less that it would be studied by ethnographers or debated in theoretical terms by anthropologists who live with people rather than above them. 'Indigenous culture' proved stronger than German military might.

The reason for the continued existence of Himba 'culture', and indeed German 'culture', through apartheid times in Namibia and since (Namibia gained full independence from South Africa in 1990), is that Himba and German culture are not identical in 1910 and today. The idea of culture as process rather than a thing preserves it as an analytical possibility for anthropology, against the earlier German-Austrian anthropological tradition or its American or Afrikaner derivatives.

Full Circle: the Return of Culture and Indigenousness

If the difference between apartheid and the indigenous peoples' movement has nothing to do with firstness, what has it got to do with? The one legitimate sense in which apartheid differs from the indigenous peoples' movement is definable in terms of the relative position of South Africa's white population and, in general, international terms, the relative position of so-called 'indigenous peoples'. The latter, very simply, are oppressed peoples, and therefore resemble in this sense the majority rather than the minority in the 'old' South Africa. So-called 'indigenous peoples' are oppressed by governments, by stronger economic interests, or whatever, and they have chosen to call themselves 'indigenous' as a means to redress their rightful grievances, because the outside world recognizes 'indigenous' as a category (cf. Saugestad 2001). Some of Adam Kuper's critics make the assumption that the argument of his paper 'The Return of the Native' (2003) has to do with representations: that he is arguing for a rebranding of 'indigenous peoples'. But he is, of course, not arguing that. He opposes the very existence of the category. My argument in a previous paper (Barnard 2006) was that he is right to challenge the category within anthropology, but that beyond anthropology we are stuck with it.

There is no legitimate category 'indigenous' in anthropological language. However, 'indigenous' is a real term, a legal fiction if you like, in the outside world, because it forms the basis of claims against illegitimate authority in the hands of governments and economic forces. In her introduction to the Richard Lee festschrift, Jacqueline Solway puts it more strongly: 'Thus instead of "primitiveness" being the underlying characteristic of indigenism as Kuper asserts, encapsulation, marginalization, disempowerment, cultural and livelihood difference from the dominant society are considered by many activists to be the defining characteristics of the indigenous' (Solway 2006: 8). All Solway's characteristics of indigenousness are interactive, and she highlights complexity too. Similarly, Russell Taylor describes his own Australian 'Aboriginality' as complex in meaning and emotive, and indeed evolving:

> In contemporary Australia the notion of Aboriginal identity, or Aboriginality, is for many including myself an intensely personal concept. It is not only extremely complex and emotive but, in the context of its construction, usage and definition, by both Aboriginal and non-Aboriginal social actors, it is still evolving. The concept is applied in a wide range of social, political, academic, scientific, judicial, governmental and other contexts, in attempts to articulate a complexity of meanings. (Taylor 2001: 133)

'Indigenous', non-academic San seem to see it all more in spiritual terms, with language often the key. Certainly this is the case among those whose N/u or ≠Khomani language was only rediscovered in 1997, and who have found a new surge of identity consciousness since South African democracy in 1994 and also since a major land claim went in their favour in 1999.

> I am very proud of being a San. From my mother's womb I came, from the land. San milk I drank from my mother's side, from my father's side, my grandmother and my great-grandfather's side. This language of ours, it comes from our great-grandfather, my mother's father's father. A language that came forth from the world, the spirit of the world. (/Una Rooi, quoted in Le Roux and White 2004: vii)

In that key South African 'indigenous peoples' case, the rights of the ≠Khomani in their land claim were ordinary rights, whether defined in human terms or in civil terms. The courts upheld the claim to land because the ancestors of present-day ≠Khomani had been wrongfully dispossessed a hundred years ago, not because they were collectively 'an indigenous people'. The South African constitution twice refers to 'indigenous' people (Articles 6 and 26), but it means this merely in the sense of people of African, as opposed to European, origin (see Robins 2001: 235–6). And of course the very notion of 'indigenous' in a southern African context has special problems, due not only to conflicting claims to land and 'firstness' in local contexts, but also to relations between the descendants of Khoisan groups and descendants of other Africans who migrated from farther north more than a millennium ago.

It is similar in Botswana (see Saugestad 2006). The Botswana government had for more than a decade tried to encourage the two thousand inhabitants of the Central Kalahari Game Reserve, an area larger than Switzerland, to leave – and in particular to abandon the large settlement that had grown up around the borehole at Xade (≠Xade). Former residents of the reserve were finally denied government provision of health, food and water and relocated, mainly in 1997, with the remaining few hundred being moved out in 2002. In 2004, 243 of them sued the government for permission to return and to have these services re-established. After 134 days in court, in December 2006 three

High Court judges each delivered separate judgements. The first was largely in favour of the government position, and the second and third largely in favour of the position of the G/wi and G//ana applicants, at least with respect to their rights to occupy traditional territory on grounds that it was indeed their traditional territory. However, although the court ruled that the population had been unlawfully denied the right to occupy the land, they held in favour of the government that it had no obligation to provide health services or food and water. The government accepted all provisions of the ruling and decided not to appeal. Yet the day after the ruling, Botswana's attorney general (who had formally been the respondent) ordered that only those listed as applicants in the case, and their dependents, could return to the reserve without permits. He further demanded that they would have to produce identity documents in order to do so. The drama, including the court decision, was all played out in civil-rights and constitutional terms, there being no special rights recognized or accorded on the basis of indigenousness.

The fact is that 'indigenous peoples' are not real entities at all except as defined by context, or more particularly as defined through self-ascription. To my mind, 'indigenous' is not a legitimate category of ethnographic description, and its use in political contexts of self-identification is phenomenally difficult (Barnard 2006: 10). Contrary to his critics, Kuper does not really see 'indigenous' as nothing more than a postmodern way of saying 'primitive', but as a rather a more complex phenomenon (Kuper 2003, 2006). Kuper's solution, abandoning the category 'indigenous' altogether, is the most clear-cut and simple. Yet it is not the only possibility. I have argued instead (Barnard 2006: 18) that we can never prevent others from using 'our' terms (if indeed 'indigenous' is partly the product of anthropological thought), and that we have no right to do so. We should instead allow 'indigenous' as appropriate in political contexts, as self-ascription dictates, and try to understand it anthropologically in those contexts, while at the same time ceasing to allow it as an objective, analytical term in anthropology. In other words, in political contexts I disagree with Kuper's solution to the problem of indigeneity, while in purely anthropological contexts, if these exist, I agree with him.

Much the same goes for culture. The final chapter of *Culture: The Anthropologists' Account* (Kuper 1999b: 226–47) is the most powerful, with attacks not only on American cultural anthropology but also on cultural studies and the ideology of multiculturalism, which is seen as an anti-Enlightenment project. Yet 'indigenous peoples' and other self-defining cultural groups tend to like diversity. 'Culture' is their term as well as ours. Let me explain with an anecdote. I took my Ph.D. under Adam Kuper's supervision at University College London in 1976. I began fieldwork for that with Naro (Nharo) in Botswana in 1974, and at that time only one Naro out of a population of about 15,000 spoke English. Only a handful, perhaps a few dozen, could then read or write at all (in Setswana). Since those times, schools have been built and hundreds of Naro children have learned literacy skills in

Naro, Setswana and English. Upon publication of *Voices of the San* (Le Roux and White 2004), a group of Naro signed a copy which is in my possession. In it are written the words (in English), 'I still honour my culture, pride and dignity, so what about you?' Whether we think Naro have 'Naro culture' or not, *they* think they do. And who are we to deny it to them?

If a 'people' can have culture, then what about governments? In August 2006, the Minister of Youth, National Service, Sport and Culture in Namibia not only proclaimed the existence of national culture, but expressed policy on it and presented his definition of the 'culture' concept. Speaking at the Polytechnic of Namibia's Eleventh Annual Cultural Festival, John Mutorwa said that culture consists of 'people's shared and learnt values, worldviews and ways of knowing and understanding their existence' and emphasized that 'culture is not static'. He added:

> Cultural relativism and ethnocentrism are, in my view, dangerous and destructive to the noble policy and cause of national reconciliation, national unity, stability, peace and development … Culture is thus a shared way of living. Culture is not and cannot be a fossil from the past. Culture is a vibrant, dynamic and constantly changing complex of ideas and interactions.[2]

Adam Kuper's work has alerted us to both the dangers and the complexities of accepting received notions of 'culture' and 'indigenousness'. Where I find difficulty is in defining such concepts for non-anthropological constituencies that have laid claim to them. These constituencies include both individuals who wish to define themselves as 'indigenous' and others, including politicians, who use the terms without either malice or attempts to gain advantage over others. Just as anthropologists operate in the contexts of political forces and ethical constraints, politicians and ordinary people operate in anthropological contexts. Our concepts and some of our professional concerns are theirs as much as they are our own.

Conclusion

Like the separate black and white stripes in the Botswana flag, the assignment of people to cultures, whether by governments, by anthropologists or by themselves, stresses difference over common humanity. As Kuper says, culture theory 'tends to draw attention away from what we have in common instead of encouraging us to communicate across national, ethnic, and religious boundaries, and to venture between them' (Kuper 1999b: 247). Yet I would still have it both ways: anthropology has come to the point where we would be best to jettison altogether the notion of cultures as wholes, while still recognizing the presence of what Radcliffe-Brown saw as interrelated and individually manipulable cultural traditions. How inclusive these traditions become remains a matter of political debate. If President Kennedy could be a Berliner, then perhaps President Mbeki can be a /Xam.

Today southern Africa has no colonies and no apartheid, but it still has inequalities, and some of the poorest and formerly most oppressed, or their representatives, cling to the status 'indigenous'. It may not be as easy a route out of their troubles as they think, but some of the most previously marginalized groups – like Bushmen or San, and their descendants especially in the Northern Cape – have become 'indigenous' (cf. De Jongh 2002). This is all the more ironic when the cultural traditions which link them to their San or Khoe ancestors seem thin, and their parentage is mixed. In my 1992 book *Hunters and Herders of Southern Africa*, I employed a rather extensive definition of 'Khoisan' (Barnard 1992: 193–8), and I am happy that I did. Following the ethnographic account of Peter Carstens from the 1960s (Carstens 1966) and the historical studies of J.S. Marais from the 1930s (Marais 1939), I included these so-called 'Coloured people' as Khoisan. I am less happy now about my overuse of the culture concept (Barnard 1992: 294–302 passim), which I used within a framework of regional structural comparison. For me Khoisan was one great 'culture', of which each form (Ju/'hoan, G/wi, Naro, Nama, Damara, and so on) was a transformation. But what kind of structures are they if not cultural? The real problem, as I think Radcliffe-Brown knew, was in thinking of cultures as countable things. The use of the adjective rather than the noun allows vagaries which are easier to get away with, hence either what Radcliffe-Brown called a 'cultural tradition' or what I in my structuralist framework thought of as a 'cultural system' (ibid.: 302).

Perhaps all concepts in social anthropology are somehow problematic, especially if they remain in our vocabulary as our theoretical positions change. Both 'culture', at least in the plural form common in the American tradition, and 'indigenous peoples', are particularly so. It is far more difficult for us to get rid of such concepts than it was for our intellectual ancestors to invent them. And it is of course neither possible nor (if it were possible) desirable to aim to get rid of every problematic concept. Let me conclude with the suggestion that if the concept of indigenousness is not about claiming rights against other people, but simply claiming rights to cultural tradition itself, then there is no harm in it. The imagery of national identities in the 'new' South Africa and in post-independence Namibia draws on many cultural traditions, and it seems to me that this can be no bad thing: the creation of a world in which we all have a claim, one in which 'race' is irrelevant and exclusion has no place.

Notes

1. Botswana Press Agency, quoted in the *Daily News* (Gaborone), 7 September 2007.
2. John Mutorwa, quoted in *New Era: Newspaper for a New Namibia*, 8 August 2006.

Chapter 6

We are All Indigenous Now: Culture versus Nature in Representations of the Balkans

Aleksandar Bošković

In this chapter, I look at a case in which a myth about a specific region was transformed into an anthropological reality. While I take my cue from Adam Kuper's *The Invention of Primitive Society* (Kuper 1988), my use of the term 'culture' is almost completely opposite to what he had in mind. I cannot imagine abolishing it, although I agree with Pina-Cabral (this volume) that it has been used uncritically. Words and concepts that we use should be taken in the context where they appear. Understanding Balkan societies, their self-representations, and the ways in which they want others to see and interpret them would be very difficult, if not impossible, without taking into account their perceptions of culture. In this region, as in other former communist-ruled countries, the term culture meant something very different from what it implied in Western industrialized societies (Wachtel 2003): it was and remains an important marker of ethnic and national self-awareness, of the degree of national development, and of distinction. It thus defines and determines 'stories we want to tell others about ourselves' in a very particular way. Conversely, and in almost equal measure, representations of the Balkans in mainstream Europe carried the implication that Balkan peoples had little or no culture.

Taking as read anthropological writings on the problematic character of representation in general (de Coppet 1992; Marcus and Fisher 1986; see also Pina Cabral, this volume), I will concentrate here on the issues raised by the representation – and self-representation – of 'the Balkans'. Speech marks are necessary here – though they will be omitted in the remainder of the chapter – since the term, concept and geographical area has been both invented and contested in the fiercest of terms. Mention of the Balkans provokes strongly-felt and loudly-expressed opinions; representatives of the countries concerned periodically either fiercely oppose or eagerly assert their inclusion in this overarching unit. Such assertions of inclusion/exclusion have serious political, ideological and cultural implications (cf. Todorova 1994, 1997; Ristović 1995; Karakasidou 2002; Jezernik 2004).

This region became especially interesting for outside observers following the bloody dissolution of the former Yugoslavia in the 1990s. Throughout that decade, wars in the former Yugoslavia were predominant in media coverage and preoccupied public opinion throughout the world (Baskar 1999; Muršič 2000). The sheer amount of violence broadcast on television was shocking for audiences: atrocities unheard of since the end of the Second World War were being acted out dangerously close to home, and mass murders and rapes were being committed in Europe for the first time since 1945. How was this possible? And what kind of people were able to commit such horrible acts?

Explaining violent conflicts has never been easy for anthropologists. As enlightened professionals mostly based in non-conflict societies, we tend to see ourselves as somewhat superior to our subjects. The lack of enlightenment of these natives, in turn, is evident from the fact that they appear to be able only to solve their differences through violence. But this does not mean that anthropologists are unwilling to take sides: when conflict began in the former Yugoslavia in the 1990s, some anthropologists rushed to the aid of 'their' ethnic groups – the ones in which they had done fieldwork, or where they had friends and colleagues (see Simic 2000; Denitch 2000). Their adoption of this insider stance inevitably complicated readings and relationships. While the issues of who was fighting whom, where and why, and what was actually going on, seemed quite clear to outside observers, these new insiders felt the need to justify the stance of those they were supporting by using a variety of sometimes quite quirky and distinctly unscholarly explanations. Alongside the more usual legacy of the Second World War and of various earlier conflicts, these included ancient hatreds, self-defense, and a genetic predisposition toward killing and destruction. Some of these became manifest in debates at the American Anthropological Association (AAA) meetings of 1992 and 1993, at which many anthropologists took sides, based on where they had done their fieldwork in the former Yugoslavia.[1] The consequences of these debates and attempted explanations were worrying, since some authors' explanations were then used as a means for extreme nationalists to justify 'their cause'. In the case of Robert Hayden, involvement in the struggle was taken even further. A specialist in the anthropology of law, professor in the Department of Anthropology at the University of Pittsburgh, and (at the time of writing) head of the AAA's section on Eastern Europe, he appeared as an expert witness at the trial of Dušan Tadić, one of those accused (and eventually convicted) of genocide at the International Criminal Tribunal for the Former Yugoslavia in The Hague.[2]

What anthropologists do, or believe in, therefore, is not always neutral or purely theoretical. Even – or especially – where they claim or attempt objectivity, this can result in rejoinders, angry rebuttals or threats of legal action. The aftermath of the publication of a paper by Cushman (2004) is a case in point. Cushman accused some anthropologists of siding with the Serbians and of supporting genocide in former Yugoslavia during the wars of the 1990s. While it is easy to understand his moral outrage, Cushman's vehemence evoked heated responses (Denich 2005; Hayden 2005) and got the editor of the journal at the time into trouble. Such a case does not, of course, distinguish anthropologists from professionals in other academic fields or disciplines, but as my primary interest here is in explaining certain models of culture and behaviour, I will leave issues of morality to people with more interest in the ethics of academic work. The crucial point is at the same time the most obvious one: when writing about politically charged situations, anthropologists should try to stick to the facts; 'reality,' no matter how apparently elusive (see Pina-Cabral, this volume), is what anthropological writing should be about. Writing about actual (observed) ethnographic situations, and trying to make the points of view of the underrepresented clear, should also clarify the most important issues about the ethics of research.[3]

Models for Explanations

One possible way of explaining anthropologists' partisan involvement with those they study, while simultaneously seeing them as 'less evolved', can be developed from Kuper's account of the invention of primitive society (Kuper 1988). Many anthropologists needed different, distant, exotic others as the basis for their explanatory models – from the totemic system of Australian Aborigines, through Amazonian Indians who lived 'close to nature' (and hence were supposed to fully understand it), to the present.[5] As the world became more globalized, and 'natives' increasingly participated in First World debates and discourses, it seemed natural that these distant and exotic others should be found in Europe. These 'new primitives' were to be located in the Balkan peninsula.

Some geographical reconceptualizations occurred in this relocation of the primitive. First of all, a new and different geography had to be invented. It was possible for the then British prime minister, Tony Blair, to declare in 1999 that the West would not tolerate crimes in Kosovo, 'on the borders of Europe'. A similar representation was present in the abstracts of a recent anthropology conference (the 2006 European Association of Social Anthropologists conference in Bristol), where it was stated that Slovenia was 'on the periphery of Europe.' These statements, reflecting a European Union-centred view, show profound ignorance of the historical and political processes which have shaped the subcontinent over the last several hundred years. The 'West' is a product of relatively recent history (Toulmin 1990), and the Western political and economic powers and the discourses which justify and legitimate them were acquired in the course of great colonial expansions by the nations of the north-western edge of the European peninsula (cf. Bauman 1993: 135–6) in the last three centuries.

Such remappings, then, refer to a symbolic geography in which the centre is Western Europe and everything beyond it is considered distant, marginal, exotic or even 'non-European' (see also Živković 2001). Such statements are not, however, held only by outsiders. In the case of Slovenia, there is also a sense of self-doubt about the extent to which Slovenian identity counts as fully European, despite the fact that the capital of Slovenia, Ljubljana, is physically much closer to most Western European capitals than, for example, Budapest in Hungary. An explanation can be sought in the oppositional character of the cold war. Although Slovenia was considered to be the most 'pro-Western' of all the states of the former Yugoslavia (1918–1991), its having been ruled by the Communist Party between 1945 and 1990 still made it distinctly 'non-Western.'

This symbolic remapping involved considerable reinvention and re-explanation, as Maria Todorova's book *Imagining the Balkans* (1997) makes clear. On the one hand, Todorova rightly points to the stereotypes traditionally present in Western descriptions and interpretations of the Balkans.[6] She demonstrates how the myth of the Balkans was constructed from literary accounts, both those of nineteenth-century travellers and adventurers and those of the Balkan wars of 1912/1913. The wars in particular created a powerful image, and a stereotype, of the Balkans, one which was further reinforced when the post-First World War partition of the Austro-Hungarian Empire gave rise to the term 'balkanization'. Of course, with the exception of Albania, all other countries of the Balkan peninsula had some sort of political existence even before the First World War, as Todorova points out (ibid.: 32ff). Hence, the procedure of 'balkanization' could easily be represented as a return to some pre-existing reality as it could be an unnatural and violent splintering of what properly ought to remain a single whole. Furthermore, the aftermath of the war actually saw more 'new' countries being created in Central Europe than it did in the Balkans. Nonetheless, the term 'balkanization' entered into political discourse after 1918, depicting unimaginable horrors of endless partition, and has been used to illuminate dangers in various parts of the world, from Haiti (by DuBois), through Lebanon – with the famous statement of one of its government officials in the 1980s: 'We shall not allow the Balkanization of Lebanon!' – to the former French colonies of West Africa – 'There are all the makings of a "Balkan situation" in West Africa' (quoted in ibid.: 35).

In similar vein, Jezernik's *Wild Europe* (2004) demonstrates a long history of stereotyping in representations of the region, showing how the Balkans was equated with the oriental, primitive and uncivilized, and how it was shown to be devoid of any culture. The Balkans thus became an important marker of what is permissible and what is not. All that was bad and alien to Western civilization was put into the imaginary realm of the Balkans, transferred into another place, another reality, where different principles of cognition and different modes of behavior were seen to be located. This mythical place was taken to represent the developing stages through which Western Europe – signifying the member countries of the European Union – had passed en route to a civilized status. As such, people from the Balkans were, and are, seen as being something like children: not quite on the same intellectual level as adults, and always in need of being told how to behave and what to do. These points reveal the evolutionist biases behind representations of the Balkans.

Unfortunately, in Todorova's construction of the concept of balkanism, inspired by Edward Said's *Orientalism* (1978), she fell unintentionally into the trap of simplification and essentialization.[7] Indeed, her book served as an important tool for those authors who were trying to put into context, justify or relativize Serb aggression in Croatia and Bosnia, as they claimed that this was all a problem of perception. According to representations like those by different Serb authors in the volume edited by Bjelić and Savić (2002), or by Bakić-Hayden (1995), the Serbs were presented as genuinely evil, when all they were trying to do was to fight for their homeland, freedom and basic human rights.[8] In an unexpected twist, these essentialized representations allowed other authors (see the examples in Cushman 2004) and, later, Western politicians and the media, to orientalize and subsequently dehumanize the Serbs. They showed how such stereotypes were taken as justifying anything that they did in their struggle, and as absolving them of any responsibility for their actions.

This particular way of representing was based on a particular and somewhat idealized point of view, as exemplified by Kate Hudson: 'Yugoslavia – the south Slav state – symbolized a progressive and open socialist society, held in high regard internationally for its monumental struggles for unity and independence and its role as the key leader of the Non-Aligned Movement' (Hudson 2003: 1). As this heroic place ceased to exist, its disappearance provoked strong reactions and fervent attempts to place blame on those deemed responsible. Just like any other human beings, anthropologists tend to react emotionally, and then to proceed in their arguments from emotions, not necessarily from the 'facts'.

Other Explanatory Models

Similar types of explanation were used in other parts of the former Yugoslavia, using different theoretical models. For example, some authors in Croatia claimed that anyone condemning the crimes of the Croatian army against Serbs in Croatia or Muslims in Bosnia were orientalizing Croats (see Bošković 2005a).[9] Using an essentialized explanation of the kind so roundly criticized by Kuper (1994b, 2003), the argument was that no foreign or outside observer could possibly comprehend what was going on in Croatia, so their explanations were obviously biased and wrong. That is, 'it takes one to know one'.[10]

This does not mean, however, that all representations of any parts of the former Yugoslavia endorse essentialist models of insider or authentic knowledge. For example, there is an excellent overview of recent Croatian ethnology and anthropology, with some important critical observations, by Prica (2005). In her paper, Prica, one of the most prominent Croatian ethnologists in recent years, took issue with some of the representations contained in her colleagues' writings since 1991. Emphasizing gendered scholarship in particular, since most contemporary Croatian ethnologists are female, Prica discussed the thematic and methodological problems of some recent ethnographies, including those dealing with war, suffering and refugees. She also criticized some Serbian interpretations of Croatian ethnology for their bias.

In general, however, the orientalization of the peoples of the Balkans means that the concept of indigenism is transformed into an important political and epistemological category in this part of Europe. The natives are somehow supposed to have a privileged insight into how things are, and how they should be. This is very similar to what Plaice (this volume) refers to, when she mentions the Labrador Inuit Association and their insistence on the geographical and historical bases of belonging. In practice, the implication is that any criticism from the outside is unacceptable. Taken in this sense, indigenism in the Balkans provides a position of absolute intellectual and moral superiority, an assertion of immediate access to the truth.

The proponents of this concept – the great majority of ethnologists in Serbia – find their natural allies in some strange places. Besides approving of Todorova, they were also very pleased with Glenny's book on the role of the Western powers in the Balkans (Glenny 1999). Its argument is not controversial in itself: the claim is that, given that foreign powers meddling in Balkan affairs were looking to promote their own interests, as great powers usually do, their intervention had disastrous consequences. Such an argument, however, suggests that if one blamed foreigners – the great colonial powers of Western Europe – for all the evils that happened in the region over the last two centuries, this not only absolves local populations and their political elites of any responsibility for their actions, but also paints a somewhat bleak picture of Balkan peoples as passive and unable to take the initiative, always waiting for something to be decided by others.

When it comes to representations of the Serbs, the 'it takes one to know one' argument has been used frequently. Several authors in the book *Balkans as Metaphor* (Bjelić and Savić 2002) argue along these lines. The claims made by one of them – Vesna Goldsworthy – are critically evaluated by Nankov (2002: 364–5), who shows how Goldsworthy would like to have it both ways. She is right when she objects to the deliberate simplifications of her people (the Serbs), but then uses the very same stereotyping strategy when referring to 'the West'. Even well-meaning outsiders can be complicit in this type of claim. An example can be found in the catalogue for the exhibition of Balkan artists in Graz in 2002 (Conover, Čufer and Weibel 2002). The curators of this exhibition, despite being outsiders themselves, used culture and cultural representations in order to promote stereotypes of Balkan peoples as distant and exotic. For example, exhibitions 'typifying' different places (of Romas for Romania; for Slovenia, a 'Retro-avantgarde' project by the Neue Slowenische Kunst (NSK); for Serbia, a video installation with a popular folk singer) were put on in separate pavilions, thus demonstrating their unique and exotic character. The curators further emphasize this in the catalogue, by offering 'a short test':

> First, take the four or five criteria most widely used to define the Balkans. Many people would place on their list such things as: place of ethnic tensions, place where old traumas are replayed again and again, place which fears dangerous neighbours across the border, place where people like to complain endlessly, place which overvalues its ancestors…. Now, take that definition you have – whatever that is – and apply it to Austria, France, Italy, United States, whatever country you are from. Warning: the surest sign of Balkan identity is the resistance to Balkan identity. (ibid.: 5)

This use of stereotypes as 'official' representations creates an interesting situation in which any point of view dissonant from what 'the natives' say or think (or believe is politically appropriate), or put forward by an outsider, should be ignored, regardless of its actual merit(s) or arguments. A good example of this is way in which Serbian scholars have ignored the work of Dutch anthropologist Mattijs van der Port (1998). Van der Port did his fieldwork in the Vojvodina region in the north of Serbia, learning the language and doing detailed research into different aspects of Serbian social and cultural identity. However, as local ethnologists did not like the way he wrote, they simply chose to ignore him, without entering into any debate or argument, or trying to prove him wrong. This dislike was not based on anything factual, but simply on the fact that he was a foreigner and, as such, threatened to bridge the insider–outsider divide. This was a matter to which he referred with some irony, noting that 'it takes a Serb to know a Serb' (Van der Port 1999).

As in the case of Greece (Gefou-Madianou, this volume), ancient civilizations and artefacts have played a role in endorsing present day ideas of culture. Some of the intellectual responses to the perceived 'orientalization' or 'balkanization' of the Serbs has to do with the insistence on the glorious aspects of ancient culture(s) in the region – such as the site of the first monumental sculpture in Europe (at Lepenski Vir, on the banks of the river Danube, a settlement which flourished *c.*6500 BCE), or the largest neolithic site in Europe (Vinča, on the outskirts of Belgrade, *c.*4000 BCE). Unfortunately, this celebration of ancient culture did not translate into increased state funding for research in these important archaeological sites:[11] until the fall of the nationalist regime in Serbia, official authorities were primarily interested in ideology, not scholarship. On a symbolic plane, the insistence on the antiquity and importance of these sites was supposed to be the decisive argument that the Serbs are more ancient and more civilized than those – the others – who have no proper past or history, and hence no culture. More colourful and historically less accurate examples were drawn from the Middle Ages. There were stories of how medieval Serbian peasants had used knives and forks while Western European kings ate only with their hands, like true barbarians. Such stories, although unverified, nevertheless played their role in the popular Balkan imagination of the backwardness of others.

Popular representations of foreigners' lack of culture, exemplified by the U.S. as well as by institutions like the EU or NATO, was also apparent inasmuch as the state-controlled media tended to report only on disasters and calamities happening in the outside world. The conclusion to be drawn was that only 'we' know how to live, how to entertain ourselves, how to stay out of trouble and, most of all, how to preserve and respect our cultural traditions.

This increasingly hardening set of stereotypes was not created in a vacuum, however. Conversely, a culture versus nature dichotomy, which fed upon and reinforced negative views of the Balkans by outsiders, was being gradually strengthened. For many so-called Western anthropologists brought up on the opinions of political analysts, and in line with what Todorova was criticizing, Balkan peoples appeared to be behaving irrationally, showing their proximity to nature. Culture, in contrast, was more complicated, more sophisticated, more distant, and reserved for more developed societies. The Balkan peoples were sufficiently 'primitive' to become objects of anthropological study by those from outside. Although anthropologists used history, demography and religion in their accounts of the Balkans (Hayden 2002), the primitive character of the inhabitants of the region – as natives on the margins of Europe – meant that 'culture' was not an obvious attribute.[12]

Some Evolutionist Theories Revisited

It is not uncommon to find evolutionary explanations paraded in the public media, and to hear anthropologists dismissing these as simply wrong and out of date. We also tend to assume that such explanations cannot be used seriously today in any context. But is it really so? As recently as 1991, the expert legal and political commission led by Robert Badinter was appointed by the (then) European Community (EC) in order to determine which countries (former republics) of the former Yugoslavia conformed to the legal and political standards of the EC, in order for them to be officially recognized by it. Badinter's Commission concluded that those countries were Slovenia and Macedonia. However, it was Slovenia and Croatia that the EC decided to formally recognize. Unlike Macedonia, Croatia was assumed by European policy makers to have culture, and it was thus deemed worthy of full recognition by the elite group of EC countries. Macedonia, less economically developed and therefore more distant from the 'enlightened West', yet having fulfilled all the legal and political preconditions of official political recognition, was supposed to wait longer.[13]

Even among anthropologists who would normally repudiate hierarchical scales of value in favour of relativism, there is an implicit endorsement of evolutionist models. This can be seen in professional anthropologists' lack of interest in developments outside their discipline's mainstream (Anglo-American, French, German). Kuper's attention to national anthropological traditions, and his co-founding role in the European Association of Social Anthropology (EASA), are distinct exceptions to the rule. While EASA has been much more open than many other professional associations to recognizing different or exotic voices, it is unclear whether many anthropologists working in Britain or the EU are aware of developments in their discipline in other countries, particularly those, like the Balkans, where the language of teaching and research is not English. This point has been raised in recent years by anthropologists like Muršič (2000) in Slovenia and Hannerz in Sweden, speaking in his address at the Durham meeting of the Association of Social Anthropologists in 2007. Despite the fact that in many such countries, publishing in English (and in foreign journals published in English) is considered a mark of distinction, and something that can significantly help one's career (Bošković 2008),[14] these anthropological traditions remain, for the most part, invisible.

The converse is also true. Whilst becoming increasingly involved in academic departments in the former Yugoslavia in recent years, I have been struck by their lack of interest in what is going on in the outside world. The virtual ignoring of Van der Port's work is only a symptom of a much wider situation affecting the system of education in the former Yugoslavia. As political relations with Western countries become strained, education programmes tend to be more nationalist in orientation, and information regarding other parts of the world becomes increasingly unavailable. In Serbia, for example, obligatory foreign language courses were scrapped from the school curriculum after the nationalist government came into power in 2004.[15] Perhaps this is some kind of ideological preparation for the isolation upon which some leading Serbian politicians thrive: they sense that they can realize their potential only in a small, closed, inward-looking and xenophobic society. 'The West' is perceived to be guilty of misrepresenting natives ('us'), and as such is irrelevant. To 'their' lack of understanding of 'us,' we respond with a lack of interest in them. The end result further reinforces the 'it takes one to know one' attitude outlined above. This leads to the gradual diminution of the importance of the comparative perspective in teaching and research in anthropology, to which I recently objected (Bošković 2005b). This is in contrast to the growing public interest in anthropology, as exemplified in the increasing numbers of students entering undergraduate studies in ethnology and cultural anthropology, in both Serbia and Croatia, as well as to the prominence of events such as the Ethnographic Film Festival in Belgrade.

Particular ways of inventing and recreating cultural notions are thus at play in this part of Europe, both from the side of 'the natives' and from that of the 'outsiders'. Although the myth of the Balkans had already been constructed in a specific sense (and for particular political and ideological purposes) in the early twentieth century (Todorova 1994; Karakasidou 2002), the real primitive society invented in the 1990s was that of the ethnic communities of the former Yugoslavia, and in a struggle to explain the inexplicable, anthropologists found themselves in a paradoxical situation. On the one hand, they believed that they could somehow be objective and detached. On the other, the fierceness of convictions and conflicting accounts led to some heated debates which were anything but dispassionate (Hayden 2002, 2003, 2005; Denich 2005; Wilson 2005).

Kuper's critique of the (mis)use of the concept of indigenism (Kuper 2003) is important here. His remarks point to some of the dangers of the newly established 'it takes one to know one' attitude. If taken seriously, absolutely privileging the insider's point of view would obviously render all social – as well as many other – sciences impossible. However, the privileging of insiders is very tempting. It presents an easy way out, a perspective that would allow its protagonist simply to ignore what appears as irrelevant or, more likely, potentially dangerous to the national cause.

Conclusion

To conclude, if anthropological attempts to deal with post-conflict situations are to have any explanatory value, and if they are to approach a certain objective validity, they should be based on certain clear professional and ethical standards. Essentializations of 'good guys' and 'bad guys' do not help at all. Neither does reaching into (imagined) history and carefully selecting those facts that serve one side in whatever struggle might be going on. Although this is not easy in situations that are extremely emotionally charged, I am encouraged by the example of social scientists working in Guatemala. Still recovering from a situation of extreme and violent conflict, a network of committed foreign scholars is working there with the aim of promoting local scholars and facilitating different forms of 'local knowledge'. They are simultaneously involved in the social life of the communities where they do their research.[16] An attempt is also made, and financial means secured, to translate articles and books into local Mayan languages, which makes outside interpretations readily available to local populations. At the same time, they are not suspending more internationally recognized criteria for measuring standards of ethnography.

Taking this as an example, it would be useful to attempt something similar in the countries of the former Yugoslavia. Doing so might enable both local and foreign anthropologists, and local and foreign media, to transcend the self-perpetuating and mutually reinforcing procedures through which the category of 'the Balkans' is endlessly reproduced.

Notes

1. Some of these explanations can be found in the volume edited by Halpern and Kideckel (2000)
2. A specialist in the anthropology of law, Professor in the Department of Anthropology of the University of Pittsburgh, and (at the time of the writing of this chapter) also head of the AAA's section on Eastern Europe.
3. Hayden (2003: 274, 278, and in particular 282, n.57); see also Wilson (2005).
4. This does not imply that anthropologists should not take active part and serve as witnesses in legal cases, merely that the giving of 'expert opinions' can be motivated by partisan convictions.
5. For the examples of the First Nations in Canada and 'indigenous people' in South Africa, see Plaice and Barnard (this vol.) I am not interested here in discussing actual quality or (lack of) depth of these types of explanations, only in the fact that they were present (and quite influential) in the history of anthropology.
6. Klaus Roth, a German scholar, told me in a personal communication (2007) that German descriptions of 'the Balkans' from the same period, which lack these essentializations, are absent from Todorova's account.
7. Todorova did not explain why there were no different, 'native,' or 'insider' attempts to explain the Balkans. For an extremely interesting and ethnographically based account of the topic, see Živković (2001).
8. In television reports from the 'Balkan wars' in the U.S. in the early 1990s, stereotyped depictions of Serbs sometimes resembled cartoon characters.
9. For examples of some Croatian controversies dealing with geographical (dis)locations, see Rihtman-Auguštin (1999).
10. Although I admire Bringa's (1995) ethnography of the war in Bosnia, I am also aware of the potent criticism of her position by a leading Croatian 'ethno-anthropologist,' the late Dunja Rihtman-Auguštin (2004: 122–4). On potential problems with anthropologists as 'expert witnesses,' see also note 4.
11. Only Vinča remains today. The site of Lepenski Vir has been relocated, its fabulous triangular dwellings moved to higher ground during 1960s to make space for the Iron Gates hydroelectric dam on the river Danube (Srejović 1981; Tasić et al. 1990).
12. Few anthropologists explored the consequences of these explanations or their implications for 'locals' (but see Van der Port 1999; Bringa 2005).
13. Following this there were disputes over the country's constitutional name which demonstrated more about the EU's incapacity to deal with problems in an efficient and rational way than about the 'Macedonian question' (Bošković 2006: 81–83).
14. Among notable exceptions are Brazil and Japan, countries with large anthropological communities (professional associations in each country have around 2,000 members) and distinctive research traditions.
15. In 2005, the former Minister of Education, Ljiljana Čolić, also proposed abolishing the teaching of classical evolutionary theory. Fortunately, her proposal did not pass, and she was eventually forced to resign.
16. See, for example, Fischer and McKenna Brown (1996) and Fischer and Benson (2006).

Chapter 7

Which Cultures, What Contexts and Whose Accounts? Anatomies of a Moral Panic in Southall, Multi-ethnic London

Gerd Baumann

In studying a seemingly irrational phenomenon such as a moral panic – an apparently spontaneously generated and widespread idea that a minority group (for example) is dangerously deviant (Cohen 1980) – the gulf between insider and outsider contextualizations and accounts must appear as an epistemological chasm. How can 'they', the insiders and experts in 'their culture', so complicate their social lives by a moral panic? How can 'we', the outside experts on culture and comparison, explain their seeming irrationality in rational terms that are recognisable to insiders too? By means of a case study of 'Asian gangs' in late 1980s Southall (London), this chapter argues that the boundaries between insider and outsider understandings are fluid and that the interactions between these heuristic opposites are best understood as dialogical, indeed dialectical.

My case study begins with four observations, and proceeds from insiders' to outsiders' perspectives, in order to show how a moral panic in a peaceable town condensed highly disparate fears, but then spawned the most implausible social folk theories. My argument then proposes four distinctions and suggests some differentiations that are neither exclusively insider nor outsider in perspective. They integrate the knowledge and assumptions of outsiders like the media and the police and, at the same time, they often invoke locally generated categories. The final step recontextualizes all accounts, whether generated within or outside the local context, and argues for four connections in order to analyse the moral panic about the 'Asian gangs' as a series of local transformations of much wider conflicts and constellations.

Observations

A Moral Panic ...

'Four out of five young people out on the streets tonight will be carrying knives'. This was Her Majesty's Home Secretary Douglas Hurd's dire statistic about the youngsters of Southall, Britain's most densely populated immigrant ghetto on the western outskirts of London.[1] When I heard this about halfway into seven years' field work, I went white with ethnographic rage.[2] Admittedly, this was a suitable propaganda lie as the third Thatcher government faced a parliamentary revolt against a new Criminal Justice Bill which radically extended police powers to 'stop and search' on suspicion alone. Yet the ludicrous statistic reflected not only narrow parliamentary and widespread civil rights fears, but also a momentous moral panic sweeping Southall and its 60,000 citizens – roughly speaking 50 per cent Sikhs from the Punjab and East Africa, 15 per cent Hindus, 15 per cent Muslims, and 20 per cent Irish and English people (Ealing Council 1982). The local press carried bold headlines such as 'Asian Gang Warfare! Parents Told to Keep Kids in the Home', a call endorsed by 'community leaders', and a police photo of the 'Terror Weapons of a Holy War', including confiscated knives, 'Sikh ceremonial swords' and the holiest of British artefacts, some cricket bats. The 'kids kept in the home' were turned into 'Prisoners of the Gangs' within a week, and there was even a 'Chicago-style street attack', though closer reading revealed pigeon-shot pellets instead of Chicago bullets. Yet as the moral panic spread through the media, even the BBC painted Southall as 'a prolific breeding ground for gangsters', where locals spread stories about 'gang members' being initiated by committing gang rape, and even level-headed school teachers saw 'a third of them' as 'members of the Tooti Nung or the Holy Smokes'.[3] As the newspapers accelerated their 'Calendar of Terror' over a summer heated up by their own hot air, there was indeed a 'street battle in Southall – two stabbed. Revenge car ambush catches four alleged Tooti Nungs ... In addition to this catalogue – sometimes involving people with no known gang connection – there have been two kidnappings'.[4] Needless to say, the 'kidnappers' did not know what to do with the kids and all were home for dinner. Yet the media mention of 'people with no known gang connection' is an apt clue. With the moral panic taken for granted, one must ask: were there gangs at all? And if so, did crime increase? And if so, by whom, when and why?

... in a Peaceable Town ...

To gather evidence on crime in Southall, let us start with the police statistics of 'All Notifiable Offences recorded for 1987 and 1988', and then calculate the corresponding percentage increases for the panic year, 1988.[5] The figures show a remarkably low offence rate and a remarkably non-violent offender profile for an industrial British suburb (Home Office 1988). Before and after the panic, 90 per cent of offences were property-related, in effect theft or burglary; only 7 per cent involved violence. Even when violent offences increased by just under 20 per cent in the panic year, the absolute figures (rising from some 600 cases to some 700) suggested a village-like safety in a post-industrial suburb of 60,000. This was clearly a case for Sally Engle Merry (1981), who sees 'urban danger' as an urban myth, and juvenile referral statistics in Southall tell the same story. Even in this immigrant town, where 50 per cent of the population at the time were under 24 years of age, juvenile offences and referrals were remarkably low, given London-wide comparative figures. None of this could have surprised any local resident or even an anthropologist, aware as we were of the tightly knit networks of social control in 'our town'. So how could so many reasonable people go in for a moral panic about 700, as opposed to the previous year's 600, people hitting each other over the head once a year? Any statistics on pub brawls and even juvenile vehicle crime show greater fluctuations and vastly higher absolute figures per head of population in any working-class district of London. So did the natives take leave of their common sense under the influence of a moral panic inspired by the police, the Home Office or the local press; and if so, what is the anthropologist's account?

... condenses Disparate Fears ...

Since the fears expressed about 'gang violence' were clearly irrational, let us briefly distinguish the constituencies of this moral panic. First, there were the local media, double-quick to cash in on the 'ethnic' dimension of the supposed 'Asian gangs'. The following analysis in the local press made it into the national headlines too:

> Both the Holy Smokes and the Tooti Nungs have been revealed as powerful criminal organizations with memberships well in excess of 1,000 and branches among the large Asians communities in [many British cities]. The Holy Smokes, the larger and better organised of the warring fractions, [are] formed mainly from the Jat caste – a proud and fierce warrior race [sic] from the Punjab.... Their rivals, the Tooti Nungs – the name translates as Worthless Ones – are generally drawn from the lower Sikh castes.... Both gangs are organised on the tiered structure operated by both the Mafia and the Chinese Triads.[6]

Such references to the Mafia, the Triads, and elsewhere to the 'Jamaican Yardies', implicitly reclassify youth crime as 'ethnic crime', and this in stark opposition to the local police chief's cool analysis: 'a few youngsters hitting each other over the head with cricket bats'.

Other constituencies, however, joined the fray. Feminists blamed the perceived explosion of violence upon patriarchal 'Asian' family structures; male religious 'community leaders' blamed it on a deeply immoral British society; youth workers castigated a lack of public funds; social workers documented an increase in poverty, including child poverty, in Thatcher's Britain; trade unionists chided a government bent on breaking the back of a united working class. Southall was in a state of mayhem amidst all these disparate moral fears and righteous concerns about social cohesion and moral responsibility. While hardly anyone had ever seen a 'gang fight' or even knew a 'gang member' from more than rumour, everyone's dissatisfactions with the nation-state of Britain and its local control over a presumed immigrant local state could coagulate into this one bloody blister: 'Southall's Asian gangs, The Holy Smokes and the Tooti Nungs'. Still, no one knew which was which or what they wanted.

... and Spawns Implausible Theories

Effectively, there were three theories that Southallians could use to make sense of the gangs: territory, caste and criminal instigation from above.

Local evidence did not suggest that territory was a fruitful line of investigation. True, Southall was and is divided into two halves, an 'old' and a 'new' Southall, by a narrow bridge over a dozen railway lines and shunting yards connecting post-industrial ruins. Yet although white youth gangs in the 1930s and 1950s had confronted each other on territorial grounds on the bridge, this did not apply to the 'Asian gangs'. Admittedly, there had once been a 'gang fight' over a snooker hall near the bridge, much desired by all as a place for obtaining soft drugs, but membership in one or another 'gang' could not be traced to dichotomies of territory. Still, the theory persisted among those older Southallians who would rather see their old territorial conflicts again than face some new 'Asian caste war'.

Caste, the second folk explanation, was a locally prevalent, yet in most ways an equally unfounded, line of enquiry. The Holy Smokes were thought to be Sikhs of the Jat caste, the Tooti Nungs ('Worthless Ones') to be Sikhs of the other, 'lower' castes: perhaps Ramgarhia, perhaps the lowest castes of Churhe ('sweepers') and Chamar ('leather workers'). Countless people believed that these allegiances had furnished the basis for caste conflict, but again without much evidence. The mere population statistics of Southall would make it impossible for 'lower caste' Sikhs to mobilize against Jat Sikhs; in any case, the Ramgarhia would not want to, given their own ideas about the Churhe and Chamar 'outcastes' and their vastly better life chances by education and skills (Bhachu 1985). Deductively, the folk theory was implausible; inductively, it failed to accord with the data even as I collected them, such as the example of two brothers who claimed membership in two different gangs. So, in the anthropologist's account, caste could not be the explanation either, whatever local people might believe.

The third folk theory, one concerned with criminal instigation of organized thefts and drug dealing, was even more implausible. Yet the 'gangs' were soon stylized as fully fledged top-down criminal organizations. A local journalist wrote:

> At the top of the hierarchy are the Godfathers, ostensibly respectable businessmen who travel freely between the Indian sub-continent and Britain. They deal with the main business of the gangs – heroin, other drug trafficking, and fraud ... The next tier are the operational bosses of the gangs ... They translate the orders ... when necessary ordering the troops. At the bottom are the 'soldiers'. Most are between 18 and 25 and officially unemployed. They ... act as cannon fodder in the street.[7]

These claims were unfounded. Even if 'the gangs' could have been shown to be organized groups, and even if there had been an organized fight over a share of the nearby Heathrow Airport drugs trade, it was unlikely that either 'gang' would send juvenile hotheads onto Southall's streets, merely to see them swiftly arrested for possessing dope or wielding a cricket bat. In sum, accounts spread via the media and finding some local credence ranged from theories about criminal syndicates perverting innocent Asian youth, through those about a Thatcherite government driving vulnerable youth into the arms of gangsters, to those concerning alienated youth reviving putatively traditional caste conflicts. In the absence of plausible local accounts, one clearly needed a detached analytical perspective (Kuper 1976, 1982, 1999b). The ground on which all these disparate mis-modellings had taken root was fertilized by a categorical transformation of interpreting any juvenile delinquency as 'gang crime', and then seeing the 'Asian gangs' as a hub of 'ethnic crime.' It was thus time to cross the putative gulf between insider and outsider knowledge and make some differentiations. Let me thus propose four distinctions to make some better sense of this so-called gang crime, namely: gravity versus frequency of offences; high-skill crime versus low-skill deviance; criminal networks versus 'ethnic crime'; and criminal careers versus symbolic identifications.

Distinctions

Gravity or Frequency?

An internal police report detailed 'gang crime' as follows:

a   fraud
b   rape
c   dishonest handling of stolen property
d   'ringing' [i.e. changing the identity] of motor vehicles
e   possession of firearms
f   suspected involvement in illegal drugs
g   causing serious injuries to members of rival gangs or dissenting members of their own

h offering 'protection' to traders or [threatening] violence in default
i Burglary or theft from cars.[8]

The list makes daunting reading, as it was probably intended to. Yet its arbitrary ordering (a to i) follows neither the frequency of offences, nor their severity in terms of penal or civil law. Just compare the same police authority's quantitative tabulation of:

Type of Offence:	Recorded 1987:	Percentage Change 1988:
(1) Theft and Handling of Stolen Goods	4717	minus 6%
(2) Criminal Damage	2324	plus 2%
(3) Burglary	1744	minus 7%
(4) Violence against the Person	438	plus 18%
(5) Fraud or Forgery	204	minus 6%
(6) Robbery	178	plus 17%
(7) Sexual Offences	63	plus 13%
(8) Other Notifiable Offences	37	plus 24%

Table 7.1: 'All Notifiable Offences Recorded by Southall Police' for 1987 and 1988:
Clearly, over the two years preceding 1989, reported violent offences (categories 4, 6 and 7) did increase by between 10 and 15 per cent, although precision would be presumptuous here given the ambiguities inherent in reporting violence under categories 6 and 7. But even counting any doubts as certainty against the accused, the year in question, 1989, showed a drop of 3 per cent aggregate in violent offences and a greater drop in non-violent offences recorded. From an analyst's point of view, these figures, not published then or since and unavailable to all but a few Southallians, would indicate that the extent of the violence was vastly exaggerated by both the media and most local actors.

High-skill Crime or Low-skill Deviance?

For the most insightful local-level distinction, I must thank four parties whom I met independently, but – Southall being Southall with its hyper-density of social control and gossip – with each other's tacit agreement. These were some youngsters facing a Juvenile Referral or a Youth Court, some shady adult characters well known for their experiences in court or in prison, some lawyers who did what lawyers must do, and one local policeman who shared my perplexity at this sudden moral panic. Their taxonomy distinguished offences as to the skills required, the resources gained, the risks taken and, notably, the social networks involved. On the skills, both manual and especially social, the taxonomy reflected common sense: stealing a purse merely requires individual dexterity and delivers cash or credit cards, while cracking a car or burgling a house requires a loose social network to handle the stolen goods. Without such loose networks, even credit card theft could not deliver profit for long. Before he was caught, 'One [male Southall] youngster is said to have used a credit card in the name of a titled lady for several weeks'.[9] Whether the rumour is an urban legend or an empirical fact, low-skill, low-risk and casual-network offences covered about 90 per cent of all offences recorded in any one year before or after the moral panic.

Criminal Networks or 'Ethnic Crime'?

Surveying the local scene, there had never been even a semblance of a local criminal aristocracy that could run a more than moderately complex enterprise. It was only a year after the moral panic, when Scotland Yard had finished their enquiries, that the extent of white-collar network crime in West London came to light.

> A £4 million mortgage and insurance racket, £200,000 credit card fraud and an underground network for smuggling in illegal immigrants and providing them with forged documentation are still being investigated. Five guns have been seized, along with £500,000, 20 illegal immigrants, false passports, hundreds of stolen or bogus credit cards and a selection of stolen cars.[10]

Other media reports offered different figures on the financial scale involved: 'The "mafia", controlled by seemingly respectable businessmen, netted £30 million a year and spanned three continents.... Scores of bank, building society and insurance frauds have been uncovered, one involving more than £12 million'.[11] Differences apart, all the media persisted in imputing intimate links between 'the school-age gangsters' and the 'multi-million pound Asian crime syndicate'.[12] The police investigators, however, explicitly denied this linkage which the media had propagated for over a year:

> The man leading the police investigation ... said: 'At first there was some suggestion that the organization was connected to the gangs, but after initial enquiries it turned out to be much bigger. It appears [sic] that these gangs did exist some years ago but I don't think there is any such thing as gang allegiance today.' ... A police spokesman stressed that ... 'there is no suggestion that the gangs are directly involved with organized crime.' ... The liaison officer of the operation added: 'This organization should not be seen as a Southall problem'.[13]

Yet rather than distinguishing between gravity and frequency, high-skill crime and low-skill deviance, criminal networks and 'Asian crime', the media hung on to a sheer irresistible urge to trace the 'ethnic' schoolboy with a cricket bat to the 'ethnic' drugs baron and the multi-million insurance fraudster. One reason for this insistence was clearly connected to racism and stereotyping. Speaking of young people in particular, Claire Alexander's (2000) study of South London Bengali youth stigmatized as 'Asian gangs' confirms similar points in a very different ethnographic setting. Sales-hungry media created a populist 'folk devil' (Cohen 1980) by turning Bengali-descended young Londoners into born ethnic gangsters, success-hungry social service agencies turned them into presumed cultural victims, and both of them combined with other parties to turn the triangle – youth, ethnic difference and masculinity – into an axiomatic 'societal problem'.

How could Southall's adults, both parents and teachers, fall for this? Here, it may help to stress the moral dimension of the moral panic. Since common sense has it that 'the child is the father of the man', just as 'all big crooks start small', the wanton association between the pickpocket and the fraud tycoon creates one continuous moral universe. In this universe, small failings lead straight to heinous crimes, while a benevolently strict, but also protective, education of the young promises a society based on morality. With such an interpretation the argument may stray into the realms of symbolic thinking, but these symbolics are indeed indispensable in understanding both the moral panic and the conjured-up danger of 'Asian gangs.'

Criminal Careers or Symbolic Identifications?

To the pioneers of 'gangs' sociology (Whyte 1943; Thrasher 1963), the most arresting feature of the Southall gangs would surely have been the total absence of open identity markers, badges, insignia and the like. Yet the twelve- to sixteen-year-old schoolboys I taught at a middle school nonetheless spent boring lessons adorning their exercise books with elaborate doodles spelling 'Holy Smokes' or else 'Tooti Nungs' – just as previously they had resorted to doodling 'KFC' for chicken or 'McD' for beef, depending on their preferences or dietary injunctions. In the breaks, too, they might easily claim to be 'a Toot' or 'a Holy', sometimes to pick a fight, though as often to avoid one. Since no one knew what the distinction might be based on or whether these were claims to symbolic identification or claims to actual 'membership', the local media, too, could sell any schoolboy brawl 'with no known gang connection' as a further instance of 'gang crime'.[14]

When I say that no one knew the difference, I refer to the three implausible folk theories described at the end of the section concerning my observations. Various local etymologies connected the attribute 'Holy' with Sikhs of the Jat, or farmers', caste that resented the rivalry and often greater economic success of the Ramgarhia, or craftsmen's, castes. Since 'Smokes' was usually taken to allude to cannabis, and 'Holy Smoke' was an Americanism familiar to all young people, it is likely that the Holy Smokes named themselves first, and that they indeed imposed the name 'Tooti Nungs' on any of their rivals. All local etymologies translated that second 'gang' label within the same semantic field: 'worthless people, outcasts, low castes, scum people, lowest of the low', or indeed: 'The Nobodies' or 'The Nothings'. They traced it to Punjabi: *tuti* (extremity or head), and *nunga* (bald, bare, naked). Most concretely, this could mean a Sikh without a turban, most abstractly a person ('head') without worth or even identity. These insider etymologies may or may not convince a Sanskritist, but the symbolics were plausible for the analyst outsider. The opposition between 'The Holies' and 'The Toots' contrasted 'The Pure' with 'The Nothing'.

We face a strange methodological impasse now. An outsider objectivist sociology alone cannot explain the insider symbolizations, but nor can the insider symbolizations alone guide the outsider analyst's explanation. That impasse, however, is the point, as we move to the third step in the argument. This last step, called 'connections', recontextualizes all accounts, whether offered by prima facie insiders or prima facie outsiders, and reveals the moral panic about the 'Asian gangs' as a local transformation of transnational conflicts and constellations.

Connections

'The Pure' and 'The Nothing'

The most arresting empirical question remaining concerns the social distinction between the 'gangs', or rather, the two gang identifications. As we have seen, insider social theories of a territorial division or a cleavage among Sikh castes made no sociological sense. Even so, understanding the 'gangs' does still involve caste; only caste must be located at one remove from empirical caste divides. Long late-night interviews over wholesome beers and unholy smokes revealed a superordinate pattern of gang identifications. According to this superordinate structural pattern, those who identified with the Holy Smokes were Sikhs of the Jat caste. It is crucial to add, though, that while all Holy Smokes were Jat, only a tiny proportion of Jat Sikhs identified themselves as Holies. Those who identified with the Tooti Nungs could be drawn from a wide range of caste origins, as well as from origins in which caste was an irrelevance. They included some Sikhs of the Jat caste and some of any other caste, as well as some Hindus, Muslims, Afro-Caribbeans, and even the odd white British and Irish young man.

Evidence to support this observation included two main sources, First, British law allows the public naming of defendants appearing in court, and since there are proven colonial concordances of Punjabi caste names (Rose 1911–1919), the lead was clear: Jat names for the Holies versus all sorts of names, including some Jat, for the Toots. Secondly, one of a group of local fourteen- to fifteen-year-old schoolboys, in a 1988 informal discussion at Featherstone Middle School, gave me a telling clue – one as insightful as anything in Bourdieu's *Distinction* (1984).

You can tell who is a Toot and who is a Holy by the [makes of] cars they drive and the music they play when they cruise on the Broadway. Even if they can't get the [make of] car they want, you can tell who is who by the music they play when they go cruising. The Holies go in for Bhangra in a big way; but the Toots will play Reggae as well, and pop, and even George Michael!

Bhangra, a traditional Punjabi harvest dance adapted to disco music (Baumann 1990) was associated with a masculine 'true Sikhism', whereas reggae was associated with Afro-Caribbean counter-cultures, and George Michael stood for an almost provocatively 'softie' sound. The symbolic opposition of these musical tastes could not be clearer.

Finally, confirmation of this superordinate pattern of distinction could be gleaned from the wider social field, stretching across all of West London. From Heathrow Airport in the south via Southall to Wembley Stadium in the north, and from Uxbridge in the west via Southall to Acton Town in the east, we now speak of a gigantic expanse of suburban West London, measuring some five by seven miles, or 80 square kilometres at least. When local brawls ended in a draw or demanded a rematch with enforcements, then local 'posses' could call in 'allies' from another suburb. On one occasion, the Tooti Nungs were helped by the Billy Boys, mostly Muslim South Asians from Hendon and Wembley: 'that's real low', commented a Jat friend, 'the Holies would never side with Muslims; they'd call in the Lions of the Punjab from up north: they're pure Sikhs like the Holies'. The 'gangs' pattern of 'pure' Sikhs versus anyone else, or indeed anyone at all versus pro-Khalistan Sikhs, seemed to hold as the most plausible pattern for recruitment and style, local antagonisms and outside alliances. To show this historic and local plausibility, we need to consider a second connection.

Southall; Khalistan: 1984–1988

When the first South Asians arrived in Southall in the early 1950s, they were all Jat Sikh farmers from the Punjab. Two key push factors were the partition of the Punjab between the newly independent India and Pakistan in 1947, which uprooted Sikh farmers from the western Punjab, now Pakistan, and an acute shortage of inheritable arable land in the eastern Punjab, now India. Among the pull factors was the postwar shortage of especially unskilled labour in West London's booming manufacturing and food-processing plants. Chain migration, family reunions and transnational marriages, coupled with 'white flight' – an outflow of those formerly living in the area – rendered the Jat Sikh population the largest single segment of Southall's total population by the mid 1970s.

They were surprised, however, in the mid 1970s, by several thousand South Asians escaping from or expelled by the 'Africanization' policies of Uganda, Tanzania and Kenya. These East African South Asians comprised Hindus and Muslims along with a majority of Sikhs of the Ramgarhia castes, all predominantly skilled people who had formed an intermediate stratum of clerks and accountants, craftsmen and engineers in formerly British-ruled East Africa. Soon, hierarchies of caste, in which the Jat claimed superiority, clashed with hierarchies of class. The latter often favoured the East African South Asians in Southall, since they had arrived as integral families, often skilled or highly skilled, and sometimes with investment capital (Bhachu 1985). While open resentment was contained in Southall, it was commonplace for Jat Sikhs to sneer at 'those arrogant, newly rich Ramgarhia', whose forebears had not owned their own land in the Punjab and who now established their own temples in town; just as vice versa, and for these in turn, it was normal to sneer at 'those peasants (*pindhu*) who never made it in the Punjab or even in Britain'.

Parallel antagonisms developed in the Punjab, where Jat farmers found themselves challenged by new Jat or non-Jat elites commanding commercial, crafts and professional skills (Singh 1986). These antagonisms did much to fuel the violent political conflicts over the establishment of a Sikh state, to be called Khalistan ('Land of the Pure'), intended to secede by force from the Indian Union. The presence in Southall of a vociferous faction among Jat Sikhs who supported the armed struggle for an independent Khalistan had been evident from reactions to the siege of the Golden Temple, the Sikhs' spiritual capital in Amritsar in the summer of 1984. The issue split the local Jat temple congregations in a series of dramatic confrontations and takeovers, coups and counter-coups, which eventually ended up in Britain's High Court.

The storming of the Golden Temple, occupied by the Khalistan Commando Force under Sant Jarnail Singh Bhindrawale and holding out against Indian government troops, transformed the nature of Sikh politics everywhere. The desecration of the Sikhs' holiest shrine, notably on 3 June 1984, the feast day of the Sikhs' hero-martyr guru, Sri Arjun Dev Ji, caused bloody repercussions not only in India, but also in Southall. The assassination of Prime Minister Indira Gandhi, on 31 October 1984, allegedly by some of her Sikh bodyguards, spawned riots, murders and fire bombings against Sikhs throughout India and horrendous human rights abuses (Amnesty International 1991; Pettigrew 1992). At the same time in Southall, the town saw the first of three political murders when the pro-Indira Gandhi editor of a Sikh weekly paper was killed in an arson attack. Eight months later, in July 1985, a moderate member of the Jat temple committee was blinded in a shotgun attack. Six months later, in January 1986, Southall saw its second political murder when a prominent pro-Indira Gandhi Sikh community leader was assassinated by pro-Khalistan Sikhs. In November 1987, now well into the period of the moral panic, two pro-Khalistan Jat Sikhs broke into a prayer meeting led by a heterodox Sikh reformist leader in Southall, gunning him down and injuring several of his followers.

In India, too, the conflict over an independent Khalistan took a new bloody turn with the second storming of the Golden Temple, ordered by Prime Minister Rajiv Gandhi in May 1988. In India, the showdown itself left

300 people dead, and the ensuing communal riots killed hundreds of Sikhs and hundreds of Hindu migrant workers who had come to the Punjab from Bihar. In Southall, this time coincided with the climax of the period of the moral panic, 1989. Remarkably, even my closest friends, whether Sikh, Hindu or Muslim, eschewed any discussion. The consensual taboo converged on the same few evasive phrases: 'It is terrible for everybody there! And imagine if that were to happen here! But just look around here: look at the gangs!'

The fear of communal violence along the lines of that in the Indian subcontinent breaking out in Southall was pervasive, and all but one Sikh temple, all Hindu temples, and most Christian churches held special 'Prayer Meetings for Peace', notably without specifying whether this meant peace on the subcontinent or peace in Southall. In Southall, as well as outside, the moral panic about the 'gangs' turned into a moral panic about 'the town' as a whole. The local press mediated this to both insiders and outsiders, however one might now define the terms. The delineation first phrased as insider versus outsider has become useless now. To give two examples: when does a Southallian who moved 'up the road' to a better house near Heathrow stop counting as an insider Southallian, and on what criteria would one count a local anthropologist as an outsider while counting a local journalist as an insider, or vice versa? At an analytic level of insider versus outsider, local versus supra local, or folk versus academic models, the insider–outsider distinction runs out of steam at this point. Its best purpose now is to serve as a heuristic crutch to structure data, but not to determine analysis (Kuper 1992a).

However, some national and international media – mainly the BBC and some quality papers – inserted a new variable into the insoluble equation of the 'gangs' that were not gangs. The moral panic about 'the Southall gangs' was an international affair because the British government itself was directly involved in the conflicts about the Punjab.

Precisely during the panic period 1988/1989, the British Government was conducting negotiations with the government of India, aimed at a mutual Treaty of Extradition. Pro-Khalistan Sikhs were the first to notice this constitutional aberration: British citizens could then be tried, sentenced and imprisoned in India, Indian citizens in Britain. The rationale for both states was clear: their common enemies were the pro-Khalistan Sikhs in both Britain and the Punjab, and their strategic target was the demolition of such transnational networks. It stands to reason then that one needs to broach a third connection to understand the 'gangs' panic, and for brevity's sake, one may dub it 'Sikhs and Brits'. This is, of course, a shorthand, given that almost all Sikhs in Britain are British citizens. But it corresponds to Southall folk terminology: most Southallians use the term 'Brits' when they mean white people who claim a privileged identification with Britain.

Sikhs and Brits

In the perceptions of the British media, the simultaneity of bloodshed in the Punjab and in Southall can only have contributed to the moral panic itself. When Southall youngsters involved in a street brawl not only desecrated British cricket bats, but also brandished 'Sikh ceremonial swords', the effect was certainly to exacerbate fears of 'the foreign' (Cohen and Young 1981). These fears may have been exacerbated because they went against a binary-structured stereotype that many Brits had long cherished: while Afro-Caribbean youngsters were often thought to be masculine trouble makers, South Asian youngsters were stereotyped as their binary opposite: peaceable, quiet-spoken, family-orientated and respectful, pursuing class advancement despite ethnic difference. So any word of 'South Asian gangs' was a tangible shock to the Brits' classificatory system. Yet the matter has deeper historical roots worth tracing and then applying.

Ironically, it was the Brits themselves who historically prepared the ground for a pro-Khalistan movement among Sikhs. The ascent of Sikhs, and especially Jat Sikhs, into the military machinery of the British Empire in India has been analysed in the most arresting manner by Richard Fox (1985). The British colonial authorities purposely created and enshrined an identity of Jat Sikhs as 'pure' or *khalsa* Sikhs. The crucial point of Fox's analysis is to show how, in a manner not untypical in colonial settings, the British colonial authorities created and canonized precisely that identity which would later be used to struggle against them for an independent Khalistan.

Establishing an idiom that Fox calls 'a creole of British racism with Indian caste society' (ibid.: 3), British colonial policies imposed a new and normative uniformity upon the previous 'precolonial evolution of several Sikh identities, each embracing a selected set of cultural meanings' (ibid.: 12). 'A single religious community, in the sense of a shared set of traditions, cultural meanings, and social practices, was absent among those who called themselves Sikhs in late nineteenth-century Punjab' (ibid.: 108). It was only by the recruitment of religiously and ethnically or caste-homogeneous Sikh regiments that the British army in India 'nurtured an orthodox, separatist, and martial Singh identity among Sikh rural recruits to its regiments and companies' (ibid.: 10).

The colonial authorities purposefully enlisted the symbols of Singh identity, the combined saintly and soldierly character of the baptized [*khalsa*] Sikh ... Only Singhs or those willing to become Singhs could enlist ... The British [even] labored to ensure the religious conformity of the Sikh recruit ... [and] military commanders required a strict observance of Singh customs and ceremonies afterward. (ibid.: 142)

Even Fox's most explicit critic, McLeod, confirms the gradual and deliberate creation of 'a new consistency and a new clarity of definition' (McLeod 1989: 78–80). And neither could he fail to, for the Brits themselves were perfectly aware of what they were doing at the time: 'Sikhs in the Indian army have been studiously "nationalized" or encouraged to regard themselves as a totally distinct and separate nation. Their national pride has been fostered by every available means' (Petrie, writing in 1911, quoted in Fox 1985: 142). The scale of this military operation in cultural engineering was enormous, as by 1914, the British Indian Army 'depended on these Sikhs, transmuted into Singhs by British agency, for 39.6 percent of its combat troops. The proportion of Sikh troops in the army was ... almost twenty times their representation in the Indian population. Indeed, the Sikh contingent was absolutely larger than the Hindus' or Muslims" (ibid.: 143).

First signs that British cultural and national engineering had created a formidable enemy of its own imperial interests came with the so-called Third Sikh War of 1920–1925, an extensive revolt led by the reformist Singh Sabha movement and the recently-founded Akali Dal Sikh nationalist party. It is tempting to trace further the historical dialectics of imperial Brits creating the very 'enemy' that would later frighten their 1980s descendants unsettled by a 'holy war' of 'Sikh gangs' in Southall, but suffice it to recall that the 1947 partition of the subcontinent between India and Pakistan tore right through the Sikh homeland of the Punjab and caused several million people to flee from one side of the new border to the other. If the Brits had initially styled Sikhs as the Gurkhas of the subcontinent, they had now turned them into its Kurds: people who could never have their own homeland as a state because other states had divided it up between themselves.

The oldest echoes of this history were tangible in the Southall of the panic years. The very first Sikh migrants had been called in by a British army officer who had commanded a Sikh regiment during the Second World War and now, after partition, needed 'good Singhs' to work at Southall's giant rubber factory producing tyres; other Sikh migrants of that first cohort had come directly as disowned refugees from western Punjab. In Britain, relations between Brits and Sikhs were problematic even during the times of postwar full employment, as xenophobia and the fear of 'those turbaned men' all but barred Sikhs from the housing market, educational advancement and social mobility for years to come (Pullé 1974). More recent echoes of the Brits as an active party in Sikh identifications concerned a landmark judgment by the House of Lords which, in a case known as Mandla v. Dowell Lee (1983), determined that Sikhs formed not merely a religious category, but an 'ethnic group' (Poulter 1998: 288–91). The award of this legally crucial status, recognition as an ethnic group, could only encourage those who, from the early 1980s, had reorientated themselves toward the long-suspended idea of an independent Sikh state of Khalistan, and when matters came to a head with the first storming of the Golden Temple in 1984, the Khalistan agenda began to polarize Southall's Sikhs in hitherto unthinkable ways.

Some of the ensuing splits and rifts have been summarized earlier when we discussed Southall's political murders and the acrimonious fights over orthodoxy and temple governance. Important as the British connection was in all this, however, this polarization over Khalistan must not be understood as a master narrative that could explain the 'gangs' and the moral panic about them. Rather, the 'gangs' panic can now be understood as a very peculiar constellation of highly diverse processes of polarization.

A Convergence of Polarizations

Pulling together the evidence, one may read the events of the panic period as a transformation of several mutually independent polarizations. One of these built upon the rivalry and distrust between those Sikhs, mostly of the Jat caste, who saw themselves as representing the *khalsa* and 'pure' strand of the faith, and those, both Jat Sikhs and those of other castes, who denied any demeanour of exclusivism and claims to orthodoxy. While local tensions between the two go back to at least the mid 1970s, it was the violent events in the Punjab and India which forced the issue from 1984. Sikhs, whether in the Punjab or in Southall, had to be pro-Khalistan and 'pure', or else anti-Khalistan and ready to mix – much like the gangs. The 'Holy Smokes' label, as mentioned earlier, did not succeed in attracting all young Jat Sikhs. Just as the main Jat Sikh congregation split in two after the pro-Khalistan takeover of their temple committee, so young Jat Sikhs, too, split in two over the choice between the gang labels. It was the force of the Khalistan issue that polarized the choice into an either/or: the Pure or The Nothing.

Within the realm of 'gang' activities themselves, polarization followed the usual spiral of provocation and counter-provocation, injury and revenge, revenge and retribution. At no time, however, was the polarization among Southall youth as comprehensive as it was feared to be by their parents and elders, the media and the general public. Admittedly, some 200 to 300 juveniles and young men saw the decision between Holy or Toot as the manliest response to the most adolescent question of all: 'what am I?' Yet there never existed a single proven organized 'gang' link between the 100 or so local criminals and the 500 or so boys who doodled 'Holies' or 'Toots' on their exercise books. The insider theory of two 'ethnic' or caste or politico-religious super-gangs was finally refuted by the police investigation into existing criminal networks which, as mentioned earlier, were not exclusively Asian either. However, even this refutation was not universally accepted. Let us then distinguish some more parties to this odd conjuncture of different polarizations interacting to produce the moral panic.

On the local and national media, we can be brief. Crime sells, youth crime sells better, and 'ethnic youth crime' sells best. Yet even the quality newspapers refrained from making one of the obvious connections: the simultaneity of inexplicable 'youth gang' fighting and the British government negotiating about a Treaty of Extradition aimed at quashing the Khalistan movement in alliance with the government of India. Even the quality media maintained the habitual distinction between their 'home' news, now about 'the Southall gangs', and their 'overseas' news, now with sparse allusions to confidential negotiations about an extradition treaty between Britain and India.

The police faced a dilemma. On the one hand, they wanted to damp down rather than stir up the idea of 'Asian youth gangs': any such aspersion would have caused problems for 'community relations' and effective policing based on public support. On the other hand, they could not be seen to 'do nothing about the gangs', and they had every reason to intuit that Southall, with its transnational links and proximity to Heathrow Airport, must harbour some white-collar networks. Dealing with youth, the police discovered arms that ranged from cricket bats to knives and 'Sikh ceremonial swords'; dealing with adults, they also uncovered highly skilled white-collar networks of medium-scale fraud. In the end, they pacified Southall's streets as was their job, and the youngsters could revert, after a short exciting flirt with adventure, to doodling 'KFC' (Kentucky Fried Chicken) instead of 'KCF' (Khalistan Commando Force). A more daring outsider-analyst might explain the 'youth gangs' as a youth protest, be it against parents who wanted them to succeed at school or parents who wanted them to excel in the temple. There was indeed no shortage, in the media or the public sphere, of cultural pathologizing about 'young Asians between two cultures'.

Yet the one party that remains most enigmatic in all this are the parents and the teachers of the youngsters so suddenly labelled as 'school-age gangsters' and 'street gangs'. Surely, being level-headed and used to challenges, they might have known better in different circumstances. Yet their depictions of the events served, despite all their intentions, to rehabilitate essentialized models of cultural purity. Consider this text by Sri Guru Singh Sabha which was distributed house-to-house in 1986 by the pro-Khalistan temple committee later ousted by Britain's High Court:

> We are very much conscious of the fact that our children find themselves at crossroads, due to the effects of culture fusion. Whilst we recognize the difficulties and problems experienced by our children, it is imperative that they must not detach themselves from our culture and religion. In order to attract and integrate them with our own culture ... we look forward to your continued cooperation and support.

The programmatic statement ably appealed to the widespread fear of many parents that their children might 'forget their roots' or 'lose their identity' in a diaspora threatened by indiscriminate interaction and moral permissiveness. The older generation of Southall's South Asians, however, were not the only parents, or indeed the only teachers, who feared for the future of their children in a Britain where a neoliberal Thatcher government had just celebrated its third consecutive election victory. To paraphrase some local voices, Thatcher's crooks had profited from a government war against Britain's trade unions, had liquidated the country's manufacturing industries in Southall as everywhere else, had won voluntary wars (assisting the US-

American invasion of the Caribbean island Grenada to the British re-possession of the Falklands Islands), had ruined the health service, the schools and anything else they could not privatize for the profit of their cronies, and were now hell-bent on abolishing centuries-old civil rights to introduce 'stop and search' policies based on suspicion alone. That the suspicion usually fell on 'ethnic' youngsters was an open secret even then, and it was well known to Douglas, now Lord, Hurd, the luckless Home Secretary who opened this story with his misguided demagogy about Southall youth. If 'life is one thing after another', as Adam Kuper once consoled me when I despaired of the complexities of Southall fieldwork, then moral panics are perhaps the most complex form of social interaction.

Conclusion

Moral panics need vectors of the most disparate interests and fears converging on one imagined, and thus often intangible, folk devil. This essay's first question – which cultures? – was as moot in Southall as it was in the early case studies pioneering this kind of study (Gluckman 1940; Mitchell 1956): in Southall, any culture that 'they' or 'we' might define as such was interacting with any other culture, however defined (Gillespie 1995; Baumann 1996). The second question – what contexts? – could only be answered by sorting and resorting all parties' mutually contradictory, and often self-contradictory, accounts. That second step drove home the need to disown any putative categorical boundaries between insider and outsider. To the third question – whose accounts? – the answer was easier, paradoxically perhaps, because of the very complexities of the case.

Methodologically, all accounts must count as empirical data. That much is certain, whether one studies an urban myth, as in the case of Southall, or a myth – even an anthropological one – such as Bošković (this volume) did for 'the [fractious] Balkans'. Analytically, however, the ethnographer has to weigh ethnographically plausible accounts against ethnographically less plausible ones if they strive for a 'progressive accumulation of knowledge based on the maximization of rational enquiry' (Pina-Cabral, this volume). That, too, is plain Aristotelian logic, applied by all humans, schooled or not, to all phenomena. In the present case, many local and/or media hypotheses about violent incidents, or even putatively violence-prone structures, contradicted more plausible empirical evidence, and so the ethnographer had to judge, not paternalistically but almost like an anatomist in love, which local or media accounts were data to be read as symptoms and which were hints to uncover plausible structures and aetiologies. This does not mean discounting local theories: in fact, in the present case, some of their unwarranted assumptions and shortcuts provided crucial clues to understand the moral panic about the 'gangs', whether these 'gangs' were real, imagined or latently in-between. For such an ethnographic triangulation (Pina Cabral, this volume), all the disparate data and analyses had to be put on tap, but none allowed on top. Epistemologically, such a diagnosis of social dynamics is manageable if the folk and analysts' models are treated as dialogically, and sometimes dialectically, interactive.

Notes

1. Source: interview with Douglas Hurd on the BBC Radio 4 news programme *P.M.*, 28 September 1988.
2. This long fieldwork in Southall was inspired and unfailingly supported by Adam Kuper.
3. Quotes are taken from a report on 'Southall Street Gangs' on the BBC Radio 4 news programme *Today*, 13 July 1987.
4. *Greenford, Northolt and Southall Recorder*, 14 October 1988, p.4.
5. Figures from London Metropolitan Police, Southall Division, *Information Booklet: Youth Involvement in 'Gangs' in the Southall Division*. Mimeograph, 11pp. Southall: Divisional Community Office, Southall Police Station, 1988.
6. As note 4.
7. As note 4.
8. As note 5, pp.4–5.
9. *Daily Mail*, 3 August 1989. p.5.
10. *Daily Telegraph*, 3 August 1989, p.3.
11. As note 9, p.2.
12. As note 9, p.4.
13. *Southall Gazette*, 4 August 1989, p.1.
14. See: *Greenford, Northolt and Southall Recorder*, 14 October 1988, p.4.

Chapter 8

'What about White People's History?': Class, Race and Culture Wars in Twenty-first -Century Britain

Gillian Evans

If culture, as Kuper claims (1999b), has lost its analytical utility as a concept in the tool kit of anthropologists, should we treat it as an ethnographic category, whose utility lies in its being invoked by our informants (Baumann 1996)? Adopting such a strategy in this paper, I analyse how it came to be the case that at the beginning of the twenty-first century, white working-class people in Britain are now categorized as a 'new ethnic group',[1] a people forced, in a setting which they consider to be their home, to articulate a cultural identity in order to compete in a multicultural political climate.

The analysis is divided into three sections. In the first, I explore a case study which allows me to explain how a multicultural system of social classification fails to account for social class. I show how this obfuscation makes it difficult to provide an adequate explanation of certain kinds of social phenomena in Britain such as educational failure in a fifth of the population.[2] In the second section I put flesh on the bones of this case-study explanation, relating the social and economic history of working-class community formation and disintegration in Bermondsey (where I conducted field work research during 1999 and 2000), to wider and increasingly controversial debates about multiculturalism in contemporary Britain. Via an analysis of the quarrel between two leading protagonists in the struggle for racial equality in Britain, I end by exploring the implications for the white working classes – who are just beginning to get on board the bandwagon – of the most recent call in British politics for an end to the support for multiculturalism.

Race and Culture in Social Classification

In January 2002, Diane Abbott, MP for Hackney North and Stoke Newington, wrote an article about the educational failure of black British boys. 'There is a silent catastrophe', she lamented,

> happening in Britain's schools in the way they continue to fail black British school-children. When African and Afro-Caribbean children enter the school system at five they do as well as white and Asian children in tests. By 11 their achievement levels begin to drop off. By 16 there has been a collapse. And this is particularly true of black boys – 48% of all 16-year-old boys [nationally] gain five GCSEs, grades A to E. Only 13% of black boys in London achieve this standard. In some boroughs the figure is even worse. This is not a new issue.[3]

Part of the problem of black British boys' under-achievement at school, Abbott suggested, was that black boys did not do well in a school environment dominated by women, and white women in particular. Explaining that educational achievement did not form part of the development of what most of these boys considered to be an acceptable, 'cool' style of black masculinity, which was often based on 'bravado and violence', she stressed that boys could not make a positive association between masculinity and formal learning if there were no male, and especially black male, teacher role models and if discipline was lax. The article acknowledged that similar matters of masculinity may be relevant for white working-class boys, but underlined that, for black boys, 'there are the added factors of racism and the extreme unwillingness of teachers and educationalists to face up to their own attitudes'.[4] Also relevant, Abbott proposed, was the failure on the part of schools to take into account the often very different cultural background of black boys. Describing the successes of independent black schools and self-help Saturday schools, which aimed to make up for the deficiencies in the mainstream educational system, Abbott stressed, 'What all of these schools have in common are highly motivated black teachers, involved parents, strong discipline and boundaries, and a celebration of children's cultural identities'.[5]

The ensuing debate[6] reinforced what her article proposed: problems to do with gender and educational achievement could not be adequately addressed without raising, and answering, questions about young peoples' race, ethnicity and cultural background. Problematic about this approach, however, is the way that a focus on race, ethnicity and culture tends to eclipse the overarching significance of social class (usually defined in the most basic of ways: in terms of the occupational status of the household, signified by the family's application for free school meals). Taking social class into account and leaving aside for a moment the question of what difference there is between race, ethnicity and cultural background, statistics revealed in 2000 that in comparison to social class the gender gap was relatively small; the same was also true of the 'race gap'. The OFSTED publication (Gillborn and Mirza 2000) revealed, for example, the following:

◆ When the GCSE results of white and black (African-Caribbean) young people were compared, the 'race gap' was seen to be twice as significant as the gender gap with eighteen percentage points between white and black young people's achievements.

◆ This race gap was, however, still nowhere near as important as the 'social class gap' of 40 percentage points, which meant that social class was still more than twice as significant as race when trying to assess any child's average chances of doing well at school.

Thinking about the likely educational outcomes for any black British child, it is clear that race, ethnicity and gender are important variables, but most significant of all is the issue of the child's parents' socio-economic status. As I have explained elsewhere (Evans 2006a), this is because parents occupied in manual, unskilled and semi-skilled labour are more likely to be relatively uneducated themselves and more dependent, therefore, on the schooling system to impart educational values to their children. This places the children of working-class families at a disadvantage in education compared to the children of middle-class professional parents who are more likely to be relatively well-educated and less dependent on the standard of education available in local schools. For working-class parents, reliance on the standard of education provided locally is unavoidable. Where standards in local schools are good this is not necessarily a problem, but where schools are failing, working-class children are placed at a double disadvantage.

Accounting for social class, as well as race, ethnicity and gender, we might predict, then, that white working-class boys are likely to be failing in education at a similar level to black working-class boys, which is indeed the case (see below). The similar likelihood of white working-class boys' failure at school throws into question a multicultural and racial system of social classification in education. It then becomes clear that those black British boys who fail in school are most likely to be the children of working-class parents. Such an appreciation would lead us to realize that both black and white working-class boys and their parents, living in working-class neighbourhoods, may have a lot more in common than a racial system of classification would allow anyone in Britain to imagine.

White Working-class Boys

Making it one of their lead stories on 6 March 1996, *The Times* reported on one of the key issues raised in the annual report of Chris Woodhead, who was then Chief Inspector of Schools in England. This was the problem of boys' increasing failure to match girls' achievements in school. Particularly problematic, he suggested, was white working-class boys' failure to learn. He suggested that it was, 'one of the most disturbing problems we face within the whole education system'.[7] Seven years later, in August 2003, the following trend was noted: 'Poorer white boys are outstripped academically by Indian, Pakistani, Bangladeshi and Chinese boys. The only group who do worse are Afro-Caribbean boys, where only 16 per cent of poorer pupils gain five or more GCSEs at grades A to C'.[8] The report emphasized (supported by similar reports in 2006)[9] that, in that year, only 18 per cent of white working-class boys achieved the minimum of what is expected of them: that is, five or more GCSEs at grades between A and C.[10] A closer and more recent analysis of the statistics (Gillborn and Kirton 2000) showed that while Indian (and Chinese) boys were likely to be leading the way compared to boys of the same class background, white working-class boys were, in terms of national averages, more likely than their peers of Afro-Caribbean, Pakistani and Bangladeshi descent to attain five or more higher grade GCSEs (Office for Standards in Education 1999). This does not mean, however, that this trend was mirrored in all boroughs across the nation; indeed, white working-class boys were the lowest achieving group in some boroughs (Gillborn and Gipps 1996).

Notable about these trends is the relatively similar, but nevertheless differential attainment of Asian, white and Afro-Caribbean working-class boys. This suggests that ethnicity is not to be discounted with the reintroduction of a focus on social class. Instead, the system of classification must be sufficiently nuanced to allow for a more adequate explanation of educational failure, balancing a multicultural system of classification by an account of social class. This rebalancing of class and multiculture would allow us to conceive of black and Asian boys who are failing at school as working-class as well. It would also change the way we understand white working-class boys.

In other words, a focus on race, ethnicity and culture emphasizes difference at the expense of commonality which, in turn, prevents us from investigating and understanding more about what those commonalities are. Equally, an exclusive focus on failing white boys' social class position distracts from the potential relevance of their ethnic grouping and cultural background, which makes it seem, by default, that ethnicity and culture pertain only to black and Asian people. The point, however, is not, in any simple way, to argue for the assertion of a new ethnic status for the white working classes. This would only increase racial polarization in Britain. What is required, rather, is a balanced system of social classification in education, one which:

◆ takes the social class position of black and Asian people as seriously as it does their ethnicity and cultural background – this would allow us to see what struggles black, white and Asian working-class people share in common in Britain.

◆ takes the ethnic and cultural background of white people as seriously as it does their social class position – this would allow us to appreciate the diversity of white people in Britain rather than assuming that diversity is a feature of black- or Asian-ness.

The corollary of such a shift would be the undoing of the homogeneous national identity – a seemingly straightforward British-ness – which is ascribed to white working-class boys. This unravelling would reveal a variety of locally situated histories and an appreciation of how these specific histories relate to the failure of certain kinds of white working-class boys to do well at school (Evans 2006a). So long as the historical significance of their class position is ignored and they are treated as cultural anomalies in a multicultural system of classification, diversity experts will continue to wonder and worry about why it is that white working-class young people find it so difficult to articulate their 'cultural identity' (Ajegbo 2007). Similarly, arguments will continue about the prevalence of institutional racism and the consequent failure of black boys to do well at school (Gillborn 2008). Meanwhile, the more complex challenge remains: how to understand the ways in which social class, race, ethnicity and cultural background intersect and overlap in Britain. Addressing this challenge means first having to tease apart variables which are often conflated.

Race, Ethnicity and Cultural Background

Race is generally classified in U.K. policy documents as equivalent to ethnicity.[11] This results in a schema featuring two main so-called racial categories: white and black, with black young people usually being defined as Afro-Caribbean and white young people as British (or, in some classifications, Irish). In a further residual category, that of Asian, racial and ethnic categories are conflated.[12] Young black people are racially and ethnically differentiated from their white peers, that is, further classified according to the geographical region of their or their parents' or grandparents' origin.[13] Such a scheme of place-based classification serves to obscure certain social effects, while revealing much about how social difference in Britain came to be constituted historically and how it is currently perceived.

Ethnicity and cultural background too are often conflated as if they were versions of the same thing. If ethnicity in Britain concerns classification on the basis of shared region or country of origin, then cultural background – never formally classified – concerns particular, collectively defined, ways of life associated with that place of origin. So, for example, Diane Abbott attempts to describe how, because of their different cultural background, 'West Indian' boys are unlike their white counterparts: 'Black boys are often literally bigger than their white counterparts and may come from a culture which is more physical'.[14] There are, however, several problems with assuming a synonymy between ethnicity and cultural background, and – in turn – race. Firstly, people who are associated, through ethnic classification, with a particular region of origin may in fact come to identify with a way of life which is completely different from that of their relations and ancestors. A white working-class boy from inner-city Birmingham, for example, may come, in time, to behave, in his embodied style of youthful masculinity, just like an Afro-Caribbean boy who is the son of first-generation Jamaican immigrants living in the city. Even though he does not look black, this boy may have learned how to become a man in a similar way to his Afro-Caribbean peers; perhaps he has grown up with black boys and they share a similar history and, therefore, a similar kind of embodied being. We cannot, on the basis of someone's racial or ethnic classification, make assumptions about his history or – for want of a better phrase – his cultural background. The problem with culture and its often inseparable association with race and ethnicity is that, as a signifier of collective distinction, it risks ensnaring people in bounded, unchanging, ethnic or racialized groups and associated ways of being. It is partly this essentializing tendency which caused Kuper (1999b) to raise such strong objections to the uncritical use of the term.

Cultural Difference, Prejudice and Racism

As the preceding analysis has made clear, the problem with focusing on the racial, ethnic and cultural difference of black and Asian people is the tendency, by default, to ascribe to the white people of Britain an imaginary homogeneity. This eclipses the historical and contemporary significance of regional and class-based differences between the white people of Britain which simultaneously makes it difficult for anyone to become curious about the history of how black and Asian immigrants came to live amongst and to form relations of various kinds with locally distinctive groups of white working-class people.

Through such a focus it would become clear that black, white and Asian people in Britain necessarily share overlapping histories and cultural backgrounds. We could then ask the questions that really matter in the contemporary moment and which I begin to address in the next section of this chapter: how are the tensions between similarity and difference played out in working-class neighbourhoods? What kinds of social structure and forms of collectivity govern people's sense of what it means to belong to such a neighbourhood? And could these kinds of questions help us, in any way, to understand more about educational failure among working-class boys?

Perhaps, for example, the similarly low levels of achievement for both white and black working-class boys might be something to do with similarities in their cultural backgrounds and histories, such as the prevalence among them of young, dominant, male peer groups which are formed on the basis of macho, bravado-encouraging, and often violent styles of masculinity forged on the street (Evans 2006a, 2006b). Perhaps boys from backgrounds like this also have to cope at school with similar prejudices against being working class – and working-class boys in particular (Evans 2006a). Perhaps working-class Afro-Caribbean boys struggle most against the white middle-class ideal which is embodied in didactic practice because they are furthest away from it.

Having explained some of the effects of a racially divided multicultural system of social classification in Britain, and having highlighted the importance of locally situated studies of British-ness, I now proceed to give an account of the history of a racially conceptualized understanding of social distinction in Bermondsey, a predominantly working-class area of South-east London.

Community Belonging: Class and Race in Working-class Neighbourhoods

Bermondsey's distinctive architectural features speak of an old dockside industry and proud municipal past. Victorian wharves and warehouses pack three and a half miles of Thames riverfront to the east and west of Tower Bridge; converted factories, pubs, Christian churches and ultra-classic buildings, like the former town hall, jostle for space with pre- and post-Second World War social housing estates and everywhere, since the closure of the docks and the factories in the 1970s, the evidence of profitable gentrification for new kinds of residents. These latest newcomers are wealthy young professionals from outside the area, quite unlike the dockers' and factory workers' descendants whose affiliation with Bermondsey dates back, in some families, well over a hundred years.[15] Renowned for its fiercely protective and closely-knit working-class community, Bermondsey earned its Victorian nickname as 'London's larder' because of an industry focused on the importation and processing of food from countries the world over. This was a community that imagined itself on the basis of kinship and residence or 'born and bred' criteria of belonging, and the remnants of this community are still defined in the same way.

At the height of the industrial period, Bermondsey's working classes endured the most difficult of living and working conditions. The poorest were extremely badly paid, often in casual employment, existing close to destitution in overcrowded, insanitary slums while the better-off had the good fortune to take up more skilled jobs that passed from father to son in skilled and protected trades related to the docks. The struggle to survive real hardship was typical of what the urban poor had to endure in Britain before benefits were felt from hard-won improvements resulting from the localized collective action of philanthropists, civic heroes, trades unions, socialist politicians[16] and, later, the welfare state.

Housing and Community Formation

Socially, the historical precedent concerning community formation is important. The first point to emphasize is the tremendous resilience required of working-class people struggling against overwhelming odds to earn a living, keep a roof over their heads, raise a family and to achieve anything approaching a 'decent' or 'respectable' life. The workings of the class system[17] in Britain – a social structure which meant that working-class people were treated as third-class citizens who deserved no better than they got – required of families, communities and trade guilds that they preserve any tiny advantage they could accrue. Thus, protectionism became both a necessary survival strategy and, eventually, the foundation of a way of life based on various forms of territorially-based exclusion and employment-based collective action such as Guild Socialism.[18]

The second point to stress is the collaboration between family and neighbourhood members which made survival a function of collective living arrangements: kinship-based communities and particular residence patterns developed around particular forms of industry. This is the kind of kinship and residence based community described in Willmott and Young's classic ethnography of London working-class life, *Family and Kinship in East London* (1957). This ethnography made it possible for policy makers to understand that, in the face of appalling poverty and insecurity, the poor of London were forced to survive on social wealth. However, this wealth was never evenly distributed and differentiations between kinds of working-class people were always pronounced.

In Bermondsey, before the large scale development of social housing during the pre- and post-Second World War period, women would secure housing from private landlords, preferably on the same street, for their newly married daughters. This meant that, in time, just as Willmott and Young describe for Bethnal Green, neighbourhoods became populated by people sharing dense, female-centred kinship relations. This led to a social situation characterized by low population turnover, a strong sense of community narrowly defined and an emphasis on familial reputation and duty to significant others who lived close by. An elderly white woman told me, for example, of her father's disapproval when she was courting with a white working-class man from Peckham (a neighbouring area of South-east London.[19] Her father had said to her, when she brought the young man home one day, 'What do you want to bring a bloody foreigner in the family for?' Territorial affiliations were, therefore, paramount, leading to a stereotype of endogamous marriage in Bermondsey and the development, in practice, of a xenophobic community based on what I call place-ism – strong discrimination against and suspicion of outsiders of all kinds.

One of the most important social changes of the thirty years after the Second World War was the reduction of private-renting housing tenure to residual status (Carter 2006: 1 and 2005: 66). Local authority politics (mostly Labour) in urban areas of Britain became dominated by massive public-sector construction of new social housing, the buying out of private landlords and eventually the last of the slum clearances. The challenge of public housing policies was how to solve, through new collective means imposed from above (Carter 2006: 1), the problems that tenants had been struggling with in private tenure. It was clear that the standard of private housing was often appalling and that the people of

Bermondsey deserved better all round, but how to address this problem without disrupting the mechanism of community formation from below? With the majority of housing stock held as a public good, it was crucial for politicians to be able to convince voters that distribution of this resource was being organized fairly and in their best interests.

History suggests that a harmonious match and, therefore, the forging of trust between residents-as-neighbours, and between residents-as-voters and Labour politicians, was well made because the idea of a kinship-and-residence community on the ground was reflected in the system of distribution of housing from above (Carter 2008: 165) The dominance of locally-grown Labour activists on the Council ensured that 'public provision of housing acted as a collective purchasing-club on behalf of the most respectable, prosperous and skilled members of the local working class; rents were high, and housing allocation overtly favoured the respectable' (Carter 2006: 4 and 2005: 17) This system worked well for a while because Bermondsey people trusted that they were going to be well looked after and they were. Elderly men at the dockers' working men's club spoke to me of a time they perceived to be long gone, when they were looked after by a Borough Council that fought for, reflected and defended their interests. Relatively invisible in this system of public-authority patronage was the question of who the system excluded and how, by virtue of this blind spot, Labour was unprepared to anticipate or to theorize in advance about the potentially long-term effects on community formation, of social diversity in the working class (Carter, 2006: 4)

In the beginning, pride about new social housing was high and all seemed to be well until alternative claims on provision began to be felt. When Bermondsey became part of the borough of Southwark the monopoly of Bermondsey's Old Labour influence was shaken; the metropolitan borough of Bermondsey, and the rival boroughs of Southwark and Camberwell, were fused and a huge amount of social housing was allocated to those cleared out of slums. The affluent, upwardly mobile working-class families of Bermondsey could not buy bigger property because the Council discouraged owner-occupation; there was very little private property to buy and these families were unable to get council houses instead of flats. At the same time, the cost of rents was increased to subsidize the rent of those coming in from the slums for whom the higher rent in public housing was unaffordable (Carter, 2008: 163) This caused bad feeling amongst the different sections of the working class and laid the ground for further resentment about the effects of increasingly complex forms of social diversity – racial and ethnic – to come.

Immigration and Racial Hierarchy

From the 1960s onwards, with increasing immigration into London of black and Asian people from the Commonwealth, worries were growing about racial tensions in the north of the borough of Southwark, which led the Council to house immigrants away from Bermondsey in public housing on the newer estates to the south of the borough, in Peckham (Brown 2003). The lack of a strong collective vision governing the integration of immigrants into white working-class neighbourhoods led, in some cases, to the forming of racial and ethnic enclaves. Hence, Bermondsey remained, for a long time, largely white and Peckham became known as a 'black peoples' manor'.

The arrival of black and Asian immigrants in working-class areas of the country marked an important point in the developing relationship between community formation and the class system in Britain discussed above. Their arrival created a new experiential interface at which the already beleaguered and divided white working classes were forced to come to terms with the presence, in increasing numbers, of new kinds of outsiders. These black and Asian people from the colonies of the receding Empire had, up until this point, only ever been a negligible presence in Bermondsey, as the people on the other side of those transactions which brought food into the area via the docks. Jamaica Road, for example, is a main thoroughfare in Bermondsey, its name telling of the connection with Britain's imperial outpost. But rarely was the relationship ever made explicit between Bermondsey's working classes and the labouring poor in the Caribbean. With relatively large-scale immigration, a transnational relationship with Britain's subjects from the colonies, one which had once been firmly in the background of white working-class life, was suddenly brought to the fore on home turf.

Relative to the working classes, who were already treated like Britain's third-class citizens, these new immigrants, arriving in increasing numbers after the Second World War, became Britain's fourth-class citizens.[20] Largely unaware of the social dynamics of the class system in Britain, black and Asian immigrants had, in the beginning, a primary structural relationship to 'the mother country' conceived of as a racialized understanding of hierarchy which gave them a particular expectation of the kind of patronage they could expect from white people in Britain. Little did they know that the white working classes, living in poor neighbourhoods, had already had to fight tooth and nail for what little patronage they themselves could win from their employers and government. Unsurprisingly, an atmosphere of protectionism prevailed for which immigrants were unprepared (Phillips and Phillips 1998).

Many black and Asian immigrants were surprised to discover white working-class people struggling and sometimes living in abject poverty in Britain. These people in turn were shocked to find, during the war for example, that middle-class black and Asian men were well equipped to transform their skills into professional status (ibid.) This kind of realization undermined the idea of a straightforward racial hierarchy and highlighted a complex intersection between class and race which could only be ignored so long as the groups at the bottom of both hierarchies were kept relatively segregated. This history makes clear that immigration has become a contentious issue in Britain precisely because it has foregrounded in public life what institutionalized education based on meritocratic ideals obscured: the twin hierarchies – race and class – through which the idea of British-ness has long been mediated.

For black, white and Asian people, living in the poorest urban working-class neighbourhoods, this process – of having to come to terms with what immigration meant for community formation – worked out differently in various parts of London (Brown 2003; Wallman 1982)[21] and the country as a whole. In Bermondsey, the historical precedent of a xenophobic community, an atmosphere of economic protectionism and a weak rationale in the Council about how to reconcile collective provision and social diversity, was critical to the eventual development of growing feelings of alienation among the white working classes.

Rights-based Housing and Disillusionment with the Labour Party

Overall, changes in housing allocation meant that the question of who lived where in Bermondsey was no longer under the control of its residents. They had never owned the land but they felt that the area belonged to them by right. Inevitably, their sense of community was threatened as the old order of collective provision by a Council working in their favour gave way to a system of housing 'rights'. These rights to housing were distributed in relation to the new centralized public policy imperative to provide service to those 'most in need' rather than to those with the greatest history of social investment in the area. Alongside a gradual diminution in the numbers of new social housing projects, there were, then, competing claims to, and divergent rationalities about, allocation of precious housing stock.

Eventually, this led, in 1983, to the wholesale defection of Bermondsey's more well-to-do white working class from Labour to the Liberals, with an outcome that could never have been predicted in the 1950s: the Liberals, as elsewhere in Britain, like Sheffield (Carter 2006, P.7), took control of what had always been Labour-dominated wards. However, this was no reflection of a 'liberal' (that is, tolerant) stance since many Bermondsey people continued to be preoccupied with excluding outsiders, and especially black and Asian immigrants. The outcome of this profound suspicion from below of social diversity, and the chronic state failure to provide the rationale for a new formation of multiracial working-class communities on housing estates, further undermined the Labour movement.

Under Thatcher's Conservative Party government, many well-to-do working-class people in Bermondsey bought their council flats under the 'right-to-buy' scheme and moved out of the area, mostly to Kent, where old ideas about community formation began to be reinvented anew. The New Labour government inherited social tensions which were becoming characteristic of urban neighbourhoods. Needs-based housing allocation policies, associated with Labour, meant that the most socially diverse, often poorest and least able to cope families, were now concentrated in the biggest and often most unpopular estates. More desirable estates, in contrast, tended to have long-term residents who had bought their flats and either rented them out to private tenants or decided to stay and continued to exert, thereby, a strong social influence on the residential profile. The knock-on effect of this division in neighbourhood politics was that Labour votes became concentrated only in the poorest areas. The Liberals in Bermondsey won the day by reproducing the leadership style of the Labour politicians of old but the social problems associated with the mismanagement of diversity proliferated from below. As Carter observes: 'It was precisely when the Labour leadership stopped being narrow, inflexible and exclusive that the Old Labour project collapsed. Its successors have had great difficulty in finding an alternative vision' (Carter 2006: 8).

The result of these processes, in areas like Bermondsey, is an ongoing contestation about the basis of community belonging, especially in relation to increasing immigration and allocation of housing which is the foundation of local residence. The Council lacks a rationale for imposing community solidarity on working-class tenants from above and the basis for community belonging from below has been damaged, perhaps irreparably. Once proud of a community forged out of collective action, many white working-class people in Bermondsey continuously lament the death of their community. Whereas territorial divisions among the working classes were once counterbalanced by collective struggles in industrial trades unions and in the Labour movement, which provided the means for creating solidarity in the workplace and in politics, the working class, nationally, is now fractured more than ever. The growing economic and political pressures associated with de-industrialization and immigration, and what has come to be perceived as the abandonment of the working classes by a New Labour government that supports multiculturalism, have made for growing feelings of betrayal among the white working classes (Hewitt 2005).

In local talk of community demise, much anger and resentment is directed down the social hierarchy, mostly at black and Asian people. Comparatively little focus is placed on the failures from on high to support working-class communities; to provide for the economic transition to a service-based economy; or to imagine a collective vision that might have made negotiations about the integration of immigrants a necessity or a social good. Trying to explain to me what housing estates in Bermondsey are like now, a middle-aged Bermondsey father suggests, 'What you've got in these blocks [of flats] now are collections of individuals thrown together, no one knows anyone else, no one cares about anyone else'.[22] Ironically, it is precisely at the moment that all the collective integrating movements of the past have been undermined in working-class neighbourhoods that the government has proposed a 'community cohesion' policy.[23] The necessity to introduce this policy derives from the perception that tension about social diversity will undermine the possibility of communal living on housing estates; alienate people from a sense of national belonging or affiliation with the state and make impossible a way of life which requires a degree of cooperation and agreement about shared values concerning the question: 'how shall we live together here?' Exactly how this new vision of cohesion will be imposed from above remains to be seen. There is little state acknowledgement, however, that this policy may be already fifty years too late.

Cleaning the Neighbourhood into Existence and Excluding Outsiders

Explaining how community cohesion worked in the past, an elderly lady speaks to me of how proud Bermondsey people once were of their council flats: the women literally used to clean the neighbourhoods into existence. On each landing women would take it in turns, no matter how hard a day's work they had already done outside the home, to clean the communal areas. It was through this turn-taking cycle of exchanges that the standards of 'decency' required for communal living were created and maintained. In addition, on some estates, a resident caretaker would police behaviour to make sure that errant residents fell into line. When new families moved in, one of the women would go to the family and let the mother know, in no uncertain terms, what day she would be taking her turn to clean and what standard of cleaning was expected. 'You could eat your dinner off the stairs in them days,' the woman emphasizes. She explains that female neighbours were judged on the basis of how clean they kept their flats and especially the visible parts of the home – the net curtains, windows and door step.

The problem, however, was that when the first Jamaican families were housed in the flats, the Bermondsey women refused to include the mothers of the families in the cycle of turn-taking exchanges. This is how racism worked on the ground: it was a refusal to enter into exchange relations with black and Asian people. This refusal was made on the basis of their difference: a difference which, compared to that of other kinds of white outsiders – like the Irish – was perceived to be extreme because of the association made between degree of foreignness of place of origin and skin colour. Racism was, therefore, inseparable from place-ism – discrimination on the basis of where a person comes from.

The elderly Bermondsey woman explains to me how the first Jamaican woman to move onto the estate, eager to fit in and to join the neighbourhood, tried to clean the stairs on the Sunday, which was a day of rest for the other women and, for some, church. The Jamaican woman would throw her dirty water, from cleaning the landing, down the stairs as she had seen the Bermondsey women do on other days. Returning to the flats, the Bermondsey women would discover their precious stairways sullied from the Jamaican woman's effort to clean the landing. Rather than noticing the woman's effort to do her best to work out what was required of her, the Bermondsey women took her failures as the evidence they needed to confirm what they felt they already knew about her: that this 'coloured' woman wasn't 'decent'. The Bermondsey woman who relates this tale says to me, in retrospect, 'Why didn't we just show her [the Jamaican woman] how to do it? It seems silly now.'

Cultures of Resistance: Ethnic Community Formation

Accounts from black people in Bermondsey about the failure to come to terms with the implications of immigration, are similarly distressing in their revelation of causes that are foundational, yet in retrospect relatively simple. A Jamaican woman tells me of the humiliation she experienced in church. She describes how she had spent the whole journey to England dreaming about how she was going to worship in England, in 'a real Church of England church'. When she got dressed up on the very first Sunday and went proudly into church expecting to be welcomed she was told abruptly: 'Your sort are not welcome here'. Leaving the church in indignation, she was, she says, filled with sadness and rage, feeling that she could never forgive the racism she had experienced in England from 'so-called Christians'.

In the factories too, racial segregation was, in some cases, the outcome of the way that community relations were structured. An Irish woman tells me how in the Peak Freans' Biscuit Factory production was hierarchically organized so that grandmothers of long-standing Bermondsey notables worked on the 'posh biscuits' conveyor belt while the Irish women worked on the least-favoured – the broken biscuits – conveyor belt. Meanwhile, upstairs, out of sight, the Jamaican women were making Christmas puddings, filled with Jamaican rum. Such hierarchies did not always go unchallenged, however. The Irish woman explains how her father had made a point of teaching her not to be prejudiced against black people so she made a fuss about the racial segregation in the factory and was punished for her resistance by being put to work on the puddings too. At first, she says, the Jamaican women were suspicious of her because they assumed that because she was white she was going to start telling them what to do, but once they realized she wanted to get on with them, all went well.

The exclusion experienced by immigrants from white working-class communities, was what led groups of them to come together, usually in networks of ethnic solidarity, to support one another as a means to survive racism in Britain. This tendency was supported by government policy when Roy Jenkins, Labour home secretary from 1965 to 1967,[24] made it clear that integration did not necessarily mean assimilation but support for 'cultural diversity' and a commitment to providing 'equality of opportunity' (Sivanandan 2006). In turning to their own resources and forming their own networks of social wealth, black and Asian people redefined the essence of community belonging in ethnic rather than residence-based or shared social class terms. This interrupted the idea that communities necessarily had to be mapped onto localized spaces of residence, and further differentiated the working class, undermining any idea that class solidarity between black, white and Asian people living in poor neighbourhoods was necessary – or possible.[25]

Founded on a combined sense of desire for belonging and for connection with the 'mother country' and, at the same time, of alienation from Britain and its often racist people, multiculturalism came into being. This was a generalized political collectivity forged out of the fight for racial equality (a fragile solidarity felt between black and Asian people as a result of not being allowed to belong to Britain), but in a setting where particular groupings were at times antagonistic towards each other. Such groupings were ethnically and/or religiously distinct transnational communities that shared, with other immigrants from the same point of origin, a sense of being at home while abroad.

Culture

With the development of a politics of multiculturalism, culture emerged as that which defined black and Asian people as different. They belonged now to collectivities all of their own, collectivities understood as a diverse set of ethnically and/or religiously defined groups marked by different ways of life.[26] Similarities, intersections and overlaps with white working-class communities were, therefore, obscured. I will return to this point in the next section of the chapter, but want to note here the corollary of this new, racially distinctive system of classification which made it seem as if what defined white people was their *lack* of cultural diversity. Where struggle for multiculturalism could, at best, have been coordinated with the fight against class inequalities, at worst it was separated from it, so that when the political and economic base of working-class neighbourhoods was undermined, the white working classes were left in a political vacuum, feeling like the only 'ethnic group' whose culture didn't matter.

Without a viable Labour movement, all that remains in relatively poor neighbourhoods is multiculturalism, which teaches people to trade on their differences, leading white working-class people to feel that their only option is now to compete against black and Asian people for resources and recognition. This is a situation which leads to the question I often heard during my fieldwork in Bermondsey: 'What about our culture?' 'What about white people's history?' The political history of community formation in Bermondsey is one of splintering and separatism: through this process the working class in Britain became racially and ethnically segmented. Thus, the dream of greater equality became the object in a racially divided and divisive tug of war. It is the outcome of this battle that is currently at stake in twenty-first-century debates about whether or not multiculturalism has outlived its political utility in Britain: debates like the longstanding argument which raged between Trevor Phillips and Ken Livingstone.

Nationalism and Multiculturalism

Sir Trevor Phillips, Britain's Chair of the Commission for Equality and Human Rights, and Ken Livingstone, formerly London's mayor, had been engaged in a high-profile conflict since 2006. This, by January 2008, resulted in demands for an independent inquiry into whether or not the latter had used public funds to support a campaign to undermine the former's position as a leading campaigner for racial equality. In the initial stages of the dispute, which led to them bickering in the media, Livingstone accused Phillips, who was then Britain's race equality chief, of 'becoming so right-wing that he could join the BNP [British Nationalist Party]'.[27] This was no idle remark since the BNP was, at that time, gaining in momentum in its expression of the increasing disquiet of a growing number of white voters. These were white people in predominantly working-class and northern areas of the country struggling to cope in a post-industrial economy; straining to accommodate to the growing influence of non-white immigrant communities in their midst and feeling abandoned by a New Labour, centrist government which no longer seemed to represent their interests.[28]

The success of the BNP, in this rapidly changing social and political climate, lay in its ability to make it seem as if the nationalist agenda was necessarily, simultaneously, a white and therefore right-wing one. This made Livingstone's proposition – linking Phillips with the far right and with the white agenda – much more than a personal insult; it also represented a serious division in the left wing of British politics about how best to tackle the thorny issues of immigration, multiculturalism and racial equality. Livingstone's rhetoric implied that the nationalist/culturalist agenda was necessarily a racist one and that to become allied with it represented a betrayal of the anti-racist struggle in Britain. Quick to reiterate his credentials in relation to the anti-racist movement, Phillips refused to acknowledge that a move towards nationalism was an inevitably white or extreme right-wing strategy. While the two men slugged out their differences, which were really all about the question of what integration means, the fracturing of the left wing served the ends of the BNP.

What heightened the sense of tension was that these events followed hard on the heels of the race riots in the north of England in 2001 and the London bombings of 2005, both of which added a much heightened and highly significant religious, faith-based, particularly Muslim, dimension to the issues at stake (Modood 2005).[29] Fearing that Britain was in danger of 'sleepwalking [its way] to segregation', Phillips, a black Briton himself, had had no qualms about provoking debate concerning the question of the relative importance to British people of their shared national as opposed to multicultural identities.

What had so annoyed Livingstone was that Phillips, following previous pronouncements about the necessary end of multiculturalism, was doggedly sticking to his repudiation of the concept. In the wake of the previous summer's successful Notting Hill Carnival, which was hailed by many as a triumph of multiculturalism in London, Phillips continued to express his misgivings, suggesting that multiculturalism, where he imagined it to be successful, ought to be about the *coming together* of different people of all kinds – black, white and Asian – rather than a matter of communities developing in isolation and celebrating their distinctiveness in separate festivities. His argument linked to talk elsewhere in government about the creation of new national symbols and celebrations that might bring all kinds of people together to affirm their shared British-ness. Also at stake, then, in the latest phase of Britain's race and culture wars, was the meaning of the prefix 'multi'. What did 'multi' now mean for left-wing protagonists – a set of diverse cultures, or one new national culture that somehow had to be merged and homogenized out of a mix of diverse elements?

British-ness

Arguing that the old liberal agenda had led, in the worst case scenario, to voluntary segregation and alienation from the values of mainstream society, Sir Trevor Phillips called for its end. This agenda, he argued, had misguidedly encouraged the integration of immigrants via policies promoting sensitivity to, tolerance of and financial support for communities developing on the basis of racial, ethnic, cultural and religious distinctiveness. Encouraging a new focus on citizenship and civic responsibility, and reflecting the policy commitments of the government's new Commission on Integration and Cohesion, Phillips hoped to improve community relations by emphasizing what the citizens of Britain share in common. In so doing he questioned whether it was possible for nationalism and multiculturalism to coexist and provoked a whole new round of discussions on a familiar theme: exactly what is British-ness?

In response, there was much talk from politicians about a vision of British-ness centring on shared or 'core' values (yet to be clearly defined) and civic obligations (now a legal object of reflection for new immigrants) extending across communities of ethnic difference and supposedly uniting people. The BNP, meanwhile, emphasized their very different mission which was to defend the interests of 'indigenous' Britains defined as, 'the people whose ancestors were the earliest settlers here after the last great Ice Age and complemented by historic migration from mainland Europe [Celts, Anglo-Saxons, Danes, Norse, and so on]'.[30]

Not surprisingly, this move, on the far right, towards emphasizing indigeneity and associating it with white-ness (without having to use the word and risk being accused of racism), raised some fresh concerns. It was not difficult to draw worrying parallels with fascist movements of the past; with the rising popularity of far-right movements in Europe and – perhaps counter-intuitively – the growing success of 'indigenous' movements around the world which were making an instrument out of culture to successfully fashion a politics of native rights (Kuper 2003). British belonging, for the BNP, thus lay in the murky, mythical Celtic-type past, while for New Labour politicians, in contrast, it was to be found in vague notions of shared, 'core values'. Most interesting about these divergent perspectives is the way that both of these nationalist movements ignored relevant moments in Britain's national and transnational history. These moments included the carving out, internally, of a class structure and, externally, of a colonial Empire whose inequalities included those based upon the iniquities of slavery. The demise of this Empire had, like a centripetal force, brought to Britain the many and diverse subjects of Her Majesty the Queen: black and Asian people from former colonies who felt a strong affinity for and had been accorded rights to a place in the nation. In the light of this history there could be no simple equation either between national belonging and racial harmony or between British-ness and equality.

Ignoring Britain's transnational history, the BNP could make it seem as if Britain was an island whose boundaries have always ended where the land meets the sea. Alternatively, it dwelt upon routes to and from Northern Europe where other 'indigenous' white people were located. This vision of history makes it harder for disgruntled white voters to work out why the presence of black and Asian people in Britain is an inevitable and inseparable aspect of what it means to be British. By the same token, while Ken Livingstone and Sir Trevor Phillips continued to fight about how best to advance the struggle for racial equality, it became difficult for them to adequately address the grievances and increasing disgruntlement of the white working classes. Trying hard to appeal to these people, the BNP, as long as they focused on indigeneity, could ignore the similar struggles of black, white and Asian people in predominantly working-class areas of the country. Without class, and trying to move beyond multiculturalism, new political discourse became dominated by the vague idea that British-ness could be forged out of a sanitized and ahistorical citizenship. Confusion prevails, then, about how the people of Britain are to be defined.

Integration and Alienation

Where Ken Livingstone had once considered Sir Trevor Phillips to be an ally in the historical struggle to secure multiculturalism's fragile place in an often unwelcoming white-dominated British society, he was now wary of Phillips's move towards what seemed to be an uncritical societal integration model. It was because he equated mainstream British society with the predominance of racial and cultural prejudice that, for Livingstone, integration could only mean a multiculturalism in which such racism and prejudice was evident. For Phillips, however, the repudiation of mainstream British values – by Muslims in particular – had gone too far. It risked undermining national stability and causing irreparable damage to race relations in Britain. How to redress the balance? This is the question that dominates cultural politics in twenty-first-century Britain.

From Sir Trevor Phillips's point of view the problem is clear: nationalism and multiculturalism can no longer coexist; a new way has to be found to work towards racial equality in Britain. My aim, in this chapter, has been to explain why the problem of cultural politics is far more complex than racial equality experts have imagined. Without adequately taking into account the history and contemporary relevance of social class formation in Britain, politicians cannot explain why the white working classes are feeling marginalized, alienated and abandoned, nor properly theorize about the kind of social structure they are asking immigrants to integrate into. Without a sufficient sociological imagination, one that extends beyond an ahistorical utopia of meritocratic equality, and into a future that is reconciled to the influence of hierarchies forged in the past, it is difficult to imagine what form community cohesion might take. Meanwhile, exactly at the moment when politicians are attempting to bring it to a grinding halt, the white working classes are beginning to work out how to get on the multicultural bandwagon. Once they realize that in the new, post-industrial, post-social class, post-multicultural era, a 'cultural identity' is no good to them either, alienation will only increase, with potentially disastrous consequences.

Conclusion

Treating culture as an ethnographic category and investigating its peculiar resonance in contemporary British life, this chapter has revealed how the shift towards and then beyond a multicultural system of classification obscures the ongoing significance of social class in Britain. Culture in this context has a highly specific political effect. It works to obscure the commonalities between black, white and Asian people living in what can only be characterized as predominantly working-class but post-industrial neighbourhoods in British cities. In this light, history becomes not what people share in common in all the various ways that they have come to be British, but what makes them ethnically distinctive in a place-based system of belonging. Forced into the background in this short-sighted manoeuvre of contemporary cultural politics, is the inevitability that national belonging and a sense of British-ness is given not only through the promises of equal citizenship hard won through racial equality struggles or a meritocracy fulfilled, but also through integration into an enduring and complex tripartite system of social rank – social class – which defies efforts to eliminate it from the British social landscape and which continues to have implications for the likelihood of any child's chances of educational success and social esteem in Britain.

Notes

1. This kind of classification of the white working class was used throughout the BBC2 'White Season' in March 2008. See, for example, press articles entitled 'the one ethnic group the BBC has ignored' (*Daily Mail*, 29 February 2008 retrieved from website http://www.dailymail.co.uk/news/article-523351/White-working-class-ethnic-group-BBC-ignored.html 31 September 2008) by the commissioning editor of the series, Richard Klein.

2. This statistic, often quoted in the media – for example, the *Guardian*, 20 May 2008, p.8 – refers to the 20 per cent of British children who are leaving primary school unable to read and write and do numeracy at basic levels.
3. *Observer*, 6 January 2002, retrieved from website http://www.guardian.co.uk/politics/2002/jan/06/publicservices.race 31 September 2008
4. As note 2.
5. As note 2.
6. Apart from Diane Abbott, two of the lead commentators in this debate have been Dr Tony Sewell, journalist, academic, education consultant and board member of The Learning Trust which is the body set up by the government to take over education services in Hackney; and Sir Trevor Phillips. Based on his own ethnographic research (Sewell 1996) and wide ranging experience of the kinds of problems black boys face at school, Sewell argued strongly that the source of black boys' problems is not so much institutional racism or poverty, but the anti-school youth culture which is so influential and which makes a particular anti-school learning form of black masculinity dominant. Sewell's stance is that the problem of black boys' underachievement at school is to do with poverty of aspiration on all fronts: home, neighbourhood and schools.
7. *The Times*, 6 March 1996, pp.1,18.
8. *Observer*, 17 August 2003, retrieved from website http://www.guardian.co.uk/politics/2003/aug/17/uk.schools1 31 September 2008.
9. 'Breakdown Britain' Report of the Social Justice Policy Group chaired by Iain Duncan Smith. 11 December 2006.
10. This was compared with white boys in general whose achievement rate was 50 per cent. White working-class girls, in contrast, achieved 25 per cent at grade A–C GCSE compared with 61 per cent for girls overall.
11. See, among other policy documents, the Department for Education and Skills' *Youth Cohort Study 2002* (2003).
12. The confusion usefully raises the issue of what people mean when they talk about race in Britain and whether or not race is a useful category of analytical distinction at all (Sanjek and Gregory 1994; Malik 2003).
13. Of course, statistical data does not necessarily tell us very much about how young people perceive themselves. For example, do all young black people in Britain think of themselves as being specifically Afro-Caribbean or do they simply choose this option when faced with a limited selection of ethnic categories?
14. *Observer*, 6 January 2002, retrieved from website http://www.guardian.co.uk/politics/2002/jan/06/publicservices.race 31st September 2008.
15. Many of the men who built the docks, and later worked on them, were Irish immigrants, and Catholic affiliations came to dominate the way dockside labour was allocated.
16. In Bermondsey, the most famous socialist politician was Dr Alfred Salter, physician and later Councillor and Member of Parliament.
17. Social class in Britain is a category of relative and ranked distinction. It situates people in relation to economic and political history; in relation to educational and socio-cultural history; in relation to a history of housing and health spanning across three generations of family life, which makes grandparents particularly important figures in oral testimonies and which suggests that it takes three generations to completely change the class position of a family up or down the social hierarchy. In other words social class is a relative and ranked category of distinction that indexes, in a complex way, any person's historical placement in a society defined by a particular kind of moral and political economy. In a nation defined by class relations we are constantly engaged in reading each other's history, trying to work out what the body and its language can tell us about social class and all of its subtle degrees of distinction. As such class is a peculiarly British obsession, one that intersects clumsily and continuously with a more historically recent and discursively more prominent preoccupation with notions of equality.

18. Guild Socialism was a political movement organized around the idea of industry controlled by workers through trade-specific guilds.
19. All ethnographic quotes in the chapter are taken from the period of my field work from 1999–2000 in Bermondsey.
20. Although most of the black and Asian immigrants to Britain would be classified as working class, many were middle class including, for example, Indian doctors in the 1960s.
21. Whilst preparing this chapter I noticed, for the first time, in the photograph on the front cover of Willmott and Young's 1950s book, that there is a black woman standing in the doorway.
22. It is interesting to note that this is not perceived to be a problem for the wealthy young professionals in their riverside warehouse apartments. Presumably they are collections of individuals too, but they can afford the prerogative of individuality. Even though these wealthy newcomers – 'yuppies' – are resented by Bermondsey people too, not so much anger is directed at them because they do not occupy social housing estates which are the bone of contention.
23. A fixed term advisory body, the Commission on Integration and Cohesion was announced in August of 2006 to consider how local areas could celebrate diversity whilst also recognizing the social tensions which may ensue from it.
24. Enoch Powell, Conservative MP for Wolverhampton, made his notorious Rivers of Blood speech in 1968.
25. Even though the trades unions eventually provided a model of multiracial solidarity in the working class, this solidarity was often hard won with many instances of early racism which had to be overcome. The dockers and Spitalfields meat workers took to the streets to support Enoch Powell, for example, when he was forced to resign.
26. These new forms of collectivity were supported by local authority funding for ethnically defined organizations. This kind of funding is now being withdrawn as the multicultural bandwagon grinds to a halt.
27. *The Times*, 1 September 2006, retrieved from website http://www.timesonline.co.uk/tol/news/politics/article625057.ece 31 September 2008
28. Neither the National Front nor the BNP have gained any ground in Bermondsey because the activists are always outsiders who are resented for trying to impose their politics on Bermondsey people. In addition, Bermondsey people are aware that their fathers and grandfathers fought against fascism in the Second World War and are loathe to imagine that fascism is the answer to their contemporary concerns. It is important to note, however, that in Stoke on Trent, which has a recent history of sixty years of uninterrupted Labour control, the BNP now have eleven councillors and the strong prospect of a BNP mayor.
29. It could be argued that this represents another kind of split in the left wing: a rift between black and Asian Muslim protagonists in the racial equality struggle.
30. BNP website: www.bnp.org.uk/about-us/mission-statement/, retrieved 31 September 2008.

Chapter 9

A Cosmopolitan Anthropology?

Stephen Gudeman

We should once again address social scientists, and aspire to contribute a comparative dimension to the enlightenment project of a science of human variation in time and space. Our object must be to confront the models current in the social sciences with the experiences and models of our subjects, while insisting that this should be a two-way process. This is, inevitably a cosmopolitan project, and one that cannot be bound in the service of any political programme.

Adam Kuper (1994b)

Fifteen years ago, Adam Kuper urged anthropologists to develop a 'cosmopolitan anthropology'. He called for an anthropology that would draw on the voices of local people, ethnographers and social science theories to build a comparative and critical science. Distinguishing this project from that of self-referential ethnography, symbolic analysis and cultural interpretation, he argued that we must confront our accepted models with those of others (Kuper 1994b). Kuper issued his challenge partly in reference to a book, *Conversations in Colombia*, which was written by a colleague and myself (Gudeman and Rivera 1990). We presented the work as an unfinished 'long conversation' between our informants, local experts, economic theorists, and the two of us. The method was open-ended and comparative, but we did not openly critique accepted models in the social sciences. Now, responding to Kuper's call, I shall revisit the project of developing a cosmopolitan anthropology by considering the relation between ethnographic and formal models.

In my work on anthropological economics, I have had to take into account two types of models. One emerges from field work conversations with local informants and experts; the other is part of our intellectual heritage and practices. I term them local and universal (or derivational) models. But if the latter seem more persuasive and realistic to us, how can we develop a critical anthropology? Using the idea of models, I shall confront and call into question our way of framing things by bringing these differing modes of knowledge into a conversation.

Homo Economicus

For many anthropologists and most economists, the 'rational man' concept provides the touchstone for analysis: it asserts a human universality by which interpretations and explanations may be formed and judged, and it is a seemingly humble assumption. But what if the rational man idea is not universal and fails to illuminate the practices that we observe? How shall we clarify them and interpret the accepted wisdom from which they diverge?

My understanding of this puzzle had a long birth. It began during my initial fieldwork in Panama, although I did not frame it as a problem until I left the country and undertook more field studies. In Panama I lived with my wife in a small village where the people were shifting from the subsistence farming of rice, maize and beans to cash-cropping sugar cane. I wanted to study this transition and began by sketching decision trees that captured their flow of choices and by soliciting their subjective probabilities for the outcomes in order to understand their crop selections. I quickly found that my questions about rational choice did not resonate with them, nor did the concept explain the social and economic conditions in which they were living. I dropped that analysis to study their material life ethnographically as well as other aspects of the culture. But I was puzzled about the gap in our reasoning.

After this work, I realized that my puzzle about the prominence of calculated choice lies at the heart of a disagreement in economic anthropology, evokes a difference between anthropology and economics, and often separates the social sciences, if not the social sciences and the humanities. In anthropology, Bronislaw Malinowski's (1922) early critique of the concept of 'rational man' had a subterranean influence on subsequent generations of anthropologists. Were the Trobriand Islanders, whom he so carefully studied, self-interested choosers, or were they acting according to other modes of reason, such as reciprocity? Two of his students burned the candle at both ends. In the style of Malinowski, Raymond Firth provided innumerable contextual studies of the Pacific island of Tikopia, but with his early training in economics Firth emphasized how the people chose to their advantage within constraints (Firth 1951, 1964, 1965). Edmund Leach, in a famous study of politics in Highland Burma (Leach 1954), explicitly presumed that the actors were choosing and maximizing political rewards even as he presented a cultural, structural and contextual analysis of their polity. The issue was most clearly revealed in the internal anthropological debate during the 1960s between the formalists, who followed a neoclassical, deductive line centred on the supposed universality of rational economic man, and the substantivists, who were developing an institutional and inductive perspective based on Karl Polanyi's work.[1] As for the difference between anthropology and economics, the question of calculated choice surfaced in the economist Frank Knight's quarrel with the anthropologist Melville Herskovits, who then rescinded his anthropological position, to the dismay of Karl Polanyi (Herskovits 1953: 507–31; Polanyi 1968: 142).[2]

These controversies reflect a larger issue in the social sciences: whether to adopt an individualistic or a relational understanding of society, a debate that might be encapsulated as the difference between Adam Smith's *The Wealth of Nations* (1976b [1776]) and Emile Durkheim's *The Division of Labor in Society* (1933[1893]) and *The Elementary Forms of Religious Life* (1995[1912]). Leaving aside his earlier work (*The Theory of Moral Sentiments* 1976a[1759]), Smith is often seen as the founder of modern economics and is famous for his pithy statement that places self-interest with its benefits at the centre of markets: 'It is not from the benevolence of the butcher, the brewer, or the baker that we expect our dinner, but from their regard to their own interest. We address ourselves, not to their humanity but to their self-love, and never talk to them of our own necessities but of their advantages' (Smith 1976b: 18).

In contrast, Durkheim claimed that society is held together not only by a general division of labour but a sharing that he often labelled the *conscience collective*. To Adam Smith he might have replied, 'If interest relates men, it is never for more than some few moments' (Durkheim 1933: 203), and added, 'a contract … is possible only thanks to a regulation of the contract which is originally social' (ibid.: 215). But influenced by Rousseau (see Durkheim 1960), Durkheim struggled to explain the 'origin' of this collective sense. From his earlier to his later work, Durkheim suggested that it arose as the social, moral and demographic density of society increased.

My view concerning the prominence of calculated selection in many Western societies grew slowly and was marked by abrupt shifts. A few years after I tried to use rational choice theory and Monte Carlo simulations in Panama, I returned to the ethnography that I had collected about material life and drew on classical economics, post-Ricardian theory, and dependency theory to understand the economic change I had witnessed, especially since I became interested in whether the subsistence crop yielded a surplus that was extracted by the unrestrained expansion or cascading of the market crop (Gudeman 1976, 1978).

During field work I recorded the people's voices about their economy with its changes, but this ethnography did not mesh well with any standard economic theory – from classical, to neoclassical, to Keynesian, to rational choice – with which I had some acquaintance. So, I asked, what would a cultural or anthropological economics look like? This question led me to explore local models and metaphors of livelihood as reported in ethnographies and reflected in some Western constructions of economy (Gudeman and Penn

1982; Gudeman 1986). Because I found that many of the ethnographic descriptions were sketchy, I undertook more fieldwork in the Andean highlands of Colombia, which stretch from the extreme north to the south of the country. My collaborator and I discovered that the people employ a house model of economy: they use the image or metaphor of a house to arrange, talk about and make sense of their subsistence practices. For example, according to them the 'base' or 'foundation' of the house grows when the holdings of the house increase, and when goods are traded they flow through the 'doors'. When the house entertains lavishly, it throws the base through the 'windows', while snacks of food 'buttress' the workers. The project is to 'support' the house. In addition to its resonance with an Aristotelian conception of the *oikos*, we found a similarity between the Colombian model and the eighteenth-century Physiocratic conception of economy: according to both, land is the source of all wealth. This realization led us through many trails in Western economics. As interlocutors we not only brought local voices from one locality in the highlands to another but also Western voices to them for a response. This long and complex conversation led us to surmise that some Western concepts about economy might have had their beginnings in the folk communities of Europe. Of course, the highland people in Colombia also trade in markets, but they see themselves at the periphery of the larger economy. We framed this interaction as the difference between a 'house' and 'body' (corporate) model of economy (Gudeman and Rivera 1990).

After this field study was completed, I realized that a house form of economy is one example of a communal or mutual economy, which is found around the world, and I turned to developing a comparative view of this mode of economic life (Gudeman 2001). But I knew that it, too, was only one part of economic life for which a larger model was required. As I worked out the larger model, the solution to my long-time query began to emerge. Economy, I find, contains both a mutual and a market realm, and the two value domains are dialectically connected: their relations shift over time, and often they conflict. I call this model 'the tension in economy'.

Economy is made up of a contradiction. We live in a double, conflicting world, which is economy's tension. Shot through with practices and ideologies, with competition and mutuality, with antagonism and community, economy encompasses more than most economists and everyday dogmas allow, and it is more complex than most anthropologists realize. Everywhere people deploy the two coping strategies of producing for themselves and trading with others. In part, individuals live from the competitive trade of goods, services and money that are separated or alienated from enduring relationships. People exchange with others to transform or substitute what they have for something else. I term this mode 'impersonal trade' or 'market'.[3] I use the word 'trade' for anonymous, competitive interchanges in which market participants exchange or barter goods, labour, money or ideas. The term covers the notion of middlemen as well as any market consumer or producer who exchanges one thing for another in competitive conditions.

But people also live from goods and services that make, mediate and maintain social relationships. Through mutuality or community things and services are secured and allocated by means of continuing ties, such as taxation and redistribution; through cooperation in kinship groups, households and other groupings; by bridewealth, indenture and reciprocity; and by self-sufficient activities, such as agriculture, gardening or keeping house.

Trade in which goods are parted from their holders and impersonally exchanged with others occurs in all historical and ethnographic situations, though its importance in relation to other aspects of economy varies. It may be a function of curiosity and imagination about the unknown as one tries out the life-world of another, or it may express power over the material and social environs in the attempt to reduce uncertainty. Through the force of competition, the central value in this realm comes to be efficiency in exchange – and consequently in production and consumption – where rational choice is exercised to be efficient. But people also keep what they produce and transfer it through mutual relationships. Such transfers, guided by heterogeneous values and lasting social connections, offer temporal certitude but can be violated or turn oppressive. Each mode has a spectrum of appearances, for communities and markets can be large or small, and cover a varying extent of material life. Economies are shifting combinations of the two, and individuals are pulled in both directions, which they modulate, hide, disguise and veil in practices and discourse.

Long before the rise of modern economics, Aristotle contrasted activities done 'for the sake of' something else with activities done 'for their own sake' (Aristotle 1984, passim). A practice undertaken for the sake of something else is a means-to-ends act, whereas actions done for their own sake, such as maintaining social relationships, are complete in themselves. They are a satisfaction that embraces diverse actions and values. These practices may be pleasurable, ethical and moral as well as parental or bad, immoral and ugly; for example, kinship bonds enshrine what Meyer Fortes (1969) termed the 'axiom of amity' or ties of mutuality. In practice, however, the two forms of action are dialectically related: each may absorb features of the other, even while they remain distinct. For example, means-to-ends actions may come to be done for their own sake, whereas social relationships may become means for the accomplishment of something else. Weber captured this confounding of the two through his encompassing and shifting use of the word 'rationality' to cover both (Weber 1978[1956]). Even if he contrasted 'formal' with 'substantive' rationality, he well knew that formal rationality could become a personal calling or mode of substantive rationality.

Weber not only distinguished between the two modes of rationality but also observed that the calculative one had become prominent in capitalism. He linked its emergence to the rise of ascetic Protestantism and the development of the Protestant ethic among certain sects in Europe (1958[1904–1905]). Weber's thesis was a principal forerunner of cultural interpretations and the analysis of the role of religion and ideology in historical change. To be certain, he did not claim to explain the rise of capitalism by a change in religious beliefs; however, he did try to trace a link proceeding from religious ideology to everyday practice. But even if Weber's account of the rise and spread of the Protestant ethic and the spirit of capitalism helps to illuminate the incessant call to work in industrial societies and the reinvestment of profits in order to have success as a sign of election in the afterlife, he never explained how calculative or formal reason itself became the engine of markets and modern economics as well as a core practice in other social domains.

Suppose that we reverse Weber's ideological argument and cast aside assumptions about inherent self-interest, endless wants and survival value. What if calculative reason arises in practices? Could the emergence of ascetic Protestantism, as Weber portrayed it, have been a response to changing conditions and not their precursor? When the pathway to grace could no longer be bought or gained through good works, the revolutionary change was that religious position could now be known through practical success. A religious quality, or certainty of the afterlife, came to be known through material accumulation or a quantity. In contrast to Weber, Albert Hirschman (1977) suggested that a rise in trade and the market economy was presaged by a shift in written discourse from a focus on the passions to praising the interests. If passions, especially in the political domain, were seen as dangerous and uncontrollable, interests – pictured as reasoned calculation in the economic realm – were tame because commerce requires polished interaction. Impelled by 'gentle' or 'soft' commerce (*le doux commerce*), the trader was a peaceful, inoffensive and calm person. Thus, Hirschman concluded that prior to Adam Smith the concept of self-interest had become a realistic, safe and principal explanation of human action, and that the subsequent diffusion of capitalist forms 'owed much to [a] ... desperate search for a way of *avoiding society's ruin*' (ibid.: 130).[4] In his argument, a shift in political ideology accounted for the emergence of the capitalist spirit. Hirschman's account, like Weber's, starts with ideology to explain everyday acceptance.[5]

In contrast to Weber, I suggest that the rise of Protestantism did not help lead to the rationalization of material behaviour; instead, it represented a profound rationalization of the religious domain itself. Was the Protestant ethic a local story or narrative we told ourselves about the economic world we were transforming? The use of practical reason begins not in religion (such as the Protestant ethic), the loosening of production from traditional constraints (with the transformation of guilds), the creation of a free labour force and marketable land (with the demise of feudalism), the rise of individualism (as a result of ideological and political revolutions), or the changing human relationship to nature (with the growth of science and technology, and the expansion of the forces of production), but in trade. Competitive or asocial trade induces means-to-ends figuring as a personal fulfilment.

By this argument, I seemingly agree with the neoclassical economists' assumption that rational choice is the centrepiece of market activity. However, neoclassical economics does not explain and account for its presupposition that rational choice is the core of all economic and social action. The discourse simply reproduces the market's apparent reality. One might say that the use of instrumental rationality, as their explanatory tool, is the 'revealed preference' of neoclassical economists. But the neoclassical account is incomplete. Self-interested choice is universal in the market but not universal in itself, because competitive trade depends on local specifications from which it is abstracted.[6]

But if I diverge from a neoclassical analysis, I also part from a Marxist interpretation, for I do not argue that the exploitation and appropriation of labour, as well as the class struggle, define high market society. I also depart from a classical Marxist interpretation of alienation in which the labourer, through the sale of his exchange value, is separated from his productive powers and the product of his activity, for it is not only the labourer who is objectified and turned into a 'thing' or reified.[7] Trade objectifies all market participants who become separated from their mutual relationships, from goods and services that mediate and maintain social relations, and from other subjectivities. In Collingwood's succinct characterization of market trade, 'each party is using the other as means to his own ends by permitting the other to use him in the same way' (Collingwood 1989: 65). In less bleak language, Hayek, citing Dr Johnson, observes that 'competition is "the action of endeavouring to gain what another endeavours to gain at the same time"' (Hayek 1948: 96). This unravelling of sociality through trade, however, does not result in a once-and-for-all change as suggested by phrases such as 'the great transformation' or the 'disembedding' of markets (Polanyi 1944), because everywhere impersonal trade and sociality are found in uneasy conjunction. Polanyi did not envisage this unstable condition.

I understand rationality in a broad sense. It has plural meanings that include calculated selection as well as other forms of reason. Stephen Toulmin has argued that 'the Dream of a Rational Method, that of an Exact Language, and that of a Unified Science form a single project designed to purify the operations of Human Reason by *desituating* them: that is, divorcing them from the compromising association of their cultural contexts' (Toulmin 2001: 78).[8]

By reason we sometimes mean instrumental rationality, but reason can refer to deduction, induction or dialectical reckoning. We also use figurative reason, including metaphor and synecdoche, even to formulate material practices. Pragmatic practices, or trial-and-error action, might be counted as a combination of reasoned processes, while the ability to disconnect and join, to fragment and combine, is also a form of human rationality, as Locke and Diderot, among others, observed. In an echo of Diderot's (1751) article on 'art' and Locke's (1975[1690]:119, 163) description of 'simple' and 'complex ideas', Simmel referred to the 'connections with which, separating and connecting, we descend beneath the phenomenal side' of facts (Simmel 1997: 233). These analytical and combinatorial capacities facilitate creativity and innovation, and build new connections between means and ends that are used in calculated selection. The pervasive but unrecognized use of these other forms of reason suggests that calculative reason does not completely describe economy.[9]

Another reasoned practice, as I learned in Colombia and elsewhere, especially marks the limits of rational choice and the realm of market exchange: thrift. Saving or economizing frames a means-to-ends act. However, it is not focused on the difference between ends and means (profitability) or on the magnitude of the ends (productivity) but on the means with the objective of preserving them for another day or having a remainder. Thrift is a form of reason that centres on keeping things as a precaution. Parsimony marks the limits of calculated choice in exchange, because it means withholding from investment in production or expenditure in consumption. Such economizing is a key practice and narrative in communal modes of economy. If dominant in competitive exchange, rational choice encounters limits in times of thriftiness that preserve relationships, which is also why its expansion into the mutual realm 'debases' it. Parsimony corresponds closely to what Keynes called the 'precautionary motive' that is part of the preference for liquidity and a cause of downturns in the market realm (Keynes 1964[1936]: 166ff). In my view, a precautionary motive is also found in the mutual realm as a defense against uncertainty. As Keynes observed, 'in the absence of an organized market, liquidity-preference due to the precautionary-motive would be greatly increased' (ibid.: 170). From this perspective, his theory was designed to counteract the effects of parsimony in the market.

Finally, we use the word reason to justify and explain actions. We give our reasons and tell stories to persuade others and ourselves of our projects. For example, according to Weber (1958), the Protestant ethic provides a reason for the use of calculative reason in material practices. (We might say that Weber presents a narrative about this narrative to convince us of the connection between religious ideology and practice.) Hirschman (1977) offers another story (both his and Enlightenment thinkers') that justifies the same action on different grounds. Similarly, in our narratives about the need for environmental restoration or development aid we may draw on persuasions other than efficiency, such as the value of redressing the past or protecting future generations. These narratives or rhetorical uses of reason present value commitments and exemplify what Weber meant by substantive rationality. Likewise, when we tell ourselves that our actions were justified because they were calculated, we invoke a substantive commitment to formal rationality, and when we disparage non-instrumental reason we adhere to the same value.

The Dialectics of Trade and Mutuality: Different Models

If, in high market society, we exalt impersonal trade and extol rational choice, we also rely on mutuality. In ethnographic contexts as well, economic practices combine mutuality with trade. Drawing on ethnographic reports and examples from market societies, I argue that economy is built around the dialectical relation of two value realms, mutuality and trade, and contains a tension between two ways of making material life – for the self and for others. As Rabbi Hillel observed in the Mishnah, 'If I am not for myself, then who will be for me? And if I am only for myself, then what am I?'

By the word 'dialectical' I refer to concepts or tendencies that, as Georgescu-Roegen (1971) suggests, both oppose and overlap one another. A dialectically defined entity may refer to one concept or tendency, the other, or both; and it is unstable. The two value realms of mutuality and market are dialectically related in many ways. For example, in markets we value efficiency, but mutual relations embody many values, such as equity, equality, age, gender, position and merit. The realms are not comparable, but each may subsume, veil, stand off from or absorb features of the other, and the balance between them changes, which is the dialectics of political economy. For example, impersonal trade is framed by mutuality, as Rousseau (1913[1762]) and Hayek (1948: 111–18), among others observed. Competitive trade takes place within an arena provided by the sociality of communication and continuing with formal rules or informal protocols about it: regular trade requires shared agreements, from peace pacts to written laws enforced by commissions.[10] But trade and calculative reason often rupture or mask the very conditions that enable them. Economists sometimes ask how anthropology can contribute to their models, but their question precludes the dialectic. I think anthropology has more to contribute to our understanding of economy than to prescriptions about how to increase the GNP, satisfy consumers, or improve the process of development.

In developing this view of economy, I have expanded some of my earlier ideas about local and universal models (Gudeman and Penn 1982; Gudeman 1986) in order to construct a more 'cosmopolitan' view. Local models are contextual formulations.[11] Diverse and found on the ground in practices and narratives, they mobilize performance. Local models have no fixed form and are unfinished as ways of constituting action within an environment that exceeds their specifications. A universal model is self-contained, derivational in form, and apparently complete. It seems to be independent of all local conditions.[12]

A universal or derivational model expresses a particular way of organizing knowledge. It has become the dominant form of knowing for some economists (and a considerable number of anthropologists). But they cling to a questionable and dated epistemology, and most are unaware of the infection. Every disease needs a name, so let us identify this epistemological malady as the search for certainty, whose most resilient form is essentialism or foundationalism. In many cases, these practitioners adopt an older 'science' view of the non-human world. Nature consists of separate levels to be analysed by an appropriate discipline. The layers compose a hierarchy of knowledge, such as physics, chemistry, biology and their subdivisions. This Comtean image is projected on society, which is also seen to consist of separate self-organizing levels, such as the 'individual' and 'institutions', or the 'symbolic' and the 'material.' Sometimes the levels are considered to be independent, but usually they are said to be 'causally' connected. Ontological angst is banished by positing an independent bottom level (such as the self-interested individual) from which the remaining 'facts', 'variables' or institutions of social life can be derived. But there are many variations of this layer-cake view. Talcott Parsons famously divided the social world into four functions (or cells) and institutional orders, such as behavioral organism, personality, society and culture (Parsons and Smelser 1956; Parsons 1966).[13] Each cell contained four more levels, and then more in a descending and increasingly specialized order. Parsons claimed that the different levels of society were functionally related through input–output connections. One contemporary version presents society and economy as consisting of discrete sectors with continuous feedback among them (Ruttan 2003).[14] North (2005) offers a more causal view of the relation between levels in his version of the New Institutional Economics. In these models, an epistemology becomes an ontology.

A derivational model is both essentialist and foundationalist. In it, some knowledge is considered to be non-inferential or self-contained; requiring no further justification, this knowledge provides the foundation for the remainder. With its levels, the universal model has rules of formation or derivation such as causality and deduction. (Induction may be used to establish the premises.) Each level of economy or society is tied to the final one (foundationalism) that is self-organized or self-sufficient (essentialism). Euclidean geometry, with its axioms and derivations, offers a mathematical example of the consistency that makes universal models persuasive. Coherent, consistent and replicable, it has a bounded structure.

In economics, David Ricardo offered an early derivational model. In his 1815 *Essay* (Ricardo 1951a), which was written to convince parliament to lift the Corn Laws, Ricardo tried to show how the laws prohibiting the entry of foreign grains benefited landowners by providing them with increased rents, while costing the industrialists who received decreased profits due to the higher rents. His argument was derivational: as cultivated land expanded to poorer soil, rents on better land – being differentially determined by the last or marginal piece – rose, whereas profits on each of these plots (being inversely related to rent) fell. The independent or foundational variable for this derivation was land fertility, which determined rent and hence the rate of profit and the growth of capital. Two years after, in his *Principles* (1951b[1817]), Ricardo replaced land with labour at the foundation. Only toward the end of the nineteenth century was a more complete marginalist analysis applied to land, labour and capital, all as scarce means; the marginalist approach calculates the relation between the last means added to a process and the last end received to derive a point of equilibrium where the cost of the last input equals the revenue of the last output.[15]

Today, in most economic models, means-to-ends calculation provides the non-inferential basis or foundation. Making up the subjectivity of *Homo economicus* and running through the derived domains of production, trade and consumption, calculative reason makes and unites economy through the image of the efficient allocation of resources. For example, given the presence of *Homo economicus*, a market is said to clear when supply equals demand. At the micro level, partial equilibrium or stasis is achieved, nothing is left over. At the macro level, with use of the Walrasian auctioneer, general equilibrium is attained when all markets have adjusted to one another. In conditions of equilibrium the model is complete. Rational choice theory, with its reliance on instrumental calculation, represents a refined development of a derivational model; and in the New Institutionalist Economics rational choice provides the foundation from which associations, rules, norms and social relationships are derived. But as Hayek observed, 'competition is by its nature a dynamic process whose essential characteristics are assumed away by the assumptions underlying static analysis' (Hayek 1948: 94). This same epistemology of nomothetic-deductive reasoning is found in global financial policy. The 'Washington Consensus' which guides the actions of the International Monetary Fund, the World Trade Organization and the World Bank (to a degree), seems to be a collection of regulations that shifts over time. These norms, which include the financial and commercial liberalization of trade, privatization, fiscal discipline and exchange rate stability, broadly derive from the assumption of calculative reason, even if the steps from foundation to policy are not explicitly set forth. Despite local resistance, this model remains intensely persuasive at these institutions.[16]

Derivational models are thought to be general and objective, however the modeller situates them. For example, Marx offered a finely honed (and layered) model of capitalism that centres on the expenditure of labour: some might argue that it is positioned from the perspective of an industrial labourer for whom a revolution was justified (Gregory 2002). Physiocracy, in contrast, was a school of modellers, with somewhat divergent visions, who focused on the land. The Physiocrats offered a layered view of economy through their understanding that natural law, given by God, set the productive returns that accrued to landowners and should determine moral law, which framed the political order. Their model was positioned from the landowners' standpoint in pre-Revolutionary France. Neoclassical economists are positioned by their focus on choice in competitive exchanges, which is a trader's perspective. These standpoints have moral implications even if presented as objective, 'God's eye' or universal views.

Local models are worlds apart. Contingent and mixed constructions, they constitute a world of relationships, objects and beings, or ways of coping with radical uncertainty. They are unfinished as ways of knowing and experiencing the world, and do not exhaust the potentiality for reinterpretation, invention and aspirations, even as they make a necessary life-world. Local models have no given structure and incorporate many forms of reason, such as similarity, analogy, contrast, identity, metaphor and synecdoche, plus critical, dialectical, causal and reflexive reason, as well as means-to-ends calculation. Local models are heterogeneous: malleable and without limits, in the sense of being bounded by rules of inclusion, local models are a creative mix of voices, tropes, images and ways of doing. For example, the layered Physiocratic model combines metaphors of the human to build a picture of the functioning economy (Gudeman 1986). The Physiocrats overlapped three body metaphors – circulation, reproduction, and mind – to construct their model. The image of circulation was drawn from the blood, that of reproduction from the female body, and that of mind from Locke, according to whom external sensation precedes internal operations. The point of overlap was the land, which was considered to be uniquely productive because it was reproductive, supported the circulatory system of agricultural products, and was external to the social world (ibid.) In this respect, Physiocracy was a local model. But the Physiocrats also asserted that humans as natural beings had three material needs: to subsist, to preserve themselves and to continue (Turgot 1898[1770]:7; Mirabeau and Quesnay 1973[1763]: 106). Material subsistence, obtained through a self-sustaining cycle that was exemplified by Quesnay's *Tableau Économique* (1972[1758–1759]), was supported by the land, which provided the foundation for their model. In *Rural Philosophy*, for example, Mirabeau and Quesnay proclaimed:

> We must consider the common weal in terms of its essence, and humanity as a whole in terms of its root, *subsistence*. All the moral and physical parts of which society is constituted derive from this and are subordinate to it. It is upon subsistence, upon the means of subsistence, that all the branches of the political order depend. Religion, in a sense, is purely and simply spiritual, but natural law inspires us and also tells us about duties relative to our needs; the civil laws, which originally are nothing more than rules for the allocation of subsistence; virtues and vices, which are only obedience to or revolt against natural or civil law; agriculture, trade, industry – all are subordinate to the means of subsistence. This is the fundamental force. (Mirabeau and Quesnay 1973:104–105)

The Physiocratic model was formed through the use of overlapping metaphors but also brought into play the notion of a self-sustaining essence, which provided the foundation for the model that had levels and derivations running from a material base to civil law, the polity and religion.

Ethnographically, I have found local models presented in discourse, myths and rituals. Consisting of practices and narratives, they may be sketched in the earth, written or verbal as in the case of the rural Colombian house model that drew on local experience. Like universal models, local models are positioned, but the same people may deploy several in a context, and if they have diverse justifications or local claims to legitimacy – expressed through narratives – that range from invoking the gods or God, to the ancestors and nature, their construction is a transcendent necessity.

But what is the relation between derivational and local models? Is one superior to the other, as logic supposedly stands to narrative, or prose to poetry? Is each appropriate for different contexts, or are they equal and opposite? In my view, universal models are abstractions because they constitute relations and entities removed from any local specifications, which must be deduced from them. For example, in discourse the universal modeller abstracts levels (such as individuals and institutions), posits a self-contained foundation or point of derivation (such as land, labour or the rational chooser), derives the levels (such as prices, institutions or a theorem), and re-presents the result as a totality: poof! the economy is created. This culturally familiar way of arranging knowledge is persuasive; however, it creates knowledge boundaries, closes out the possibility of other experiences, and makes local models disappear. Universal or derivational models create a breach between the actions they describe and other economic practices. They are also incomplete, because they require locally specified conditions and mutuality as their transcendent conditions of existence.

Even if the borders of a universal model and a market look firm, cascading continuously expands them. Cascading occurs when market participants, through the search for profit, extend their reach to noncommoditized things and services – such as forest preserves and domestic work, as anthropologists and feminist economists have observed. When markets expand, local constructions of economy are fragmented as calculated relationships replace mutuality. In discourse as well, universal modellers try to create a seamless economic totality by cascading the limits of their model. For example, exogenous variables not included in the model are separated from endogenous ones that are: social events, such as unpredicted innovations that drive change, may be excluded from the model. As one illustration, in his elegant theory of growth as an endogenous process, Solow assumes 'that there is an erratic stream of innovations, each of which, when it occurs, permits a major increase in productivity…. these can be treated as exogenous' (Solow 1997: 21). In market terms, exogenous variables do not respond to market incentives, whereas endogenous variables do.

Similarly, externalities are separated from internalities. Externalities are effects of market acts that fall outside market exchange and the calculations of profit and loss rather than being traded, such as the uncontrolled dumping of rubbish in the oceans. Internalities are transacted. But events and acts categorized as externalities or as exogenous variables do not make up a local model, because they are constituted as unexplained remainders in relation to an abstracted, derivational model rather than as parts of local constructions. To encompass these leftovers, universal modellers often extend or cascade the borders of their model. For example, Solow 'would invite any do-it-yourself endogenizer to add links in the other direction from the economic environment to the rate of innovation' in order to fill out his endogenous explanation (ibid.: 21). Likewise, externalities may be commensurated and commoditized to encompass a larger range of behaviours. In the process, universal modellers hide, silence, invade or derive local models in order to be complete in discourse and to realize their formulation on the ground. I call this process debasement, because it converts shared benefits and social relationships to market transactions.

The concept and 'reality' of the rational actor, which posits the individual as an autonomous unit who makes and orders preferences, and chooses independently of others, is an abstraction from human qualities and social relationships. As this presentation of human action is increasingly enacted and enforced through market activity, it subsumes cultural relations and often mystifies them as if they were calculated selections. For example, reciprocity and gift giving may be interpreted as aggrandizement, or mutual ties may be used to cloak calculative reason. This appropriation of mutuality for instrumental purposes occurs in formal models and in practice when corporations – as one example – represent themselves as solidary groups (a family) yet lay off workers when the market environment demands. In such cases the more powerful appropriates the features of the less powerful as it dresses itself in the latter's clothes to claim legitimacy. Veblen (1914) termed this sort of appropriation 'derangement', but we can also view it as a dialectical relation by which the qualities of one thing or category are mystified as those of another for material and control purposes.[17]

Conclusion

To conclude, we must reassess the labels of the two models. A derivational model is actually a 'local,' historically situated way of arranging things or epistemology that is legitimated by stories about its universal presence and completeness. Conversely, local models are unfinished because they can never fully describe the world within which we live, but they are universal or transcendent in the sense of being necessary for experience. Even if the market dynamic, with its reverberations, cascading and habit-forming practice, is powerful, it requires the communality that it would also contradict.

I thus return to the project of building a cosmopolitan anthropology in the sense of combining voices, subjecting our work to the critical scrutiny of the people we study, exploring the history of our research areas, and undertaking research as a conversation. Cosmopolitan anthropology also means seeing human capacities as universally shared but with differing local expressions. I have argued that we can compare, contrast and reciprocally critique these differing expressions – whether from small economies, markets or academic discourse – as local models. This is my response in a long conversation with Adam Kuper.

Notes

An earlier version of this chapter was published as the introductory chapter to my book *Economy's Tension* (New York: Berghahn, 2008). I gratefully acknowledge the permission given by Berghahn to use this version here.

1. For a recent review of this debate, see Carrier (in press).
2. In more recent times, Marshall Sahlins (1976) expresses a variation of the controversy when he contrasts culture to practical reason or utility theory.
3. For a related argument, see Gregory (1997), who distinguishes between House and Market as coeval value systems, just as he differentiates between 'savage' and 'domesticated' money.
4. But Hirschman also concluded that '*capitalism was supposed to accomplish exactly what was soon to be denounced as its worst feature*' (Hirschman 1977:132).
5. Muldrew (1998), from a different perspective, also reverses the Weberian thesis by arguing that the development of commercial transactions and the extension of credit originally depended on social relationships that provided a reputation for reliability; shifting social practices furnished the vitality for the new commercial outlook.
6. Žižek refers to:

   the Hegelian logic of the retroactive reversal of contingency into necessity: of course capitalism emerged from a contingent combination of historical conditions; of course it gave birth to a series of phenomena (political democracy, concern for human rights, etc.) which can be 'resignified', rehegemonized, inscribed into a non-capitalist context. However, capitalism retroactively 'posited its own presuppositions', and reinscribed its contingent/external circumstances into an all-encompassing logic that can be generated from an elementary conceptual matrix (the 'contradiction' involved in the act of commodity exchange, etc.). In a proper dialectical analysis, the 'necessity' of a totality does not preclude its contingent origins and the heterogeneous nature of its constituents – these are, precisely, its *presuppositions* which are then posited, retroactively totalized, by the emergence of dialectical totality' (Žižek (2000: 225).

7. I follow here Kolakowski's (1978) masterful account.
8. Toulmin also contrasts a 'balanced approach to the function of Reason and one in which that balance is upset.... In an unbalanced account, there is a systematic preference for the kinds of knowledge that are articulated in language, and most of all in the language of formal theory' (Toulmin 2001: 177).
9. Others might expand this list to include social, emotional, spiritual and communal reason (Gardner 2004), while Markus and Kitayama (1998) argue that 'rational choice' itself is socially embedded. See also Markus, Mullally and Kitayama (1997), Hutchins (1995), and Hayek (1967: 86–88, 90; 1978: 71).
10. As I explore elsewhere, this arena has many forms and scales, from a political order and laws to civic associations, family ties, ethnic identity, friendship and fictive kinship; and it is infused with mutuality expressed as shared languages, relationships, body gestures and ways of doing (Gudeman 2008).
11. Similarly, in speaking of models of agency, Markus and Kitayama state that 'these models are both forms of knowledge and social practices; they have both conceptual and material elements' (Markus and Kitayama 2003: 46).
12. Some time after I formulated with a colleague the idea of local and universal or derivational models (Gudeman and Penn 1982) and used it in a book (Gudeman 1986), I discovered that Stephen Marglin had proposed a similar epistemological divide (Marglin 1990, 1996). Originally he termed these modes 'techne' and 'episteme'. Recently he has labelled them 'experiential' and 'algorithmic' knowledge (Marglin 2007).

13. The four functions were adaptation, goal attainment, integration and pattern maintenance. These social functions were principally carried out through different institutions, such as the economy, the polity, the social order and religion.
14. Some years ago, Milton Friedman urged: 'A fundamental hypothesis of science is that appearances are deceptive and that there is a way of looking at or interpreting or organizing the evidence that will reveal superficially disconnected and diverse phenomena to be manifestations of a more fundamental and relatively simple structure' (Friedman 1953: 33).
15. I have discussed Ricardo's model elsewhere; see Gudeman (1986).
16. For descriptions of the Washington Consensus and its recent augmentations, see Green (2003), and Baumol, Litan and Schramm (2007).
17. Veblen (1914) also referred to this process as 'imputation' and 'contamination'.

Chapter 10

The Door in the Middle: Six Conditions for Anthropology

João de Pina-Cabral

Some of the best minds in anthropological theory over the past decades have been warning us that modernist anthropological theory has come to a serious impasse.[1] Modernist anthropological theory comprises the conceptual frameworks that emerged in the late nineteenth and early twentieth centuries, reaching its peak in the 1930s and 1940s, and then entering into a process of critical self-questioning around and after the 1960s. Fifty years after the optimistic formulations of Parsons, Kroeber, Fortes and Gluckman, the central concepts that laid the ground for the development of our discipline are viewed with suspicion by most anthropologists today. In this paper, I argue that we can neither deny the value of the critique nor resign ourselves to the air of gloom that results from it. I suggest some ways out of the impasse.

'Is the concept of society theoretically obsolete?' One might lean towards either side of the famous Manchester debate,[2] but one has to acknowledge that it makes sense to ask the question. Similarly with the concept of culture. Having examined its history, Adam Kuper concludes that 'it is a poor strategy to separate out a cultural sphere, and to treat it in its own terms' (Kuper 1999b: 247).[3] In a related vein, Marilyn Strathern (1992a, 1992b, 1999), Eduardo Viveiros de Castro (2002b) and Roy Wagner (1981) argue that the modernist theoretical mould depends on three essential sets of polarities that can no longer constitute pillars of our thinking. But they have also shown how those polarities have surreptitiously survived in the categories we continue to use and in our modes of acting as anthropologists. These are, to use Viveiros de Castro's summary: primitive versus civilized; individual versus society; and nature versus culture.[4] In his history of the concept of the 'primitive', Adam Kuper (1988) laid out the historical ground for such a realization.

Despite being very much alive, relevant and active as an empirical discipline, anthropology has for too long been theoretically gagged in relation to the other social sciences, sociology in particular (cf. Pina-Cabral 2005a). Although our research areas expand and we are making significant contributions to the understanding of the central problems facing our contemporary world – such as AIDS, homelessness, terrorism, to name just a few (see Bastos 1999; Hannerz 2004; Passaro 1996; Donahue 2007) – our capacity to intervene theoretically has been diminished by our persistent attachment to formulas of disciplinary definition that are no longer scientifically defensible (cf. Pina-Cabral 2006).

It has been argued that the problem lies in the very nature of these pillars, in that, as with all modernist thinking, they have written into them a utopian disposition. Modernist thought was driven by what we might call expectation concepts (cf. Bolle 2004: 273, see also Latour 1993). The dynamism of such notions lies in that they describe by reference not to what is (or was) but by reference to an expected future. Thus, the opposition between primitive/ civilized assumes the eventual victory of civilization; the opposition between individual and society assumes both the eventual victory of the individual (as Mauss and Durkheim clearly stated) and the future coming of a fuller condition of sociality (as Marx predicted); finally, the nature/culture opposition assumes the victory of culture and science over nature.

Dystopian Modernism

If we remain bound by such expectation concepts, even though we may well lose faith in the future, we still have not freed ourselves from the framework they imply. We move from a utopian posture to a dystopian posture, but we are still in the shackles of a futuristic expectation. Over the past ten years, anthropology has given signs of this type of gloom (Pina-Cabral 2007b). Many adopted deflationist attitudes, giving up on or being agnostic about the possibility of knowledge of the real; many accepted discursivist descriptions of socio-cultural life, slipping into a rhetorical game of liberated meanings; many continued to call themselves social scientists but abstained from knowing what science is, and some even raised the possibility of there being alternative anthropologies and alternative sciences. Some gave up on generalization grounded in ethnographic observation. Finally, some entertained the notion that there may be no such thing as a 'human condition'.

Such attitudes are essentially negative. Instead of opening up new paths of empirical and theoretical exploration, they remain trapped within the terms set by the modernist oppositions which caused our initial dissatisfaction. They are the posturings of those who, faced with the discovery that the expected future has not materialized, have despaired of the future overall. This, however, is not a tenable position. It makes more sense to follow the lead of Adam Kuper (1988, 2005; see also Mintz 1994: 290) and question the bases of the 'primitivist' hypothesis that supported the scientific project of twentieth-century anthropology.

In order to do so, however, we also have to query some of the central presuppositions that underpinned it – most particularly the metaphysics of group-ness that accompanies the utopian disposition: that is, sociocentrism. The term – coined by Durkheim and Mauss in the last pages of their essay on primitive classification (Durkheim and Mauss 1963) – points to some of the sets of oppositions mentioned above. It reveals three tendencies: firstly, to treat social entities as unitary and self-defined (individual/society); secondly, to approach modernity as a uniquely creative move (primitive/civilized); and thirdly, to reify ideas as representations outside the world (nature/culture).

The problems we face today are largely derived from our unwillingness to shed the utopian dispositions we inherited from the early modernists. This applies not only to the anthropological theory that we produce, but also to how we produce it. In an insatiable search for yet another 'master' thinker who will take us to a higher level of theory, we continue to search for yet another paradigmatic shift that will free us from the perplexities of the past.[5] But this is a quest for a mirage. As Adam Kuper has shown, we cannot afford to cut loose from our anthropological heritage, but we should not remain bound to those aspects of it that cause us problems (Kuper 1988, 2005). There is no contradiction in looking for 'a door in the middle': that is, in giving up on radical breaks and searching for humbler solutions that will allow us to practise anthropology and ethnography in new ways whilst building on our distinguished heritage. The six conditions that I outline below are not seen as definitive answers to old quandaries, but as paths out of this dystopia.

Realism

The real is neither at the point of arrival nor at the point of exit: it poses itself for us, rather, midways.

João Guimarães Rosa, *Grande Sertão: Veredas* (2001)

It is important to continue to hold that, in ethnography, we can capture the real. Ultimate truth will always evade us but lesser truths – which, over time, accumulate – do not. Empirical research is a complex and exacting task. But the difficulties in undertaking it are worth overcoming because the knowledge that results from it proves to be more resilient and less prone to observational disagreement than our everyday knowledge of our surrounding world. Despite many circumstances which mediate such knowledge, the ultimate value of empirical observation and theoretical rationalization cannot be denied.

We must learn how to distinguish epistemological relativism from methodological relativism, since, whilst the former is a dead end for our discipline, the latter is its basic trademark. Anthropologists have often been tempted to conclude from the fact that the lived world is historically constituted, that the constituting process is all there is; that is, that there is no world. Some claim, emphatically, that since anthropology is a Western system of knowledge it cannot presume to be better or more embracing than the local knowledge systems it studies. According to this view, any claim of scientific status or of a form of progressive accumulation of knowledge based on the maximization of rational enquiry is taken to be demeaning of the people anthropologists study and thus morally suspect.

This argument assumes that to favour a scientific approach is to make claims to its being morally superior to everyday means of knowing the world. In other words, it assumes in modernist fashion, firstly, that everyday life can be lived according to science, and secondly, that such a life would be somehow morally superior. If these assumptions were valid, then the peoples being represented in our studies would be entitled to complain about the scientific status of ethnography and anthropology. They are, however, unfounded. Further, it is anthropologists rather than the people they want to represent who are despondent about modern science. Such a stance represents an incapacity to distance oneself from the expectation concepts concerning primitivism and individualism. It also means a continued embracing of modernist sociocentrism.

Moreover, the posture presumes a moral obligation to represent the people studied. Anthropologists speak for 'their' people. Thus, sociocentrism meets paternalism in a narcissistic discourse which ultimately privileges the ethnographer over their informants. If anthropology *were* 'Western' and I *were* 'Western', then it would not be morally suspect for me to prefer 'my own' discourse over that of another.[6] But the wider world in which anthropologists are situated is far more complex than their local everyday context. Their participation in a global ecumene[7] brings with it an obligation to respect the views of others. Anthropology is not 'Western'; it is an intrinsic part of that global ecumene that is the reason for anthropologists' sense of responsibility to respect the ideas of others.

In a postcolonial setting, the practice of ethnography has altered fundamentally. This is so, not only because ethnography and anthropology are now routinely practised by people whose identification as Western is doubtful, but also because the people anthropologists study have found new ways of negotiating the knowledge anthropologists produce (Ramos 1998). The paternalistic assumption that anthropologists' methodological mandate to respect the people they study extends to a right to represent 'their people' (a collective constituted out of ethnographic practice) is highly suspect. The world where ethnography is practised today is one where the ethnographer is likely to encounter anthropologically trained 'natives'. A new condition of mutuality is, thus, inscribed into the ethnographic encounter that makes for a far more complex political engagement of the ethnographer in his or her field.

Deflationism (the belief that truth is not a valid category) is thus something to be avoided if we want to pursue our activities as anthropologists and ethnographers. In anthropology, Kuper warns, relativism goes hand-in-hand with a form of implicit idealism (Kuper 1999b: 19). To question the possibility of access to truth – or to pluralize truth – is to retreat into the realm of pure ideas. Whilst this might appear to liberate one from the pitfalls of ethnocentric interpretation, by opening the way to a plurality of perspectival approaches, it actually reconstructs the problems of sociocentrism by reifying the groups or peoples that are supposed to hold such views.

The move to idealism, and the retreat to the realm of ideas, eats away at the possibility of anthropological knowledge. If we want anthropology to be possible and ethnography to thrive, we should avoid such forms of dystopian depression. But this does not mean that we should engage in blind positivism. Some of the recent attempts to revive robust types of scientistic realism are just as much acts of despair as culturalist deflationism. As contemporary philosophers have shown, we do better to steer towards the 'door in the middle'; that is, some form of minimal realism that will allow us to operate methodological relativism whilst avoiding epistemological relativism (see Lynch 1998).

Limited Interest

Ethnography and anthropology are not and have never been a discourse on the native's discourses (see Viveiros de Castro 2002a). As was stressed by earlier anthropologists, neither society nor culture offered themselves ready-made for the anthropologist to describe. Rather, anthropologists had and still have to construct their object from observations of everyday, taken-for-granted events, many or most of which are not discursive in the sense of being planned acts of communication. And because events are constitutive processes, acts of communication and social categories of action (persons, groups, and so on) are profoundly intermeshed in historically complex ways.

Two central aspects mediate our ability to observe and describe human lives as they are lived: firstly, the play of intersubjective relations, both as they operate in the production of local meanings and vis-à-vis the ethnographer; and secondly, events in the surrounding or environing world whose parameters may remain implicit (Davidson 2004). These inform what ethnographers can understand of the human setting in which they find themselves, including those explicitly formulated events in terms of which they interpret locally recurrent forms of historically constituted engagement. Moreover, understanding intersubjectivity necessarily entails an analysis of its political, economic and other dimensions; that is to say, an analysis that reveals the constituting forms taken by social relations in any given case.

Analysing the play of intersubjectivity in the environing world provides for a more thorough and subtle understanding of domination, for example, than is available by means of discourse analysis. The idea of discourse, in Foucauldian or Deleuzean terms, of course includes power (cf. Lutz and Abu-Lughod 1990; Viveiros de Castro 2007). But all discursivism ultimately implies a dystopic denial that the world outside of human sociation impinges on human sociation and that our shared or surrounding world is also part of our ethnographies. The very acts of practising and of writing ethnography would be impossible without decisive attention both to this environing world and to the way in which earlier acts of communication have been reified in each particular setting. It is essential to recognize the complex process of triangulation which occurs between interpreters, their human others, and the surrounding world. Mintz gives an example of this relationship when he observes that:

> a profound difference between the history of our discipline in Europe, on the one hand, and in the Western Hemisphere on the other, inheres in the simple fact that our [American] subjects of study, our 'primitive' peoples, were our neighbours – our ill-treated, indeed often persecuted, neighbours. In this instance as in others, the anthropology we do and have done is conditioned by the history and social complexion of the society whence we come (Mintz 1994: 290).

Triangulation occurs at all levels: the ethnographic encounter is shaped by it at both ends. It is shaped, on the one hand, by the local, historically informed relations of triangulation and, on the other, by the complex process of historical constitution of disciplinary agendas. As Davidson put it, 'relativism about standards requires what there cannot be, a position beyond all standards' (Davidson 2005: 181).

Like all human action, anthropology is interested, in the sense that it is engaged in the world; it has implicit within it an investment on the part of the agent (personal or collective). Bourdieu, in his treatment of the notion of habitus (Bourdieu 1980), shows that the border between conscious and unconscious interest is of little heuristic use when studying human action (see also Davidson 2005: 286–7; Pina-Cabral 2007b).

Interest is related to motivation which, in turn, is defined by two central parameters: on the one hand, the categories of identity that inform an agent's motivational perceptions and, on the other, the intersubjectively produced categories that characterize the field of action. The central value of the notion of interest is that it allows us to understand social action as a constant negotiation of the future and the past in intersubjective terms. The issue of simultaneity, to be discussed later, is relevant inasmuch as it limits the directedness of interest. No person bears only one identity. Diverse forms of investment in the world combine in any particular social action; interests limit each other and compound one another, way beyond the capacity of unilinear or single-minded intention (whether this be individual or collective). The concept of interest, then, is only useful to the extent that it is seen as limited. It is possible to investigate the limits of interest in any specific case of human action, thus gaining some insight into the complex process of triangulation that characterizes it (see Pina-Cabral and Bestard Camps 2003). That, too, is a door in the middle.

Meaning

The proclivities of sociocentrism to treat both social entities as self-enclosed units and categories or ideas as things (as actual pictures in the mind) appear to be independent of each other. They are, however, determined by the same modernist need to separate subject from object, action from thought, fact from value (cf. de Coppet 1992: 70). The fact that the two tendencies appear mutually independent merely contributes to their mutual validation. This is argued cogently by de Coppet in his historical account of the evolution of the concept of representation. It is difficult to follow him to his ultimate conclusions, however, because of his continued attachment to a hard concept of 'society/system'. This runs counter to my present argument: that modernist sociocentrism is best eradicated from the study of what it is to be human. The critique of such a notion of society does not, contra de Coppet (ibid.: 70), necessarily imply a retreat into individualism. It is erroneous to attribute a separate ontology to personhood and to collectivities (societies, cultures, groups, systems), since to do so is to reproduce the metaphysics of group-ness that characterized the thought of Comte, Durkheim and their followers, one of the greatest hurdles that social anthropology has met with throughout the twentieth century.

To overcome this hurdle it is necessary not only to transcend the dichotomy which counterposes individuality and group-ness. Existing ideas about meaning also need to be interrogated. Anthropologists have been working for too long with a semiotic theory of representation that is arguably dependent on an 'essentially incoherent picture of the mind' (Davidson 2001: 52). More sophisticated theories of meaning are required, which emphasize both the socially relational aspect and the fact that meaning is dependent on practical experience. Giddens points to anthropologists' implicit adoption of a theory of meaning that is epistemologically unsound: 'those who speak of a crisis of representation in anthropology, or who see anthropological work merely as a species of creative fiction, are the victims of a false theory of meaning'. He traces the origin of this to the structural linguistics of Saussure and the way in which 'meaning is understood [there] in relation to a play of signifiers, not – as it should be – in the context of practical experience' (Giddens 1996: 124–5).[8]

This 'picture of the mind', as Davidson calls it, has become so deeply engrained in our philosophical heritage[9] that we find it almost impossible to escape its grip, even when its noxious effects become apparent.

In one crude, but familiar, version it goes like this: the mind is a theatre in which the conscious self watches a passing show (the shadows on the wall). The show consists of 'appearances', sense data, qualia, what is 'given' in experience. What appear on the stage are not the ordinary objects in the world that the outer eye registers and the heart loves, but their purported representations. Whatever we know about the world outside depends on what we can glean from the inner clues. (Davidson 2001: 34)

Contrary to this, Davidson argues, we have no use for the notion of 'purely private, subjective "objects of the mind".... Beliefs are true or false, but they represent nothing. It is good to be rid of representations, and with them the correspondence theory of truth, for it is thinking there are representations that engenders intimations of relativism' (ibid.: 46).

To reject such a theory of meaning does not mean that we must reject the need to understand the processes of semantic integration that constitute the favoured paths in our universe of beliefs. These, ultimately, are what the ethnographer searches to identify (Pina-Cabral 2004). The ethnographer's method is essentially to make sense of what others are doing and saying in terms of an assumption of human similarity and of a world that is common at once to self and other. And here we return to the notion of triangulation:

We are bound to suppose someone we want to understand inhabits our world of macroscopic, more or less enduring physical objects with familiar causal dispositions; that his world, like ours, contains people with minds and motives; and that he shares with us the desire to find warmth, love, security, and success, and the desire to avoid pain and distress.... [U]nless we can interpret others as sharing a vast amount of what makes up our common sense we will not be able to identify any of their beliefs and desires and intentions, any of their propositional attitudes. (ibid.: 183).

This passage deserves the attention of anthropologists, since few have chosen to give attention to the simplest processes that make for the possibility of their favoured form of empirical knowledge – ethnography. By these means, rather than taking for granted the possibility of simple human communication in the face of interpretative indeterminacy, many might have avoided the destructive and deeply unsettling slide from methodological relativism to epistemological relativism that has so troubled the discipline since the 1960s.

To this must be added something that is implicit in the passage of Mintz's quoted earlier: ethnographers do not work in a private individual setting. They are never alone with their subjects of study except if and when they choose to discard their professional robes. Ethnography and anthropology are processes within a collective pursuit with a collective past and a presumed collective future. And that is not 'the history of the West', whatever that might mean. Rather, it is the complex and ongoing history of the constitution of a global ecumene that is increasingly becoming available to all.

Such a global ecumene is, of course, structured by shifting relations of domination because the process of making meaning always implicates the form of relations it engages. But there is no point in despairing of this. On the contrary, we must take the fact that our own scientific activity is immersed in human history as the very starting point of our efforts to know more and better. As Merleau-Ponty pointed out:

> Since we are all hemmed in by history, it is up to us to understand that whatever truth we may have is to be gotten not in spite of but through our historical inherence. Superficially considered, our inherence destroys all truth. As long as I cling to the ideal of an ideal spectator, of knowledge with no point of view, I can see my situation as nothing but a source of error. But if I have once recognized that through it I am grafted into every action and all knowledge which can have a meaning for me, and that step by step it contains everything which can exist for me, then my contact with the social in the finitude of my situation is revealed to me as the point of origin of all truth, including scientific truth. (Merleau-Ponty 1964: 109)

Here, too, is a door in the middle that allows us to avoid both the utopian and the dystopian fantasies of completeness.

Freedom and Necessity

'Human sciences', claims Fernando Gil, 'have taken on the task of resolving the paroxysmal antinomy of Kantian freedom and necessity' (Gil 2004: 11). He defines 'necessity' by reference to determination: that is, in Aristotelian terms, the condition that something comes next unless something else prevents it from doing so. Curiously, anthropologists in the twentieth century have avoided this antinomy – perhaps because of the theoretical paroxysm it implies.

Freedom of the will has played a very small role in anthropological theorizing, despite having permeated all good ethnography. The few exceptions can be seen in those writings where anthropologists talk about the actual people from whose behaviour they try to abstract; for example, through situational analysis (e.g., Van Velsen 1964) or methodological debate (e.g., Casagrande 1960). The notion of determination is, however, either taken for granted in generic terms or too easily derided. In anthropological literature, necessity in human behaviour is most often linked to Malinowski's theoretical blunders concerning 'needs'. This word has a bad name in anthropological theory, being used most often as a blanket term in order to iron out some logically unsatisfactory theoretical jump.

When Boon and Schneider, for example, justify their culturalist reading of Lévi-Strauss's oeuvre by trashing the notion of 'the hypothetical "social needs" of the group' (Boon and Schneider 1974: 807), they close off important doors to interdisciplinary debate concerning relative human determination. Worse still, they manage to sidestep the issue of the freedom of the will, ignoring the fact that one cannot be considered without the other. Cultural determinism comes to be hidden beneath a thin veneer of liberal goodwill. They try to clean up Lévi-Strauss's arguments about the atom of kinship by transposing these to culture – which they understand in purely semiotic terms as the realm of 'ideas.' They complain that, as a response to his British critics, Lévi-Strauss has (correctly, they argue) 'shifted his kinship models to their *proper* cultural level' but (unfortunately, in their view) he 'left the *vestigial* social cohesion arguments' (ibid.: 816, my emphasis) in *The Elementary Structures of Kinship* (Lévi-Strauss 1969).

Contrary to Boon and Schneider, however, such an option would not have resolved the problem of the ultimate social import of kinship. It would continue to be necessary – ultimately – to talk of 'groups' and 'units', as indeed they do: 'Societies do not *have* patrilateral or matrilateral systems; rather groups or parts of groups reveal ideas of such marriages which might be carried out to various extents' (Boon and Schneider 1974: 810). Thus, their culturalist reduction to ideas only succeeds in delaying, postponing or obscuring the inevitable talk of group-ness – raising the far more problematic notion of knowing what exactly is an idea as held by a group.

This is a problem with all culturalist anthropology, as is apparent, for example, in Ortner's most recent attempts to integrate power and practice into culture (Ortner 2006). Her efforts are genuine and valuable but they remain constrained by the fact that, concerning culture, no dependence on ideas is possible that does not ultimately postulate the group that holds them. Talk of material 'needs' is avoided, but cultural determination rules and freedom of the will is neglected. In any case, since groups always lurk behind cultures, we are bound by theoretical honesty to enquire what these groups are, how they are formed, and how these ideas relate to the groups or units that hold them.

Again according to Boon and Schneider, 'in myth, man's analogical capacity ... is portrayed as being dependent on its materials only insofar as it must have something ... to work with.... [Similarly] we might relax our preconceptions as to the genealogical and social organizational nature of "kinship" data as well' (Boon and Schneider 1974: 815). The dependence on previous interpretation in order to recognize the occurrence of myth or kinship, and the dependence for that on triangulation with others and the world, are simply taken for granted, as if they were matters of small concern. Man's materiality is taken to be secondary to his ideas – merely the wall on which the cultural shadows are reflected. This is as extreme a form of idealism as anthropology will ever manage.[10] The hegemonic position that Schneiderian idealism has assumed in global anthropology over the past two decades is surely one of today's principal theoretical hurdles. It does not help us to ease any of the perplexities caused by sociocentrism, neither those concerning 'group-ness' nor those concerning 'representation'. As Davidson warned, 'the notion that our will is free from physical determination has prompted many to hold that the mental and the physical must be discrete realms, but if they are somehow decoupled, it is a question of how knowledge is possible. Skepticism and the problem of free will are symmetrical problems' (Davidson 2005: 277).

In fact, the antinomy between freedom of the will and determination only becomes troublesome to the extent that we avoid it. Anthropologists ought boldly to address the issue and develop ways of mediating it. Humans are subject to determination both to the extent that they live in a material world and to the extent that they are constituted by a human environment where rationality and language operate. The latter institute new forms of causality, new 'needs'; the two forms of determination converge. This is what Davidson calls the anomaly in our ontological monism: there is only one world, but rationality sets in motion new styles of causality within that world.[11] This means that all human action is confronted both by its 'underdetermination' (e.g., ibid.: 318) and by its 'unpredictability' (see Arendt 1958: 233). That is, we are incapable of determining not only the causes of our actions, but also what their impact will be on the world. Again, in Gil's formulation, 'the unpredictability resides less in the mere intersection of causal series than in the *simultaneity* of occurrences in the particular here and the particular now' (Gil 2004: 5). Hazard accompanies our every move.

Thus, the fourth condition highlighted here is that, when considering human thought and action (that is, when interpreting the actions of humans in the world), the anthropologist should be satisfied neither by talk of random choice nor by talk of absolute necessity. We cannot settle either for a Sartrean notion of freedom or for a Malinowskian notion of need. Freedom and necessity do exist in the human condition but, due to the anomaly in our monism, they have to be seen as mediated. We must avoid anthropological determinism, whether this be positivistic or, as is the case with the example presented above of Boon and Schneider, idealist in character.

If human action is underdetermined and unpredictable, any unmediated notion of necessity is invalid. But the idea of necessity has a number of distinct implications (see Gil 2004) depending whether it is seen as opposed to what is possible (i.e., capable of happening), to what is contingent (i.e., determined by circumstances not yet established), to what is free (i.e., unconstrained), or to what is indeterminate (i.e., not capable of being determined as, for instance, in the above example of simultaneity). Theorizing the determinations of human action in a world characterized by anomalous monism requires a search for a mediation to these antinomies.

Thus, we observe occurrences that are not merely possible but probable; not merely contingent but frequent; not merely free but relatively unconstrained; not merely indeterminate but spontaneous. When these four conditions meet, we are faced with observations that have a high level of generality and a special relevance for the study of the human condition.

Anthropology has long silenced the discussion of universals of the human condition. When the topic surfaces, it is usually met with dystopian derision. The reason for this is that, despite some useful insights by Needham (1981: 20–24) concerning 'primary factors',[12] most anthropologists have understood 'universals' in terms of 'needs'. It has been thought that if something were to be a universal then it would have to be observable always and permanently in all historically known instances of human sociation. This, however, is a mistake, since it implies that phenomena of human thought and action are subject to the same type of causality that characterizes inert substances. The anomaly in our world means that no such causation will ever be found in matters of human thought and action.

A universal of the human condition, therefore, can usefully be redefined to cover what Needham (1978) called 'proclivities' – that is, dispositions of thought and action that are probable, frequent, spontaneous, and for which there seems to be an inclination. Through this 'door in the middle' we can search for instruments of interpretation that do not imply an abandoning of generalization. In many ways, this position is not only akin to Adam Kuper's advocacy of a universalist viewpoint but also very similar to that espoused by Maurice Bloch in his recent essay on seeing and lying, where he argues that 'we might attempt to generalize about a phenomenon such as the recurrence of the association between truth and sight without ignoring important anti-universalist points' (Bloch 2008: 22).

Alterity and System

Modernist sociocentrism relies on a contrastive notion of alterity that sees it as a relation between two or more entities that stand apart from each other. Societies and cultures, as much as individuals, are assumed to be closed upon themselves and oppositionally related. This kind of sociological monism, however, is unwarranted. Alterity and identity in human affairs are not symmetrical (Levinas 1996; cf. Pina-Cabral 2005b). Alterity both creates identity – in the ethical face-to-face relation that constitutes persons ontogenetically – and reflects it. Social entities (persons or collectives) are not elemental units, for they are mutually constituted. Similarly, 'mental categories' are also not subject to treatment as things or pictures, due to the ultimate indeterminacy of interpretation (Davidson 2005: 316).

Thus, for example, to accuse anthropology of focusing on continuity to the exclusion of change (Robbins 2007) does not really address the issue, since it focuses exclusively upon only half of it. There have, indeed, been many anthropologists over the past decades who have focused on change at the expense of continuity, but that did not solve the problem. Anthropologists lack a socio-cultural language for dealing with change. But we also lack a language to describe long-term fixity and continuity in anything other than a unitary manner (Pina-Cabral 1992). The problem has to do both with schism *and* continuity, to quote Victor Turner's famous title (Turner 1957). The basis of the problem is that the emphasis on sameness has prevented a more complex understanding of alterity.[13] We must abandon the notion that societies and cultures (and the groups that hold them) are *things* to the extent that they are identical with themselves. Identity is produced by alterity and, thus, it is always preceded by it.

Embracing processualism will not, in itself, resolve the problem if one remains trapped by a sociocentric concern with unitariness. Instead of seeing social entities as enclosed units, we must understand that they are the result of continual processes of identification. No identity is ever fully accomplished, as identity is a momentary crystallization of the processes of identification and differentiation that are constantly going on in human settings. Identity is not a 'picture in the mind'; rather, it is the historically specific observable effect of these processes. Being the sediment of history, identity is constantly challenged by it – that is, by the continuation of the very same processes that produce it. This must prompt us to give up our unitarian concept of identity. Modernist thinking tended to see the unitariness of groups and societies as equivalent to that of individuals. Thus, sociocentrism and individualism usually converged: in Fortes's work on kinship this is explicitly elaborated in the notion of the 'juristic person' (Fortes 1969: 301). Calling our attention to this, Marilyn Strathern claims that 'in anthropological discourse, systems, like conventions or like societies and cultures, were frequently personified as agents with interests of their own – an image laminated in the picture of corporate groups as juristic persons' (Strathern 1992b: 97). However accurate, this formulation raises further problems, since it presupposes that all agency must be limited to individuals, to physical persons, and hence that no suprapersonal entity can be attributed with it. This presupposition is not only empirically erroneous but theoretically disturbing, as it suggests a re-entry of individualism by the back door. As de Coppet (1992) warned, it presumes the greater unitariness of the person as a level of social identity.[14]

The presumption of unitariness has implications for our daily activities as anthropologists and ethnographers. Our main instrument of analysis is the search for system in empirical fields that we have delineated on the basis of earlier analyses. The notion that the ethnographer's task is one of interpretation is yet another instance of a half-truth that, through a fallacy of all-or-nothing, is taken to represent the whole (Pina-Cabral 2007b). Interpretation is merely the beginning of an ethnographer's task, as they have to place the interpretations they gather into some sort of analytically relevant whole. The relevance of such a whole will not emerge from everyday interchange or be limited to the ethnographic present, but rather builds upon the history of anthropology.

When we look for patterns, correlations, or correspondences, we are in fact looking for system within fields that we, or our predecessors, previously outlined. Anthropology is familiar with such pursuits, and has made its greatest achievements precisely when carrying out this type of exercise. Major discoveries – such as that of the existence of classificatory systems of kinship, of rites of passage, of segmentariness, or of matrimonial strategies – have depended on the postulation of system and on the identification of forms of structural causality and structural transformation.

One of the conditions for the continuation of anthropological thought is to accept certain lessons from our predecessors regarding how systemic analysis yields insights into how we humans live in our environing world. In doing so, unitariness should not be granted to socio-cultural entities; entity status should not be given to 'ideas'; and structures should not be viewed as complete and self-regulating. The structuralism of the 1960s and 1970s is no longer a possibility, and removing it to the realm of ideas, as Boon and Schneider (1974) would have it, is unhelpful. Once more, a mediation or 'door in the middle' will allow us to profit from anthropology's accumulated methodological legacy, and to arrive at a mitigated structuralism.

If, as Gil claims, 'to be able to conceive a mobile order is the ambition of all great philosophy' (Gil 2004: 17), it should also be the ambition of anthropology. Following a suggestion laid out by Musil (1995), Gil defines 'mobile order' by reference to three great aporias – or contradictions – of human action: power and limitation, arbitrariness and law, freedom and measure. These may not be easily resolvable, but if engaged with boldly they will allow for an acceptance of the open-ended and incomplete character of anthropological enquiry. They will enable the realization that domination, though it is a founding element of human thought and action, will never be absolute; that normativeness, although a permanent feature of social life, will never be fully enforceable; and that freedom is matched by measure at all levels. Human imagination is free, creativity exists, but always within the bounds established by the fact that persons and collectives have been historically constituted.

Affects

Finally, anthropologists must come to terms with the fact that humans cannot leave their skins. Our human condition is the ethical base of our scientific thinking. All forms of thinking are both in the world and human, that is they are ethically geared to action.

This focus on ethics – and, consequently, on affect – is in sharp contrast to prevalent modernist sociocentric attitudes, which have encouraged one to see the relation between social entities as one of conflict – either between units or between independent partners. They do not focus on the limits of interest but presume interest to be incumbent upon elemental units (persons or collectives) and, thus, univocally determinable.[15] The result is a cynical model of social existence which is essentially conflictual, and of unequal power as a form of violence, in which there is a constraining of the interest of someone by someone else. The particular version of this that has become hegemonic in anthropology over the past decades is largely due to the vulgarization of Michel Foucault's so-called 'Nietzsche's hypothesis' (Foucault 1977; cf. Hoffman 2007: 757). This amounts to the notion that 'the history that bears and determines us has the form of a war rather than that of a language –

relations of power, not relations of meaning' (in Chomsky and Foucault 2006 [1971]: 147).

Since the publication of Foucault's final lectures at the Collège de France, however, it has become possible to trace the evolution of his thought during the late 1970s. Foucault's formulation of Nietzsche's hypothesis arose from his direct and active engagement in politics, particularly the politics of race (Hoffman 2007). As the latter evolved, Foucault started to understand that 'the discourse of race war which had served as the harbinger of his own thinking about power [was being] transformed into an integral, biologically driven "state racism".' (ibid.: 758) Thus, finally, he came to ask himself, 'can war really provide a valid analysis of power relations, and can it act as a matrix for techniques of domination?' (Foucault 2003 [1997]: 46).

The concern of Foucault's more mature years was to query this overt and warlike domination. In this way he approaches Emmanuel Levinas's concern that 'it is by no means certain that, at the beginning, there was war' (in Finkielkraut 1997: 12). This is an area of anthropological thinking which requires further theoretical elaboration since, as Foucault discovered, this kind of formulation often turns out to be the harbinger of the very processes that it aims to critique (see also Fry 2005). Rather, once we question the modernist sociocentric mould, we are faced with a totally new picture of the relationship between power and sociality. Inequalities of power must be identified with war, and domination seen as brutal violence, only if identity is seen as symmetrical with alterity. But such a perception is challenged if we recognize that 'Human experience is social before it is rational' (Finkielkraut 1997:10). The roots of domination are present at the very moment of the constitution of the person. The first person never existed; all people were created by other people. The very possibility of understanding depends on sociality as much as sociality depends on understanding – and, at the root of it all, on the learning of a human language.[16]

Wittgenstein's enigmatic comment that 'meaning something is like going up to someone' (quoted in Davidson 2001: 107) thus makes more sense. We see more clearly now the origin of Boon and Schneider's (1974) error: they wanted to separate meaning from sociality; ideas from persons. But persons are constituted by meaning and meaning can only exist in the 'surrounding' world: 'The basic situation is one that involves two or more creatures simultaneously in interaction with each other and with the world they share' (Davidson 2001: 128). Communication requires that a person must agree to follow the paths that he or she perceives others to be tracing (ibid.: 114).[17] If anthropologists are to escape the trap laid out by modernist sociocentric conceptions of social entities, and of meaning as representation, they have to start working empirically, that is ethnographically, with the notion that at the root of all sociality lies not conflict/war but docility/negotiation. This can also be called 'charity' (Quine 1969: 46; Davidson 2005: 211), 'coresponsibility' or 'fraternity' (Levinas 1996; Finkielkraut 1997). Ethnography would not be possible if we did not recognize humanity in others and if we and they were not essentially, fundamentally, formatively docile. This may be why ethnographers are so keen to call their subjects of study 'friends': such a term may be a euphemism, and paternalistic, but at the root of it lies a real sense of empathy based on a shared feeling of coresponsibility, an ethical relation of co-constitution.

When I call on docility as the root of sociality, the reader might be led to think that I have stopped watching the news on television. Not at all. It is not necessary to forget the horrors, the betrayals, the heartlessness, to come to terms with the fact that domination does not arise between social entities violently. Rather, that which allows for the constitution of social entities can later turn to violence (Finkielkraut 1997).

To persist – dystopically – in finding solutions that rely on sociocentrism and on a semiotic theory of representation, is to make it more difficult to understand social relations. Instead, it is at the level of affects (ethical dispositions, not to be confused with morals) that the meaning of such relations must be sought. This will allow a reconstruction of the conditions of possibility of anthropological analysis and of ethnographic enquiry.

The Door in the Middle

By using the phrase 'the door in the middle' I aim to capture the spirit of the six conditions outlined above. Seen together, they represent an argument in favour of a new form of classicism, a new engagement with the historicity of anthropological knowledge. Such an engagement is opposed to the modernist model of knowledge construction as being based on leaps towards new 'paradigms', a model which Martins (1974) calls caesurism. Curiously, most authors that left their marks on anthropological theory in the 1990s and the early twenty-first century, whilst being explicitly post- or non-modernist, continue to conceive of their activity as producers of anthropology in vanguardist modes. The procedure involved is the following: firstly, to postulate a break in understanding at a certain moment in history, corresponding to some sort of new theoretical insight marked by a master – be he Marx, Lévi-Strauss, Lacan, Foucault, Schneider, or Deleuze – and then, secondly, to cast into irrelevance all that went before.

This procedure typifies and catalogues, in a linear process of overcoming, the various modes of carrying out anthropology as if they were unitary and indivisible, as if they were 'prototypes' or *episthèmes*. Thus, it produces ahistorical critical objects that, much as they may be useful for the teaching of undergraduates, are difficult to identify with any intellectual honesty: 'structural-functionalism', '1980s relativism', 'classical kinship theory', and so on. My argument, to the contrary, is anti-caesurist (Pina-Cabral 1992, 2007a): it denies that there can ever be any decisive break, any paradigmatic shift, any radical theoretical caesura in the thinking of social scientists.

The pretension that such breaks can exist is often self-interested and derives from a type of academic anxiety of influence mixed with a desire not to consider the arguments of 'old timers'. For example, if all that went before Schneider's critique of kinship (Schneider 1984) becomes 'classical kinship theory', or all that went before 'postcolonial studies' is 'colonialist anthropology', these bodies of knowledge can be safely ignored. But if, instead of claiming decisive breakthroughs, it became possible to build upon anthropology's established claims, then the 'door in the middle' would be our way. This would make it possible:

(1) to assume a position of minimal realism,

(2) to work with a notion of limited interest in the study of human action,

(3) to capture the process of triangulation in the constitution of meaning,

(4) to open once again the debate concerning universals by a more complex approach to the issue of determination,

(5) to re-engage creatively with systemic analysis through a mitigated structuralism, and

(6) to approach a theory of relations of domination that avoided the pitfalls of the notion of power as violence.

In this way, we might be able to bring to fruition in our empirical research (both ethnographic and comparative) the profound critical discoveries that have characterized anthropology since the late 1950s without being imprisoned by its sociocentrism.

I propose that we should stop looking at the future, in a utopian way, as if it was incommensurable with the past. We should embrace the historicity of social knowledge not as a condition but a desideratum. Following Merleau-Ponty's injunction quoted above – and much like Quine when he formulated the notion of the indeterminacy of translation – we must realize that the historicity of knowledge is not a limitation; rather, it is the very ground of the possibility of social anthropology.

Adam Kuper's lifelong engagement both with our heritage from the past and with our active contemporary debates is, to my eyes, one of the best models that we could follow for a truly creative practice of our discipline.

Notes

1. An earlier version of this paper was presented at a seminar on 'Anthropology, Now and Next', organized by Christina Garten and Helena Wulff in honour of Ulf Hannerz, at the University of Stockholm, September 2007. I am grateful to all the participants for a fascinating debate. Later, I also gained considerably from the symposium 'An Epistemology for Anthropology' (sponsored by the Wenner-Gren Foundation and the Institute of Social Sciences, Lisbon, and held in September 2007). I am indebted to critical comments by Peter Gow, Dominique Boyer, Luis Vasconcelos and Catarina Frois. Christina Toren's intellectual friendship has been a special privilege.

2. This debate was between Marilyn Strathern and Christina Toren, who supported the motion, and J.D.Y. Peel and Jonathan Spencer, who rejected it whilst agreeing to the relevance of the topic: see Ingold (1996: 55–98).

3. In the face of the author's prudent conclusions, the anger with which this book has met is to me a clear sign of how academics are more afraid of what threatens their jobs than what threatens their ideas.

4. Source: http://www.ppgasmuseu.etc.br/museu/texto/Curso-2006-1_EVC-MG_MNA-806.doc.

5. See Hermínio Martins's classical criticism of 'caesurism' as a theoretical disposition (Martins 1974).

6. This represents a qualifier to the perspectival identification of 'anthropology' with 'Euro-American' that has characterized Marilyn Strathern's Schneiderian turn in the 1990s (see Strathern 1992a: 98).

7. See Hannerz (1992, 2004). However, I see this concept first as an instance of sociation rather than merely in terms of 'culture', thus diverging from Hannerz's 'ongoing effort to explore what social anthropology can credibly contribute to the understanding of global or transnational cultural processes' (Hannerz 1992: 34; cf. 2004). Second, these processes are rooted in the history of the modern era (Mintz 1994) rather than being limited to the twentieth century.

8. Viveiros de Castro points to something similar: 'the old postulate of the ontological discontinuity between sign and referent, language and the world, which guaranteed the reality of the former and the intelligibility of the latter and vice versa (and which served as the foundation and pretext for so many other discontinuities and exclusions – between myth and philosophy, magic and science, primitives and civilized – appears to be in the process of becoming metaphysically obsolete; this is the way in which we are stopping to be, or better, are stopping to ever-having-been modern' (2007: 95). See also Gudeman (this volume).

9. In the case of anthropology, the most important influence is probably Durkheim's dependence on a French style of academic Kantianism.

10. Perhaps this is why Lévi-Strauss (1984, 1988) never took their advice in the matter of kinship studies.

11. In this matter, Davidson follows both Aristotle and Spinoza in arguing that 'there is only one substance [but] the mental and the physical are irreducibly different modes of apprehending, describing and explaining what happens in nature'. Thus, together with these philosophers of the past, he sustains 'the conceptual irreducibility of the mental to the physical' (Davidson 2005: 290).

12. Cf. Needham's belief that these 'elementary forms of thought and action' are direct responses to 'properties of the cerebral cortex' (Needham 1981: 25), which was ultimately unuseful.

13. This might be another way of seeing Hannah Arendt's argument that modernity has witnessed the triumph of the notion of 'sameness' (Finkielkraut 1997: 103).

14. This would explicitly go against Strathern's treatment of the Garia person in the same paper (e.g., 1992b: 101, n.13).

15. This is one of the reasons why the concept of 'interest' was treated with suspicion (see Mauss 1950: 271).

16. The requirement of having learnt a language in order to be able to think does not mean that communication demands the sharing of a natural language (Davidson 2005: 89–108).

17. This has been corroborated by the recent identification of the neurophysiological mechanisms underlying the understanding and imitation of action, António Damásio's 'as-if-body loop' (2003: 125–6).

Chapter 11

Adam Kuper:
an Anthropologist's Account

Isak Niehaus

In a characteristically provocative essay, Leach (1984) suggests that an understanding of the personal background of anthropologists may shed useful light on the history of their ideas. In this respect, observers frequently comment upon the Jewish origin of so many prominent anthropologists. The popular stereotype posits some kind of elective affinity between Jews as 'ethnic outsiders' and anthropologists as 'professional strangers'. MacMillan (2000) sees this affinity as being more profound. He argues that experiences of the diaspora, anti-Semitism and nationalism made Jewish scholars particularly sensitive to questions of race, tribe and ethnicity. Jewish anthropologists working in Africa, such as Max Gluckman, A.L. Epstein, Philip Mayer and Abner Cohen, played an important role in developing theoretical orientations on these topics: moving beyond an insistence on the immutability of race and tribe towards an emphasis on ethnicity. Living 'in the shadow of the Holocaust', MacMillan maintains that they formulated the now commonly accepted view of ethnic identities as being fluid, optional, multiple and selected in the context of specific situations. This is most apparent in Epstein's comparisons of the survival of Jewry in the United States despite the loss of the Yiddish language, and in many instances also the belief in Judaism, with that of Bemba identity on the Copperbelt, removed from the rural centres of Bemba traditions (Epstein 1978).

Likewise, Adam Kuper's background as a Jewish South African had a very significant impact upon his subsequent anthropological work. Adam was privileged in having had a large and supportive Jewish network that aided his intellectual development at various crucial points in his life. But of equal significance is that he grew up in a liberal Jewish family under the shadow of apartheid, an oppressive political system that was not only profoundly racist but also based upon the premises of essentialist ethnic and cultural differences. Hence, Adam's intellectual trajectory led in a slightly different direction from that of his illustrious predecessors. It led towards a more profound theoretical critique of ethnographic particularism, of the romantic appreciation of ethnicity, and of the very concept of culture. As more acceptable alternatives, Adam defended positivism, embraced cosmopolitanism and devoted analytical attention to universalistic and comparative concerns.

Background and Early Education, South Africa

Adam Kuper's paternal great grandfather, Chaim Kuper, came to South Africa as a Jewish refugee from Lithuania in 1882. Chaim settled in Oudtshoorn, a town in the southern Cape renowned for its ostrich-farming industry. Chaim and his siblings worked as ostrich-feather traders and Chaim soon distinguished himself by leading a breakaway faction from the town's synagogue. Adam's grandfather, Moses Kuper, was sufficiently integrated into the local rural Afrikaans-speaking society to be arrested by the British as a spy during the Anglo-Boer war of 1899 to 1902, and imprisoned on St Helena.

During the twentieth century, South Africa's Jewish population drifted to the cities and became English-speaking. Moses Kuper moved to Johannesburg, where he worked as a circumciser and ritual slaughterer. The High Commissioner, Sir Alfred Milner, had conducted a vigorous Anglicization policy to boost the English vote by importing Scottish teachers and by establishing excellent grammar schools. This enabled Moses's children to secure a fairly decent education in English.

In 1948, Daniel Malan's National Party defeated Jan Smuts's United Party and a more repressive system of racial discrimination soon came into being. South Africa's new Afrikaner nationalist government (which included former Nazi sympathizers) vigorously propagated apartheid in all spheres of life. Although South Africa's Jews continued to occupy important positions in commerce, medicine, law and science, they were increasingly marginalized from government. Johannesburg's Jewish community had a particularly close connection to the University of the Witwatersrand (Wits), whose students included famous anti-apartheid activists such as the liberal Helen Suzman, and Communist Party leaders Ruth First and Joe Slovo. It also included leaders of African nationalist movements such as Nelson Mandela and Robert Sobukwe.[1]

Adam's father, Simon Kuper, studied law at Wits and his mother, Gertrude Hesselman, was one of the first women students at the university. Simon initially worked as a lawyer representing big business, and played an important role in Jewish politics. He became chair of the South African Jewish Board of Deputies and also of the South African Zionist Federation, later resigning from these positions when he became a judge. Gertrude Hesselman taught mathematics at the Helpmekaar High School.

Adam was born in Johannesburg in 1941. He recalls that his friends were largely Jewish boys, who were not greatly concerned with the lives of other communities. Religion was not a matter of faith. Adam went to synagogue on Sundays, studied Hebrew and belonged to a Zionist youth movement. But his parents travelled by car on the Sabbath, and nobody in their circle of friends was a true believer (Kuper 2007a).

However, whilst studying history and social anthropology at Wits from 1959 to 1961, Adam developed a passionate interest in South Africa and in Africa, which soon eclipsed his earlier Zionist concerns. This was a particularly volatile period in South African history, marked by campaigns against the passbooks, the Sharpeville massacre and also by the crystallization of opposition to apartheid.[2] Adam's cohort included many Indian and African students. They talked politics continually and marched in protest to the Johannesburg Fort, where some of their colleagues were imprisoned without trial (ibid.: 3–4). Adam encountered an array of different political positions at Wits, but identified most closely with a liberal approach that emphasized individual rights rather than ethnic, nationalist or socialist ones. He was – and remains – suspicious of social engineering by strong government.[3]

At Wits, his most inspiring teacher was Etienne Marais, an Oxford-educated Afrikaner of the Cape liberal tradition, who had written important historical works on the colonization of New Zealand, the Cape Coloured people, Kruger's republic, and on the Anglo-Boer war. Marais promoted rigorous scholarship and believed that one should approach historical material with the detached, objective spirit of a scientist.[4]

Social anthropology, like history, had a distinguished record at Wits. Winifred Hoernlé, who was one of the first women to do ethnographic fieldwork in Africa, introduced the subject to the university in 1926. A brilliant teacher, she was a proponent of the structural functionalism of Alfred Radcliffe-Brown. Her students included Max Gluckman, Eileen and Jack Krige, Hilda Beemer (later Kuper) and Ellen Hellman, who wrote classical ethnographic studies on the Zulu, Lozi, Lobedu, Swazi, and urban slums of Johannesburg respectively. Hoernlé and her students viewed South Africa as a single society in rapid transition, a vision best illustrated by Gluckman's (1940) famous analysis of the opening of a bridge in Zululand. This placed them at loggerheads with the Afrikaner volkekundiges who, like the apartheid government, propagated a romantic, primitivist view of separate, bounded cultures (Sharp 1981; Gordon 1988). Many of Hoernlé's students subsequently played important roles in setting the agenda for British anthropology.

At Wits, social anthropology subsequently stagnated under M.D.W. Jeffreys, a former colonial administrator in Nigeria, who taught a rather outdated brand of diffusionist theory (Murray 1997: 255). Adam's teachers were Max Marwick and John Blacking. Marwick had written a competent study of sorcery amongst the Cewa of Zambia, but lacked detailed knowledge of anthropological history and theory. John Blacking, more charismatic, was a

Cambridge-trained ethnomusicologist who invited students to parties at his home and supported them in their studies.

More decisive than these figures in prompting Adam to become an anthropologist, however, were those linked to him through kinship. Adam's mother was a close friend of Hoernlé's student, Eileen Krige, and his father's brother, Leo Kuper, was a well-known sociologist who wrote influential works on South Africa's black bourgeoisie, African nationalism, passive resistance and genocide. Leo married Hilda Beemer, who lived at the home of Adam's parents whilst Leo served in the allied forces. Both Eileen Krige and Hilda Kuper proceeded to study anthropology under Malinowski at the London School of Economics (LSE).

Adam tells a mythical story about his conversion. His uncle Leo and aunt Hilda were teaching at the University of Natal and Hilda was conducting fieldwork in Swaziland. Because of Hilda's poor driving record, the university opted to have her nephew, Adam, act as her chauffer. In Swaziland, Adam stayed with the regiment that guarded the queen's village, where he had a particularly memorable conversation with a prince. The prince had been educated in England, but was wearing Swazi attire. Whilst he and Adam were drinking beer together inside a beehive hut, he asked, 'Do you believe in witchcraft?' 'No', Adam answered. Hereupon the prince quoted Hamlet, 'There are more things in Heaven and Earth, Horatio, than are dreamt of in your philosophy'.

When Adam told his mother that he wished to become an anthropologist, she was disappointed (Kuper cited in Fausto and Neiburg 2002: 305).

Cambridge and the Kalahari, 1962–1966

In 1962, Adam registered for a Ph.D. in social anthropology at Cambridge University. Pessimistic about the country's political future, and desiring to escape from a parochial world, Adam had decided to leave South Africa. By now there were spies on university campuses, and the National Party government had banned Leo Kuper's book on passive resistance. Since there was a gap between the end of the South African term and the beginning of the British one, Adam took an extended vacation, during which he visited Israel and Europe. In Paris, Adam attended French classes, and read Durkheim and Lévi-Strauss in the original French. *Le Totémisme d'Aujourd'hui* and *La Pensée Sauvage* were both published that year and greatly impressed him.

At the time, the anthropologists at Cambridge were Edmund Leach, Meyer Fortes (also a South African Jew), Jack Goody, Stanley Tambiah, Reo Fortune, Ray Abrahams and Audrey Richards, who was attached to the Centre for African Studies. Where Leach informed Adam that he regarded Cambridge as a lower-middle-class institution, Fortes confided in him that the university was anti-Semitic. He discovered that there were many other matters on which they did not see eye-to-eye (Kuper 1992b). The social anthropology department admitted only six Ph.D. students per year, who received hardly any instruction but read and attended seminars.

Cambridge, besides showing evidence of scholarly divisiveness, was by South African standards very conservative. Most staff members worked on classical topics like kinship and ritual, and had little interest in politics. (The only exceptions were Edmund Leach and Audrey Richards, but she was interested in politics in a rather colonial sort of way.) Anthropology was also narrowly conceptualized. Upon hearing that Adam was reading Jan Vansina's studies on oral tradition, Fortes warned him: 'You can't be an anthropologist and be interested in these sorts of things! If you want to study history, be an historian!'

Cambridge, nonetheless, served as a nodal point for scholarship and produced impressive students. Adam's coevals included Maurice Bloch, Susan Drucker-Brown, Jim Ferris, Steven Gudeman, Keith Hart, Tim Ingold, Johnny Parry, Peter Rigby, and Andrew and Marilyn Strathern. Perhaps the Department's success lay in the fact that no single professor indoctrinated junior members of staff and students into their theoretical approach. Instead, students encountered constant debate between Leach and Fortes, and between the rival theories that they presented.

In 1963, whilst in his first year at Cambridge, Adam received the traumatic news that his father, Simon Kuper, had been murdered. He was brutally gunned down whilst working at his desk at home in Johannesburg, apparently by a criminal gang whose members were on trial.

Whilst at Cambridge, Meyer Fortes referred Adam to Isaac Schapera – another Jewish South African who was, at one stage, engaged to Adam's aunt Hilda. As doyen of Tswana studies at the LSE, Schapera advised Adam to work on the Kgalakgadi, who reside on the western fringe of the Kalahari Desert in Bechuanaland (now Botswana). Adam's field work there coincided with the well-known Harvard Bushman Studies project, but was conducted from a very different standpoint. As a supporter of the African independence movements, he wished to show that African societies were fully amenable to democratic processes and institutions.

These researches culminated in the publication of *Kalahari Village Politics: An African Democracy* (Kuper 1970). The monograph describes the Kgalakgadi as pastoralists, horticulturalists and migrant labourers whose public affairs were ordered by the *kgotla*, a forum for village decision making. Discussions in the *kgotla* were fairly open and criticisms were freely expressed and tolerated. Adam offers a detailed analysis of the various levels of politics operating in the village, Kuli. Though a segmentary lineage system did not prevail, kinship relations were politically important. The village was made up of agnatically related groups, of which the one providing the headman was predominant. Attached to these groups were segments related by ties of kinship and affinity, and also Bushmen serfs. He shows how shifting alliances operating in the village limited the headman's power and also how local level politics were embedded in larger colonial administrative structures.

Although *Kalahari Village Politics* was praised as a novel analysis of the colonial bureaucracy, in retrospect it can be argued that it painted too optimistic a picture of political processes amongst the Kgalakgadi. At the village level, women and Bushmen serfs were excluded from popular decision making and lacked jural rights (Vengroff 1971: 146).

Extending this work, and evidencing his commitment to the comparative approach, Adam collaborated with Audrey Richards to edit a book on how councils reached decisions through processes of debate and joint discussion (Richards and Kuper 1971). The volume includes comparative ethnographic material on village assemblies in Botswana, Madagascar, Nigeria, Zambia, Ghana and Uganda, as well as an English town council.

Working in Uganda, 1967–1970

Adam married Jessica Kuper (née Cohen) in 1966. At that time the labour market was very favourable and the demand for anthropologists exceeded their supply. Adam turned down job offers from University College London and the University of Cape Town in favour of a teaching position at Makerere University in Uganda.

In retrospect the newly married couple's decision not to return to South Africa was a wise one. Students and staff were now being excluded from admission to the country's universities on racial criteria. In 1968, Monica Wilson appointed Archie Mafeje, an African, as senior lecturer in social anthropology at the University of Cape Town, but the government forced the university to rescind the appointment on the grounds that no black lecturer should be allowed to teach white students. The very next year, Adam's former teacher, John Blacking, and an Indian medical doctor, Zureema Desai, were convicted of conspiring to contravene the Immorality Act, which prohibits sexual acts between individuals of different racial categories.

Makerere University had been established towards the end of British colonial rule, offered degrees validated by the University of London, and drew students from the whole of East Africa. After Ugandan independence in 1962, Milton Obote relied upon Makerere to meet the urgent demand for administrative personnel (Furley 1988: 175). Adam taught in the Sociology Department with Raymond Apthorpe, who had done a Ph.D. at Oxford, and with Peter Rigby, a fellow social anthropologist from Cambridge. He found teaching in Uganda extremely rewarding. Despite anthropology's label as handmaiden of colonialism, East African students displayed reasonable interest in the subject. Adam's best student, Hilda Kabushenga, completed a Ph.D. at Minnesota, and later pursued a career in international development. (Whilst in Kampala, Jessica did fieldwork on the Goan community, and Adam regularly visited the Kigezi district with some of his students.)

Unfortunately, their stay in Kampala was cut short. After the birth of their first son, Simon, a circular warned Uganda's expatriate community of a possible coup. The first secretary at the Israeli Embassy also advised Adam not to stay beyond the end of the year. Hence the Kupers left Uganda only months before Idi Amin's violent overthrow of Obote's government. Army officers now replaced the country's Makerere educated ministers, and West Nile troops regularly confronted students on campus. The African staff at Makerere fled into neighbouring countries, and the University's vice-chancellor, Frank Kalimuzo, met death at the hands of the army. Amin also accused Asians of sabotaging Uganda's economy and expelled them from the country (Furley 1988: 182).

Adam's most influential essay during this period was a coauthored critique of the Dar-es-Salaam 'school of historiography' (Denoon and Kuper 1970). Showing early signs of readiness to court controversy, Kuper (along with Denoon) argued that historians of East Africa have allowed their partisan obsession with the theme of nationalism to broaden the concept immeasurably, thus rendering it useless. These historians claim that various forms of primary resistance – such as the Maji Maji uprising, messianic movements, witch-cleansing cults and African Churches – served to expand the scope and scale of political activity, and thus were effectively continuous with the later activities of the modern nationalist movement, TANU (Tanzanian African National Union). These 'nationalist historians', including Terence Ranger, failed to consider the crucial impact of factors beyond the borders of Tanzania, such as resistance movements elsewhere, colonial policies and pan-Africanist ideas. They were also selective in their use of sources, privileging the writings of district commissioners and modern TANU activists over the anthropological literature. The authors warned against projecting present day ideological concerns into the past, concluding that African history 'is too important to be left to politicians' (ibid.: 348).[5]

University College London, 1970–1975

Before leaving Kampala, Adam had applied for posts in Singapore, Hong Kong and at University College London (UCL), and he was successful in his application to the latter. In 1970, the political climate at UCL was tense and intimidating. M.G. Smith was head of department and Mary Douglas had been promoted to a personal chair. Fardon (1999: 127) recalls, 'the academic staff and students were splitting into factions descended from the sociological trinity'. Smith headed the Weberians, Douglas the Durkheimians, while many of the younger staff members were Marxists. 'Personality clashes fuelled intellectual differences, so that the department seemed a close analogy of the African village, riven by accusations of witchcraft' (ibid.: 128). The different factions drank in different pubs.

In an interview, Adam recalled that a 'Marxist Cargo Cult' suddenly developed in anthropology. Activist lecturers and students spent lunch times reading Althusser, organized collective sessions like Bible readings, and branded their non-conformist colleagues as reactionary (Kuper cited in Fausto and Neiburg 2002: 309). At the time, the publication of Douglas's book *Purity and Danger* (Douglas 1966) had made her world-famous. But, given her upper-class and Catholic origins and the fact that her husband worked as a researcher for the Conservative Party, the Marxists treated her as an outcast. Being largely supportive of her, Adam was sometimes tarred with the same brush.

Adam seldom criticized the Marxists in his writings. In a review of Gellner's edited volume *Soviet and Western Anthropology* he wrote that Communists and Russian scholars are mutually exclusive, implying that large numbers of the former were to be found in the halls of British academe (Kuper 1980a). But Meyer Fortes – who had served as an intelligence officer during the Second World War, and remained aware of their operations – warned him that MI5 might pick up such ill-considered comments.

Despite these tensions, Adam's tenure at UCL was extremely productive and he wrote two further monographs. In the early 1970s, Isaac Schapera, now retired, invited Adam to write a book on the history of British social anthropology for a series of textbooks that he was editing. Adam, barely thirty years old, had done no previous research on the topic, and he thus used mainly published texts to write *Anthropologists and Anthropology* (Kuper 1973). The monograph starts in 1922, the year Malinowski published *Argonauts of the Western Pacific* and Radcliffe-Brown *The Andaman Islanders*. Adam outlines their contrasting styles, theories and their respective reigns at the LSE and at Oxford. Particularly striking is his description of Malinowski's creation of the field work tradition as a classic 'prophet myth'. He then describes the influence of Evans-Pritchard, Gluckman, the Rhodes Livingstone Institute, Turner, Leach and the British followers of Lévi-Strauss. The monograph also includes a sensitive discussion of the relationship between social anthropology and colonialism, which challenges simplistic accusations that the former is the latter's 'handmaiden'.

The academic reviewers of *Anthropologists and Anthropology* were outraged, lambasting Adam for 'reinforcing a great man theory of history', not situating his discussions in the context of British society and politics, and for providing insufficient references. He also upset sociologists by calling their discipline 'boring and sterile' (Lewis 1975: 23–26). By challenging the unspoken assumptions enshrined in the micro-politics of a small academic discipline rather than criticizing the then current 'folk devils' of apartheid or of African nationalism, Adam seems to have touched a raw nerve. The reading public, however, did not share these negative assessments. The monograph became a very popular overview of anthropological theory, running to three editions and being translated into half a dozen languages.[6]

Adam undertook his second major fieldwork expedition during a sabbatical year at UCL. He and Jessica wanted to work in Goa, India, following on from Jessica's work among Goans in Uganda, but they encountered problems due to the India-Pakistan war. M.G. Smith, who was a Jamaican, suggested that instead they do research in his country of origin. In Jamaica, Adam was attached to a planning agency in the prime minister's office, but he had sufficient freedom to conduct field work in various different locales – including a hill village, a slum area of Kingston, a sugar-cane estate, a middle-class suburb and also a tourist resort in Montego Bay.

The resulting monograph, *Changing Jamaica* (Kuper 1976), combines data derived from participant observation with more macro-level historical and sociological material to present a holistic picture of contemporary Jamaica. Adam argues that Jamaica faces many characteristic economic problems – such as growth benefiting foreigners, an uneven distribution of land, an excess of imports over exports, and migration from country to city. Despite the shortage of agricultural labour in the countryside, people continued to move into the slums of Kingston, which exhibited a high rate of unemployment. The book analyses this trend in terms of landholding and inheritance patterns in rural areas, and in terms of the availability of jobs in the informal economy, jobs which established Kingston residents would not stoop to.

Despite the legacy of slavery, the book suggests, a simple racial model does not adequately describe social status in Jamaica. Whilst there is a relationship between race, social position and class, few social groups are consciously built upon racial divisions. Social status is rather defined in various ambiguous ways – through style, education, wealth and morality. Political leaders nonetheless use African symbols to rally supporters and to convey messages about the Jamaican nation.

Adam sees the most significant polarization of Jamaica as being its division into two well established political parties – the ruling People's National Party (PNP) and the opposition Jamaican Labour Party (JLP). The country was a patchwork of villages, and if your rival village supported one party, you belonged to the other. During field work, people in one village would not talk to Adam, whereas those in another warmly invited him for drinks and for meals. This was because the first village supported the opposition, the second the ruling party, and residents of both identified Adam with the government. The two parties differed little in terms of their regional, economic or ideological support: party loyalty was based on personal benefit.

Leiden University, The Netherlands, 1976–1985

In 1976, Adam was appointed professor (*hoogleeraar*) at Leiden University in the Netherlands, a country with a long tradition of anthropology. During the colonial era the Netherlands had a far-flung empire, encompassing Indonesia, the western half of New Guinea, Suriname and the Antilles, and anthropology had evolved in the context of training courses for civil servants in the colonies. In the postcolonial era, the Netherlands retained strong global commercial interests, and the Dutch government outstripped most other countries in foreign development aid. New programmes were launched in non-Western sociology and Development Studies, and anthropological interests broadened into Africa, Latin America, the Pacific, South Asia and the Mediterranean. During this period of expansion, Dutch universities increasingly hired foreign scholars.

The 1970s also saw the emergence of new theoretical paradigms such as transactionalism – which focused on networks, coalitions and patron–client relationships – and the very same brand of Marxism that Adam had encountered at UCL. Certain academics staunchly believed in the genius of Mao: students took anthropology as a means to liberate the oppressed, distrusted their professors, and insisted that their work should be peer graded. At the University of Utrecht, Communist Party members were even assigned to monitor the correct teaching of Marx (Thoden van Velzen cited in Kruik and Veernis 2005: 99–100).

However, Adam found Leiden's anthropology department very conservative: 'The Marxists were in Amsterdam and in the Centre for African Studies. I did not have much to do with them'. The department had been founded in 1877 and taught a version of structuralism and intra-regional comparison known as the *Leidse Richting* ('Leiden Orientation').[7] Under the leadership of scholars such as Patrick de Josselin de Jong and Andre Köbben, Leiden was an ideal place for exploring structuralist concerns to which Adam had long been sympathetic.[8]

In 1981 Adam spent his sabbatical at Stanford University's Centre for Advanced Behavioural Sciences and wrote *Wives for Cattle: Bridewealth and Marriage in Southern Africa* (Kuper 1982). This monograph is a comparative study of kinship among the Bantu-speakers of South Africa, and is influenced by Isaac Schapera, Radcliffe-Brown, Lévi-Strauss and the Leiden orientation.

Given that Lévi-Strauss examined marriage only as indirect exchange rather than seeing bridewealth as providing for a more direct form of exchange, Adam resolved to explore this question. He asks why the custom of exchanging wives for cattle varied within pre-industrial South Africa. Beyond the bewildering diversity of practices recorded in the ethnographic literature, he discerns a systemic *combinatoire*, of which the Nguni, Sotho-Tswana, Venda and Tsonga form clearly distinguishable variables. Three factors are responsible for these variations: the relative economic importance of pastoralism, local rules governing cousin marriage, and systems of political stratification. Bridewealth does not merely transfer resources between different spheres of production, but also enables elites to maintain positions of privilege. Adam shows why the Lobedu find 'marrying in' the strategy best suited for their type of succession, and why the Swazi have opted for 'marrying up' and the Tsonga for 'marrying out'. Critics welcomed *Wives for Cattle* as an extremely important work that gave new life to comparative analysis. Possibly missing the point of a structural analysis, their enthusiasm was qualified by the fact that the book deals with ideal rather than actual marriages, and neglects to explore social process (Wylie 1983).

Whilst in Leiden, Adam also wrote important essays on regional comparisons, kinship terminologies, a Lévi-Straussian approach to dream interpretations, South African ethnography, and on lineage theory (Kuper 1979a, 1979b, 1979c, 1980b, 1983a). In addition, along with Jessica he edited the *Social Science Encyclopaedia* (1985), and he also undertook brief periods of field work with students in Mauritius.

The Kupers experienced Leiden as 'a nice small town', but felt hemmed in by its increasing provincialism. During their year in California, they decided that they did not, however, want to live in the United States, and again started applying for positions in England.

Brunel University, *Current Anthropology* and the EASA, 1986–1994

In 1986, Keith Hopkins, who later became professor of Ancient History at Cambridge, invited Adam to be head of the Department of Human Sciences at Brunel University, located on the western outskirts of London. Brunel had become a university only in 1967, and though it was well known in engineering circles, arts and social sciences had not yet been well established. Hopkins had combined sociology and psychology into a single interdisciplinary department and also wished to add social anthropology. Adam accepted on condition that he could appoint additional anthropologists. He soon hired Maryon McDonald, who worked in Europe, and Gerd Baumann, who had studied Sudanese music, as well as appointing Ronald Frankenburg and Cecil Helman to teach medical anthropology on a part-time basis. Christina Toren was subsequently offered a joint position in psychology and anthropology, and established a centre for child-focused anthropological research. Soon afterwards, in 1988, Jessica became editor of social anthropology publications at Cambridge University Press, commuting vast distances to and from work each weekday. During his first decade at Brunel Adam became editor of the journal *Current Anthropology* (*CA*), was elected founding president of the European Association of Social Anthropologists (EASA), and published three further monographs.

Irven de Vore nominated Adam as editor of *CA* because the journal wished to appoint a non-American as editor whose work transgressed the narrow boundaries of social anthropology, and because Adam's writings on the 'central cattle pattern' (Kuper 1982) had had an important impact on archaeological work on Southern Africa. The Wenner-Gren Foundation paid the salaries of two editorial assistants, so editing the journal was not too tedious. *CA*, said Adam, was a 'very good graduate school'. Because the journal combines social anthropology, archaeology and biological anthropology, editorship forced him to learn about the cognate anthropological disciplines, and he soon developed a passionate interest in the works of Charles Darwin. His period of editing *CA* saw important developments in the fields of human evolution and sociobiology, and was witness to the 'great Kalahari debate'.

Through editing the journal, Adam was also able to play a crucial role in the establishment of EASA. Adam was particularly keen on the idea of establishing such an organization. Many European countries had no properly functioning anthropology associations, and British anthropology was becoming increasingly parochial. He also feared that the spread of more culturalist approaches from the United States could be detrimental to the European social anthropological tradition of Malinowski, Radcliffe-Brown and Lévi-Strauss. Sydel Silverman, then president of the Wenner-Gren Foundation, asked Adam to convene a meeting to explore the establishment of such an association, and promised start-up funds.

In January 1989, twenty-two anthropologists from twelve European countries met at Castelgandolfo, outside Rome, and decided to form EASA. It was decided that the association would serve as a professional body representing social anthropologists in Europe, and promote the classical European tradition of social sciences, through conferences, journals, newsletters, student and staff exchanges. Adam was elected as EASA's founding president. EASA's inaugural conference was held at Coimbra University in Portugal and formed part of the university's seventh centenary celebrations in 1990. Ernest Gellner gave the inaugural lecture in a provocative style, and the first two days were devoted to invited papers in sessions called 'Constituting Society', 'Constructing Genders', 'Making History' and 'Understanding Ritual'. These were followed by fourteen participant-generated workshops. Many Eastern Europeans attended and the conference was extremely successful despite complaints about language and the under-representation of women. Since then EASA has held nine successful biennial conferences, with 900 participants attending the 2006 conference in Bristol.

Where Adam's first monograph at Brunel was largely based on work he had been doing at Leiden, and was still clearly inspired by structuralism (Kuper 1987), the two which followed it (Kuper 1988, 1994a) mark a decisive shift, showing his new interest in intellectual history. Adam once used Schumpeter's *History of Economic Analysis* (1954) to get a grip on economics, and he was deeply influenced by the manner in which Schumpeter formulates theoretical problems in historical terms. In a similar manner, Adam attempts in these monographs to understand theory by seeking to elaborate a historical and an ethnographic approach to its development, asking where the ideas come from and what contexts shaped them (see Kuper 1999b: 2).

In *Wives for Cattle* Adam had come to the conclusion that lineage theory – which had made such an impact on the early history of anthropology – was practically useless for understanding South African kinship. He develops this critique further in *The Invention of Primitive Society* (Kuper 1988), arguing that the appeal of lineage and alliance theories derives from a mythical belief in the existence of 'primitive societies' in which people organized 'naturally' on the basis of blood ties and common descent. Against the backdrop of this proposition, he examines how anthropologists 'invented' evolutionary stages based on the doctrine of survival, and debated how and when the nuclear family originated. The book demonstrates important continuities between the earlier works of scholars such as Maine, Robertson-Smith, Frazer, Morgan and Westermarck; the anti-evolutionist Boasians; the theory of unilineal descent groups of British structural-functionalists; and Lévi-Straussian alliance theory.

The Chosen Primate (Kuper 1994a), however, has broader aims. In this book Adam draws on his experience of editing *CA*, synthesizing literature from different anthropological disciplines to reflect on the meanings of human nature and cultural diversity. Adam asks whether it is possible to formulate a Darwinian explanation for all ways of life that *Homo sapiens* have tried out. He argues that over the course of human history physical evolution and social development did not march hand in hand. 'The physical capacity for culture had been in place for millennia before modern human culture began its explosive development' (ibid.: 90). Neanderthals and their African and Asian contemporaries already possessed the cranial capacity and vocal apparatus that were prerequisites for the development of culture. This forms the basis of Adam's criticism of sociobiology and of various other attempts to explain culture in terms of intelligence testing, genetics and human ethology. He also reflects on the broader theme of 'nature' and 'nurture' with reference to debates on sexual differences, mating arrangements and the incest taboo.

Confronting Postmodernism and Culture, 1994–2003

In the early 1990s, the South African government lifted its ban on African nationalist movements, released Nelson Mandela from prison, and started the negotiations that paved the way for the country's first democratic elections. For three successive British summer vacations, Adam taught at the University of the Witwatersrand and desperately wanted to take up an offer to head the anthropology department at his alma mater. Yet he and Jessica decided that living in a different continent from their children and grandchildren would be too much of a wrench. As a result, Adam remained at Brunel, but now drew upon his South African experiences to write a critique of cultural relativism and of the postmodern movement that was rapidly gaining ground in the United States. He saw postmodernism as another 'cargo cult', but as more destructive of sociological and comparative anthropology than Marxism had ever been.

South African social anthropologists are generally suspicious of the concept of culture because it mistakenly suggests that knowledge systems, ideological accounts, myths and rituals hang together in some sort of unity. A similarly essentialist view of culture, with its exaggeration of the differences between people, had served as an ideological justification for the terrible political system of apartheid. American anthropologists, by contrast, are inclined to view culture as a liberating concept. Whereas 'race' suggests that the differences between people are fixed in nature, culture suggests that human ways of life are learnt and can be changed: hence, in the United States, culture has been used to fight discrimination. The agenda of multiculturalism demands that one acknowledge the voices and unique standards of marginal groups (Kuper 1999b: 4).

Adam wrote *Culture: The Anthropologist's Account* (Kuper 1999b) whilst on sabbatical at the Institute for Advanced Study at Princeton University. This work examines uses of culture in American anthropology, tracing their roots to certain strands within European thought. The German concept of culture as consisting of the subjective, spiritual properties of social groups, he suggests, had greater impact in the United States than the French conception of civilization as the highest expression of human reason.

He nevertheless credits Talcott Parsons rather than Franz Boas with creating the contemporary American concept of culture. Boas subscribed to the enlightenment vision of the unity of humankind, defined culture broadly as an assemblage of traits, and saw cultural differences as due to history and to borrowing. At Harvard, Parsons allocated each social science a designated subject matter: sociology was to examine social life; psychology, the individual; and anthropology, culture. Parsons thereby narrowed the concept of culture and used it to refer solely to symbolic discourses, beliefs and values. Whereas Parsons still saw culture as being in constant interaction with social and personality systems, those such as Kroeber treated culture itself as the principal determinant of human existence.

Adam then examines the works of three prominent theorists of culture: Clifford Geertz, David Schneider and Marshall Sahlins. He documents Geertz's intellectual transformations from his early Indonesian monographs on economic and social processes, to his more recent hermeneutic concerns with treating culture as a text. In his latter works Geertz was concerned less with what people do than with the interpretations they make of each other's actions: he offers no criteria for judging these interpretations. Schneider, meanwhile, extended culture into kinship studies and argued that nature and the facts of life have no independent existence apart from how they are defined by culture. The notion of kinship, for example, does not exist among the people of Yap, the Micronesian island where Schneider did his field work; they denied the role of coitus in procreation, had no idea of fatherhood, and used similar terms for relatives and non-kin. Sahlins, in turn, focused on history as culture, and on how myths explain the past and guide the future. Adam's critique of all three authors is similar: they reduce social life either to culture as text, as symbol, or as code and hereby neglect the social, political, economic and material factors that are indispensable for understanding social action. Culture not only blinds us to the complex dynamics of human existence, but also fetishizes difference.

Following on from this, Adam offers a reading of postmodernism. He shows how James Clifford and George Marcus turned to literary approaches and to concerns about the politics of writing and representation. These authors proposed investigating how anthropologists, in writing ethnographic texts, constructed authoritative claims and fashioned their objects of analysis. This reflexive mode and constant questioning of who can speak for others, writes Adam, have had a paralysing effect upon the discipline.

Two well-crafted essays elaborate upon aspects of this critique. In the first (Kuper 1994b), Adam claims that elements of cultural relativism and of postmodernism have acquired an elective affinity with American identity politics as expressed in the rainbow coalition of minority causes. The postmodern critique of conventional anthropology as exoticizing and misrepresenting others, and the concern to give privileged hearing to muted voices of marginal groups, leads to the proposition that, ideally, only a native can speak for a native. This was evident in the decision by the Greek Anthropology Association to preclude Greeks who had studied abroad, and foreign anthropologists working on Greece, from membership. Instead of allowing such inward-looking, self-referential writers to set the agenda for anthropology, Adam argues, we should strive to create critical openended debates, incorporating not only the views of natives, local experts and foreign anthropologists, but also those of colleagues studying other regions. Anthropology is ultimately a cosmopolitan project and our debates should range beyond our immediate fields of ethnographic study to address long running questions about general social and cultural processes.

In the second essay (Kuper 2003) Adam writes a critique of the indigenous people's movement that claims to represent the interests of 'tribal peoples', such as hunters and nomadic herders, in asserting collective rights to land and in demanding participation in decision-making processes. The rhetoric of this movement portrays indigenous people as the original inhabitants of various countries, as people who represent a natural state of humanity, who are more in tune with the environment than members of industrial consumer societies, and who are bearers of an ancient culture, associated with spiritual rather than material values. This rhetoric is often moulded to suit the concerns of environmental and anti-globalization movements.

Though generous in their intentions, Adam argues, the political motives of the movement are based upon dubious intellectual assumptions. They replicate essentialist notions about culture and identity and revive obsolete romantic notions about primitives. The argument that original inhabitants of a country should have privileged access to its resources resonates with the propositions of many right-wing parties. The suggestion that access to land be based upon a calibrated measure of descent signifies a drift to racist criteria of inclusion and exclusion. The movement also replicates the mistaken assumptions that hunter-gatherers have been isolated from farmers and other settled populations, and that they are not amenable to change. Adam also points to the tricky issue of evidence in land claims, and to the argument that myths and oral traditions should be on a par with archaeological and historical evidence. At times the movement also replicates the segregationist logic of apartheid. In Botswana, for example, Survival International has defended the residential rights of Bushmen in the Central Kalahari Game Reserve. Adam argues that the movement distracts attention from real local issues, exacerbates ethnic tensions, and promotes unrepresentative spokespersons.

These arguments have predictably aroused a strong response. Critics of *Culture: The Anthropologists' Account* have suggested that Adam misses many other important ethnographic strategies – besides postmodernism – that have been developed in the United States, and that anthropologists can ill afford to withdraw from political struggles to define culture. Sympathizers of indigenous people's movements have accused Adam of blaming the victims for using bad language, and have argued that the use of culture as a basis for rights often amounts to 'strategic essentialism' rather than a drift to racism.

Kinship in Europe, 2001–

In 2006 Adam reached sixty-five, but he was asked by Brunel's vice-chancellor to continue working for three additional years beyond retirement age. By this time the focus of his analytical attention, reviving an earlier area of interest but in a new guise, had shifted to English kinship, a focus that Schapera's stimulating paper on kinship terminology in Jane Austen's novels (Schapera 1977) might well have influenced.

One concern has been recognition of the formative role of public debates on incest and cousin marriage in early-nineteenth-century England on the origins of social anthropology (Kuper 2002a, 2008). Previously the control of sex and marriage were vested in Church authorities alone; and fornication, adultery, incest and bigamy were ecclesiastical rather than criminal offences. Incest was defined as sexual intercourse between persons prohibited from marrying by Church decree, including not only blood relatives but also relatives by marriage. But secular control was gradually established and family law became increasingly independent of religious beliefs. Biologists and anthropologists were soon drawn into public debates to work out and justify new secular concepts and principles of marriage, adultery and divorce.

Cousin marriage was of cardinal concern in these debates. Though these marriages were fairly common among English elites, there was a popular belief that close-kin marriages produced sickly offspring. Charles Darwin had observed the beneficial aspects of hybridization in animals and plants and became concerned about the effects of inbreeding in human populations, and indeed in his own family. His son, George Darwin, used statistical methods to establish the vitality of the offspring of these unions and concluded that incidents of cousin marriages were roughly the same in the general population as they were in the asylums.

At the same time, early social anthropologists obsessively debated incest taboos. McLennan and Morgan argued that promiscuity had been the rule in early human societies, and that the incest taboo marked the passage from savagery to the first stage of civilization. Tylor outlined the beneficial social, rather than biological, effects of the taboo, noting that exogamy enabled human groups to establish permanent alliances. By contrast, Westermarck argued that primitive people had gone overboard in their attempt to stop close-kin marriages and saw excessive prohibitions as a sign of backwardness.

Public opinion turned against cousin marriage during the Victorian period. These marriages had been beneficial in counteracting the division of land through inheritance, but now decreased with greater urbanization, smaller family size and women marrying later. Moreover, incest became thought of in terms of child abuse in congested family quarters in large cities.

Adam also observed that the vast majority of highly successful businesses in contemporary Europe and in the United States are family businesses. This seems to fly in the face of assumptions about the assumed rationality of capitalist enterprises, and might force us to think in a different way about capitalism. Adam seems to think that family businesses are doing something better than other kinds of businesses, and that trust and mutual services built on the ethic of kinship might produce a kind of economy within the company utterly different to that which obtains in the world outside (Kuper 2001a, 2008; Kuper cited in Fausto and Neiburg 2002: 311).

Conclusion

Although the South African policies of apartheid were predicated upon racial discrimination, the country's former Afrikaner nationalist government constantly invoked ethnic and cultural differences in their various attempt to justify these policies. Apologists for apartheid often deployed culture with the same categorical rigidity as race. These historical experiences can teach important political lessons and point to the dangerous pitfalls of ideologies of cultural particularism. This has been all too evident in various events, from the violent break-up of the former Yugoslavia to the bloodshed that accompanied the 2008 elections in Kenya. The South African experience of apartheid also prompted us as anthropologists to reconsider the use of central concepts in our discipline. Adam was a key protagonist in this process. As a member of South Africa's Jewish minority and as a liberal, he strove to transcend the narrow confines of ethnographic particularism in his thinking, and he eventually questioned the very notion of culture itself.

In conversation Adam acknowledges many mistakes that he made throughout his professional career. He has often told me that he should have been more sensitive about the position of women in *Kalahari Village Politics* (Kuper 1970), more careful when writing *Anthropologists and Anthropology* (Kuper 1973), and that *Wives for Cattle* (Kuper 1982) should have been more historical. I also personally feel that in his attempt to get to the heart of complex issues, Adam sometimes oversimplifies them. But, in a world of rapid change, most ideologies and intellectual fashions have often proven less durable than the liberalism, cosmopolitanism and positivism that he has espoused.

Notes

This chapter draws on my reading of Adam Kuper's works and published interviews, and also on my memory of the conversations that we have had from time to time. Adam was my Ph.D. supervisor and is currently my colleague at Brunel University. I interviewed Adam at his home in Muswell Hill one Sunday evening (21 April 2007), but only to eliminate some of the worst errors in my manuscript. It is from this interview that the few unsourced direct quotes in this chapter are drawn. I thank him for an enjoyable conversation and I also thank Deborah James for her perceptive and constructive comments on earlier drafts of this chapter.

1. South Africa's Jews were generally opposed to government's apartheid policies and have played an important role in enunciating left-wing policies (Campbell 2002).
2. From 1939 until the enactment of university apartheid, Wits developed as an 'open university', admitting students from all races. Through the Extension of University Act of 1959, the National Party government prohibited all 'non-whites' from attending 'white' universities, except with ministerial permission, and established a series of separate 'ethnic university colleges'. See Murray (1997).
3. Adam describes his position as a 'European' rather than 'American' version of liberalism. The latter version generally refers to any position left of the Republican Party. See H. Kuper (1984) and Butler, Elphick and Welsh (1987) for in-depth discussions on the particularities of South African liberalism.
4. See Saunders (1988: 115–17, 124–5) and Murray (1997: 247–8) for an appraisal of Marais's work as a historian.
5. See Ranger (1971) for a response to this critique, and Denoon and Kuper (1971) for a rejoinder.
6. The first edition was published in hard back by Allen Lane and in paperback by Penguin, and was translated into Spanish and Portuguese. In 1983 Routledge published a revised and expanded second edition that was translated into Polish and Greek. Another, more substantially revised, edition came out in 1996, followed by translations into Slovenian, Japanese and French.
7. See De Wolf (2002) for insightful accounts of the Leiden orientation.
8. The Leiden orientation had originally inspired Lévi-Strauss' work on kinship, and Lévi-Strauss' subsequent studies on mythology again influenced developments in this approach.

References

Ajegbo, K., D. Kiwan and S. Sharma. 2007. *Curriculum review: Diversity and Citizenship* London: DfES. http://publications.teachernet.gov.uk/default.aspx?PageFunction=productde tails&PageMode=publications&ProductId=DFES-00045-2007

Alexander, C. 2000. *The Asian Gang: Ethnicity, Identity, Masculinity.* Oxford: Berg.

Alexander, N. 1983. *Sow the Wind.* Johannesburg: Skotaville Press.

Amnesty International. 1991. *Human Rights Violations in Punjab: Use and Abuse of the Law.* London: Amnesty International.

Arendt, H. 1958. *The Human Condition.* Chicago: University of Chicago Press.

Aristotle. 1984. *The Complete Works of Aristotle.* J. Barnes (ed.) Princeton, NJ: Princeton University Press.

Asch, M. 1997. *Aboriginal and Treaty Rights in Canada.* Vancouver: University of British Columbia Press.

Babiniotis, G. 1998. *Lexiko tis Neas Ellinikis Glossas* [Dictionary of the modern Greek language]. Athens: Kentro Lexikologias.

Bakić-Hayden, M. 1995. 'Nesting Orientalisms: The Case of Former Yugoslavia', *Slavic Review* 54(4): 917–31.

Barnard, A. 1992. *Hunters and Herders of Southern Africa: A Comparative Ethnography of the Khoisan Peoples.* Cambridge: Cambridge University Press.

———. 2003. '!Ke e: /xarra //ke – Multiple Origins and Multiple Meanings of the Motto', *African Studies* 62: 243–50.

———. 2004. 'Coat of Arms and the Body Politic: Khoisan Imagery and South African National Identity', *Ethnos* 69: 1–18.

———. 2006. 'Kalahari Revisionism, Vienna and the "Indigenous Peoples" Debate', *Social Anthropology* 14: 1–16.

Barth, F. 1969. 'Introduction', in F. Barth (ed.) *Ethnic Groups and Boundaries: The Social Organization of Culture Difference.* London: Allen and Unwin.

Barth, F., et al. 2005. *One Discipline, Four Ways: British, German, French and American Anthropology.* Chicago: University of Chicago Press.

Baskar, B. 1999. 'Anthropologists Facing the Collapse of Yugoslavia', *Diogenes* 188/47(4): 51–63.

Bastos, C. 1999. *Global Responses to AIDS: Science in Emergency.* Bloomington: Indiana University Press.

Bauman, Z. 1993. 'The Fall of the Legislator', in T. Docherty (ed.) *Postmodernism: A Reader.* Hemel Hempstead: Harvester Wheatsheaf.

Baumann, G. 1990. 'The Re-invention of Bhangra: Social Change and Aesthetic Shifts in a Punjabi Music in Britain', *World of Music* (Berlin) 2: 81–98.

_____. 1996. *Contesting Culture: Discourses of Identity in Multi-ethnic London.* Cambridge: Cambridge University Press.

Baumann, H. 1934. 'Die Afrikanischen Kulturkreise', *Africa* 7: 127–39.

Baumol, W., R. Litan and C.J. Schramm. 2007. *Good Capitalism, Bad Capitalism, and The Economics of Growth and Prosperity.* New Haven, CT: Yale University Press.

Bernal, M. 1987. *Black Athena: The Afroasiatic Roots of Classical Civilization.* New Bruswick, NJ: Rutgers University Press.

Bhachu, P. 1985. *Twice Migrants: East African Settlers in Britain.* London: Tavistock.

Bjelić, D.I. and O. Savić (eds). 2002. *The Balkans as Metaphor.* Cambridge, MA: MIT Press.

Bloch, M. 2008. 'Truth and Sight: Generalizing without Universalizing' *Journal of the Royal Anthropological Institute* 14 (Special Issue): S22-S31.

Boas, F. 1938. *General Anthropology.* New York: Macmillan.

_____. 1940. *Race, Language and Culture.* New York: Macmillan.

Böhme, H. 1972. *Deutschlands Weg zur Großmacht. Studien zum Verhältnis von Wirtschaft und Staat während der Reichsgründungszeit 1848–1881.* Köln: Kiepenheuer and Witsch.

Bolle, W. 2004. *Grandesertão.br.* São Paulo: Livr. Duas Cidades.

Boon, J. and D. Schneider. 1974. 'Kinship vis-à-vis Myth: Contrasts in Lévi-Strauss' Approaches to Cross-Cultural Comparison' *American Anthropologist* 76(4): 799–817.

Bošković, A. 2005a. 'Distinguishing "Self" and "Other": Anthropology and National Identity in Former Yugoslavia', *Anthropology Today* 21(2): 8–13.

_____. 2005b. 'Antropologija i Srodne Nauke — Metodologije i Perspective' [Anthropology and related sciences: methodologies and perspectives]. In L. Gavrilović (ed.) *Zbornik radova Etnografskog instituta SANU 21*, Belgrade: Serbian Academy of Sciences and Arts.

_____. 2006. 'Virtual Balkans: Imagined Boundaries, Hyperreality and Playing Rooms', In Association Apsolutno (ed.) *The Absolute Report*, Frankfurt am Main: Revolver.

Bošković, A. (ed.) 2008. *Other People's Anthropologies: Ethnographic Practice on the Margins.* Oxford: Berghahn.

Bourdieu, P. 1977 *Outline of a Theory of Practice.* Cambridge: Cambridge University Press.

_____. 1980. *Le Sens pratique.* Paris: Editions de Minuit.

_____. 1984. *Distinction: A Social Critique of the Judgment of Taste.* London: Routledge and Kegan Paul.

Braun, J. 1995. *Eine Deutsche Karriere. Die Biographie des Ethnologen Hermann Baumann (1902–1972).* Munich: Akademischer Verlag.

Brice-Bennett, C. 1977. *Our Footprints are Everywhere.* Nain: Labrador Printers.

Bringa, T. 1995. *Being Muslim the Bosnian Way: Identity and Community in a Central Bosnian Village.* Princeton, NJ: Princeton University Press.

_____. 2005. 'Haunted by the Imaginations of the Past: Robert Kaplan's *Balkan Ghosts*', in C. Besteman and H. Gusterson (eds), *Why America's Top Pundits Are Wrong: Anthropologists Talk Back.* Berkeley: University of California Press.

Brown, B. 2003. *Exploring Ethnic Tensions Through Locality.* Institute of Community Studies Working Paper No. 4, London

Buchanan, C. 2003. 'Canada's Indian Problem: Canadian Anthropology and Ideas of Aboriginal Emendation', unpublished paper presented at Trent University, February 2003.

———. 2006. 'Canadian Anthropology and Ideas of Aboriginal Emendation', in J. Harrison and R. Darnell (eds), *Historicizing Canadian Anthropology.* Vancouver: University of British Columbia Press.

Bunzl, M. 1996. 'Franz Boas and the Humboldtian Tradition: From Volksgeist and Nationalcharakter to an Anthropological Concept of Culture', in G. Stocking (ed.) *Volksgeist as Method and Ethic: Essays on Boasian Ethnography and the German Anthropological Tradition.* Madison: University of Wisconsin Press.

Butler, J., R. Elphick and D. Welsh (eds). 1987. *Democratic Liberalism in South Africa: Its History and Prospect.* Middletown, CT: Wesleyan University Press.

Byer, D. 1999. *Der Fall Hugo A. Bernatzik, Ein Leben Zwischen Ethnologie und Öffentlichkeit 1897–1953.* Cologne: Böhlau.

Campbell, J.T. 2002. '"Beyond the Pale": Jewish Immigrants and the South African Left', in M. Shain and R. Mendelson (eds), *Memories, Realities and Dreams: Studies in South African Jewish Experience.* Johannesburg: Jonathan Ball.

Campregher, C. and D. Mihola. 2006. 'Unterhaltung für die Wehrmacht: Anmerkungen zur Entstehungsgeschichte von 'Der weiße Kopfjäger', in H. Schäffler (ed.) *Begehrte Köpfe. Christoph Fürer-Haimendorfs Feldforschung im Nagaland (Nordostindien) der 30er-Jahre.* Vienna: Böhlau Verlag.

Carrier, J.G. In press. 'Simplicity in Economic Anthropology: Persuasion, Forms and Substance', in S.Gudeman (ed.) *Economic Persuasions.* New York: Berghahn.

Carstens, W.P. 1966. *The Social Structure of a Cape Coloured Reserve.* Cape Town: Oxford University Press.

Carter, H. 2005. 'The Life and Death of Old Labour: Collective Action and Social Cohesion in Southwark and Sheffield, 1945–1997', D.Phil. dissertation. Oxford: University of Oxford.

———. 2006. 'Collective action and social exclusion in the British post-war housing programme'. http://www.ehs.org.uk/ehs/conference2006/Assets/Carter NRIID.pdf, retrieved 31st September 2008

———. 2008. 'Building the Divided City: race, class, social housing in Southwark 1945–1995'. *The London Journal*, 33(2): 155–185

Casagrande, J. (ed.) 1960. *In the Company of Man: Twenty Portraits by Anthropologists.* New York: Harper.

Chomsky, N. and M. Foucault. 2006 [1971]. *The Chomsky-Foucault Debate on Human Nature.* NY: The New Press.

Chrisjohn, R. 1997. *The Circle Game.* Toronto: Theytus Books.

Clifford, J. and G. Marcus (eds). 1986. *Writing Culture: The Poetics and Politics of Ethnography.* Berkeley: University of California Press.

Cocks, P. 2000. 'The King and I: Bronislaw Malinowski, King Sobhuza II and the Vision of Culture Change in Africa', *History of the Human Sciences* 13(4):25–47.

Coertze, P.J. 1959. *Inleiding tot de Algemene Volkekunde [Introduction to General Ethnology].* Johannesburg: Voortrekkerpers.

Coertze, P.J., F.J. Language and B.I.C. van Eeden. 1943. *The Solution of the Native*

Problem in South Africa: Suggestions Concerning the Afrikaner Standpoint on Apartheid. Johannesburg: Publicite.

Cohen, S. 1980[1972]. *Folk Devils and Moral Panics: The Creation of the Mods and Rockers*. Oxford: Martin Robertson; London: McGibbon and Kee.

Cohen, S. and J. Young (eds). 1981. *The Manufacture of News: Deviance, Social Problems and the Mass Media*. London: Constable.

Cole, D. 1999. *Franz Boas: The Early Years, 1858–1906*. Seattle: University of Washington Press.

Collingwood, R.G. 1989. *Essays in Political Philosophy*. Oxford: Clarendon Press.

Conover, R., E. Čufer and P. Weibel (eds). 2002. *In Search of Balkania: A User's Manual*. Graz: Neue Galerieam Landesmuseum Joanneum.

Cornwell, J. 2003. *Hitler's Scientists: Science, War and the Devil's Pact*. London: Penguin.

Crandall, D.P. 2000. *Place of Stunted Ironwood Trees: A Year in the Lives of the Cattle-herding Himba of Namibia*. New York: Continuum.

Cullingham, J. 1995. *Duncan Campbell Scott: The Poet and the Indians*. National Film Board.

Cushman, T. 2004. 'Anthropology and Genocide in the Balkans: An Analysis of Conceptual Practices of Power', *Anthropological Theory* 4(1): 5–28.

Damásio, A. 2003. *Em Busca de Espinosa: Prazer e Dor na Ciência dos Sentimentos*. São Paulo: Companhia das Letras.

Danforth, L. 1984. 'The Ideological Context of the Search for Continuities in Greek Culture', *Journal of Modern Greek Studies* 2: 53–85.

Davidson, D. 2001. *Subjective, Intersubjective, Objective*. Oxford: Clarendon Press.

———. 2004. *Problems of Rationality*. Oxford: Clarendon Press.

———. 2005. *Truth, Language, and History*. Oxford: Clarendon Press.

De Coppet, D. 1992. 'Comparison, a Universal for Anthropology: From "Representation" to the Comparison of Hierarchies of Values', in A. Kuper (ed.) *Conceptualizing Society*. London: Routledge.

De Jongh, M. 2002. 'No Fixed Abode: The Poorest of the Poor and Elusive Identities in Rural South Africa', *Journal of Southern African Studies* 28(2): 441–60.

Denich, B. 2005. 'Debate or Defamation? Comment on the Publication of Cushman's "Anthropology and Genocide in the Balkans"', *Anthropological Theory* 5(4): 555–8.

Denoon, D. and A. Kuper. 1970. 'Nationalist Historians in Search of a Nation: The "New Historiography" in Dar es Salaam', *African Affairs* 69: 329–49.

———. 1971. 'The 'New Historiography' in Dar es Salaam: A Rejoinder', *African Affairs* 70: 287–8.

Dertilis, G.B. 2005. *History of the Greek Nation (1830–1920)*, 2 vols, 2nd edn. Athens: Estia.

De Wolf, J. 2002. 'Conditions of Comparison: A Consideration of Two Anthropological Traditions in the Netherlands', in A. Gingrich and R. Fox (eds), *Anthropology, by Comparison*. London: Routledge.

Diderot, D. 1751. 'Art', in D. Diderot and D'Alembert (eds), *Encyclopédie, ou Dictionnaire Raisonné des Sciences, des Artes et des Métiers*, Vol. 1. Paris: Briasson, David, Le Breton, Durand.

Dilley, R. (ed.) 1999. *The Problem of Context*. Oxford. Berghahn.

Donahue, K.C. 2007. *Slave of Allah: Zacarias Moussaoui vs The USA*. London: Pluto.

Douglas, M. 1966. *Purity and Danger: An Analysis of Concepts of Pollution and Taboo*. London: Routledge and Kegan Paul.

Dracklé, D., I. Edgar and T.K. Schippers (eds). 2004. *Educational Histories of European Social Anthropology*. Oxford: Berghahn.

Dragland, S. 1994. *Floating Voice: Duncan Campbell Scott and the Literature of Treaty 9*. Concord, Ontario: Anansi Press.

Dubow, S. 1987. 'Race, Civilization and Culture: The Elaboration of Segregationist Discourse in the Inter-war Years', in S. Marks and S. Trapido (eds). *The Politics of Race, Class and Nationalism in Twentieth Century South Africa*. London: Longmans.

———. 1994. 'Ethnic Euphemisms and Racial Echoes', *Journal of Southern African Studies* 20(2): 355–70.

Dumont, L. 1994. *The German Ideology: From France to Germany and Back*. Chicago: University of Chicago Press.

Durkheim, E. 1933[1893]. *The Division of Labor in Society*, trans. G. Simpson. Glencoe, IL: Free Press.

———. 1953[1924]. *Sociology and Philosophy*, trans. D.F. Pocock. London: Cohen and West.

———. 1995[1912]. *The Elementary Forms of the Religious Life*, trans. K.E. Fields. New York: Free Press.

———. 1960. *Montesquieu and Rousseau*. Ann Arbor: University of Michigan Press.

Durkheim, E. and M. Mauss. 1963. *Primitive Classification*, trans. R. Needham. Chicago: University of Chicago Press.

Dyck, N. 1991. *What Is the Indian 'Problem'? Tutelage and Resistance in Canadian Indian Administration*. St. John's: ISER.

Ealing Council. 1982. *1981 Census: Ward and Borough Profiles*. Ealing: Town Planning Division, Technical Services Group.

Eder, K. 1985. *Geschichte als Lernprozeß? Zur Pathogenese politischer Modernität in Deutschland*. Frankfurt: Suhrkamp.

Epstein, A.L. 1978. *Ethos and Identity: Three Studies in Ethnicity*. London: Tavistock.

Evans G. 2006a. *Educational Failure and Working Class White Children in Britain*. Basingstoke, Hampshire: Macmillan Palgrave.

———. 2006b. 'Learning, Violence and the Social Structure of Value', *Social Anthropology* 4: 247–259.

Fardon, R. 1999. *Mary Douglas: An Intellectual Biography*. London: Routledge.

Fausto, C. and F. Neiburg. 2002. 'An Interview with Adam Kuper', *Current Anthropology* 43(2): 305–13.

Finkielkraut, A. 1997[1984]. *The Wisdom of Love*, trans. K.I. O'Neill and D. Suchoff. Lincoln: University of Nebraska Press.

Firth, R. 1951. *Elements of Social Organization*. Boston: Beacon Press.

———. 1964. *Essays on Social Organization and Values*. London: Athlone.

———. 1965[1939]. *Primitive Polynesian Economy*, 2nd edn. London: Routledge and Kegan Paul.

Fischer, E.F. and P. Benson. 2006. *Broccoli and Desire: Global Connections and Maya Struggles in Postwar Guatemala*. Stanford, CA: Stanford University Press.

Fischer, E.F. and R. McKenna Brown (eds). 1996. *Maya Cultural Activism in Guatemala*. Austin: University of Texas Press.

Fortes, M. 1969. *Kinship and the Social Order: The Legacy of Lewis Henry Morgan*. London: Routledge and Kegan Paul.

Foucault, M. 1977. 'Nietzsche, Genealogy, History', in D. Bouchard (ed.) *Language, Counter-Memory, Practice*. Ithaca, NY: Cornell University Press.

———. 2003[1997]. *Society Must Be Defended: Lectures at the Collège de France, 1975–1976*. New York: Picador.

Fox, R. 1985. *Lions of the Punjab: Culture in the Making*. Berkeley: University of California Press.

Friedman, M. 1953. *Essays in Positive Economics*. Chicago: University of Chicago Press.

Fry, P. 2005. *A Persistência da Raça* [The persistence of race]. Rio de Janeiro: Civilização Brasileira.

Fürer-Haimendorf, C. 1939. *Die Nackten Nagas. Dreizehn Monate unter den Kopfjägern Indiens*. Leipzig: Brockhaus.

———. 1990. *Life among Indian Tribes. The Autobiography of an Anthropologist*. Oxford: Oxford University Press.

Furley, O. 1988. 'Education in Post-Independence Uganda: Change amidst Strife', in H.B. Hansen and M. Twaddle (eds), *Uganda Now: Between Decay and Development*. London: James Currey.

Furniss, E. 1992. *Victims of Benevolence: The Dark Legacy of the Williams Lake Residential School*. Williams Lake, BC: Caribou Tribal Council.

Gardner, H. 2004. *Frames of Mind*. New York: Basic Books.

Gefou-Madianou, D. 1993. 'Mirroring Ourselves Through Western Texts: The Limits of an Indigenous Anthropology', in H. Driessen (ed.) *The Politics of Ethnographic Reading and Writing: Confrontations of Western and Indigenous Views*. Saarbucken: Verlag Breitenbach.

———. 1999a. 'Cultural Polyphony and Identity Formation: Negotiating Tradition in Attica', *American Ethnologist* 26 (2): 412–39.

———. 1999b. *Politismos kai Ethnographia. Apo ton Ethnografiko Realismo stin Politismiki Kritiki* [Culture and ethnography: from ethnographic realism to cultural critique]. Athens: Greek Letters.

———. 2000. 'Disciples, Discipline and Reflection: Anthropological Encounters and Trajectories', in M. Strathern (ed.) *Audit Cultures: Anthropological Studies in Accountability, Ethics and the Academy*. London: Routledge.

———. 2003a. 'Anastohastiki anthropologia kai akadimaikos horos: trohies, dilimata, prooptikes' [Reflexive anthropology and academia: trajectories, dilemmas, perspectives], in V. Kremydas (ed.) *To Paron tou Parelthondos: Istoria, Laografia, Koinoniki Anthropologia* [The present of the past: history, folklore, social anthropology]. Athens: Etaireia Spoudon Neoellinikou Politismou kai Paideias.

Gefou-Madianou, D. (ed.) 2003b. *Eaftos kai Allos. Eniologiseis, Taftotites kai Practikes stin Ellada kai tin Kypro* [Self and other: conceptualizations, identities, and practices in Greece and Cyprus]. Athens: Greek Letters.

———. (ed.) 2006. 'Multiculturalism and Migration in Greece: Ethnic Groups, Identities, Representations and Practices', unpublished report of an anthropological study. Athens: Panteion University.

Geisenhainer, K. 2003. *'Rasse ist Schicksal'. Otto Reche (1879–1966) – ein Leben als Anthropologe und Völkerkundler*. Leipzig: Evangelische Verlagsanstalt.

Georgescu-Roegen, N. 1971. *The Entropy Law and the Economic Process*. Cambridge, MA: Harvard University Press.

Gibb, R. and D. Mills. 2001. 'An Interview with Adam Kuper', *Social Anthropology* 9(2): 207–16.

Gibson, G.D. 1956. 'Double Descent and Its Correlates among the Herero of Ngamiland', *American Anthropologist* 58: 109–39.

Giddens, A. 1996. *In Defence of Sociology*. Cambridge: Polity Press.

Gil, F. 2004. 'Acaso, Necessidade, Acção: entre Aristóteles e Verdi' in L. Schmidt and J. de Pina-Cabral (eds), *Ciência e Cidadania: uma homenagem a Bento de Jesus Caraça*. Lisboa: Imprensa de Ciências Sociais.

Giliomee, H. and H. Adam. 1979. *The Rise and Crisis of Afrikaner Power*. Cape Town: David Philip.

Gillborn, D. 2008. *Racism and Education: Coincidence or Conspiracy?* London: Routledge.

Gillborn, D. and C. Gipps. 1996. *Recent Research on the Achievement of Ethnic Minority Pupils*. London: HMSO/Ofsted.

Gillborn, D. and A. Kirton. 2000. 'White Heat: Racism, Under-achievement and White Working-Class Boys.' *International Journal of Inclusive Education* 4(4): 271–88.

Gillborn, D. and H. Mirza. 2000. *Mapping Race, Class and Gender: A Synthesis of Research Evidence*. London: Ofsted.

Gillespie, M. 1995. *Television, Ethnicity and Cultural Change*. London: Routledge.

Gingrich, A. 2005. 'Ruptures, Schools, and Nontraditions: Reassessing the History of Socio-cultural Anthropology in German', in F. Barth et al., *One Discipline, Four Ways: British, German, French and American Anthropology*. Chicago: University of Chicago Press.

———. 2006a. 'Remigranten und Ehemalige: Zäsuren und Kontinuitäten in der Universitären Völkerkunde Wiens nach 1945', in M. Grandner, G. Heiss and O. Rathkolb (eds), *Zukunft mit Altlasten. Die Universität Wien 1945 bis 1955*. Innsbruck: Studienverlag.

———. 2006b. 'Gebrochene Kontexte einer Prekären Ethnographie: Einleitende Überlegungen zum Frühwerk von Christoph Fürer-Haimendorf', in H. Schäffler (ed.) *Begehrte Köpfe*. Vienna: Böhlau.

Gingrich, A. and R. Fox (eds). 2002. *Anthropology, by Comparison*. London: Routledge.

Glenny, M. 1999. *The Balkans: Nationalism, War, and the Great Powers, 1804–1999*. New York: Viking.

Gluckman, M. 1940. 'Analysis of a Social Situation in Modern Zululand', *Bantu Studies* 14: 1–30.

Gordon, R.J. 1988. 'Apartheid's Anthropologists: Notes on the Genealogy of Afrikaner Volkekundiges', *American Ethnologist* 15(3): 535–53.

———. 1989. 'The White Man's Burden: Ersatz Customary Law and Internal Pacification in South Africa', *Journal of Historical Sociology* 2(1): 41–65.

———. 1991. 'Serving the *Volk* with *Volkekunde*: on the rise of South African Anthropology', in J.D. Jansen (ed.). *Knowledge and Power in South Africa: Critical Perspectives Across the Disciplines*. Johannesburg: Skotaville Publishers.

———. 1992. *The Bushman Myth: the Making of a Namibian Underclass*. Boulder, CO: Westview.

———. n.d. '"Tracks which Cannot be Covered": P.J. Schoeman and Public Intellectuals in Southern Africa', unpublished paper.

Gray, G. 2006. '"The ANRC has Withdrawn its Offer": Paul Kirchhoff, Academic Freedom and the Australian Academic Establishment', *Australian Journal of Politics and History* 52(3): 362–77.

Green, D. 2003. *Silent Revolution: The Rise and Crisis of Market Economics in Latin America.* New York: Monthly Review Press.

Gregory, C.A. 1997. *Savage Money.* Chur: Harwood.

———. 2002. 'The Anthropology of the Economy', *Australian Journal of Anthropology* 13(3): 361–2.

Griffin, R. 2007. *Modernism and Fascism: The Sense of a Beginning under Mussolini and Hitler.* New York: Palgrave Macmillan.

Grillo, R.D. 2003. 'Cultural Essentialism and Cultural Anxiety'. *Anthropological Theory* 3: 157–73.

Gudeman, S. 1976. *Relationships, Residence and the Individual.* London: Routledge and Kegan Paul.

———. 1978. *The Demise of a Rural Economy.* London: Routledge.

———. 1986. *Economics as Culture.* London: Routledge.

———. 2001. *The Anthropology of Economy.* Malden, MA: Blackwell.

———. 2008. *Economy's Tension: the Dialectics of Community and Market.* Oxford: Berghahn.

Gudeman, S. and M. Penn. 1982. 'Models, Meanings and Reflexivity', in D. Parkin (ed.) *Semantic Anthropology.* London: Academic Press.

Gudeman, S. and A. Rivera. 1990. *Conversations in Colombia.* Cambridge: Cambridge University Press.

Guimarães Rosa, J. 2001[1956]. *Grande Sertão: Veredas.* 19th edn. Rio de Janeiro: Nova Fronteira.

Halpern, J.M. and D.A. Kideckel (eds). 2000. *Neighbors at War: Anthropological Perspectives on Yugoslav Ethnicity, Culture, and History.* University Park: Pennsylvania State University Press.

Hamilakis, Y. and E. Yalouri. 1996. 'Antiquities as Symbolic Capital in Modern Greek Society', *Antiquity* 70: 117–29.

Hammond-Tooke, D. 1997. *Imperfect Interpreters: South Africa's Anthropologists 1920–1990.* Johannesburg: Witwatersrand University Press.

Hannerz, U. 1969. *Soulside: Inquiries into Ghetto Culture and Community.* New York: Columbia University Press.

———. 1992. 'The Global Ecumene as a Network of Networks', in A. Kuper (ed.) *Conceptualizing Society.* London: Routledge.

———. 2004. *Foreign News: Exploring the World of Foreign Correspondents.* Chicago: University of Chicago Press.

Hauschild, T. (ed.) 1995. *Lebenslust und Fremdenfurcht. Ethnologie im Dritten Reich.* Frankfurt: Suhrkamp.

Hausmann, F.-R. 2001. 'Einführung', in F.-R. Hausmann (ed.) *Die Rolle der Geisteswissenschaften im Dritten Reich 1933–1945.* Munich: R. Oldenberg.

Hawthorn, H. 1966–1967. *A Survey of the Contemporary Indians of Canada: Economic, Political, Educational Needs and Policies,* 2 vols. Ottawa: Queen's Printer.

Hayden, R.M. 2002. 'Antagonistic Tolerance: Competitive Sharing of Religious Sites in South Asia and the Balkans', *Current Anthropology* 43(2): 205–31.

———. 2003. 'Biased Justice: "Humanrightism" and the International Criminal Tribunal for the Former Yugoslavia', in R.G.C. Thomas (ed.) *Yugoslavia Unraveled: Sovereignty, Self-Determination, Intervention.* Lanham, MD: Lexington Books.

———. 2005. 'Inaccurate Data, Spurious Issues and Editorial Failure in Cushman's

"Anthropology and Genocide in the Balkans"', *Anthropological Theory* 5(4): 545–54.

Hayek, F. 1948. *Individualism and Economic Order*. Chicago: University of Chicago Press.

——. 1967. *Studies in Philosophy, Politics and Economics*. Chicago: University of Chicago Press.

——. 1978. *New Studies in Philosophy, Politics, Economics and the History of Ideas*. Chicago: University of Chicago Press.

Heinrichs, H.-J. 1998. *Die fremde Welt, das bin ich. Leo Frobenius- Ethnologe, Forschungsreisender, Abenteurer*. Wuppertal: Edition Trickster-Hammer.

Herskovits, M. 1953[1940]. *Economic Anthropology*. New York: Norton.

Herzfeld, M. 1987. *Anthropology Through the Looking Glass: Critical Ethnography in the Margins of Europe*. Cambridge: Cambridge University Press.

——. 2003. 'Localism and the Logic of Nationalistic Folklore: Cretan Reflections', *Comparative Studies in Society and History* 45(2): 281–310.

Hewitt, R. 2005. *White Backlash and the Politics of Multiculturalism*. Cambridge: Cambridge University Press.

Hirschman, A. 1977. *The Passions and the Interests: Political Arguments for Capitalism Before Its Triumph*. Princeton, NJ: Princeton University Press.

Hoernlé, A.W. 1947. 'Foreword', in H. Kuper, *The Uniform of Colour: a Study of White-Black Relationships in Swaziland*. Johannesburg: Witwatersrand University Press.

Hoffman, M. 2007. 'Foucault's Politics and Bellicosity as a Matrix for Power Relations', *Philosophy and Social Criticism* 33(6): 756–78.

Home Office. 1988. *Home Office Statistical Bulletins, Regional Trends, 23*. London: H.M. Office of Home Affairs.

Hudson, K. 2003. *Breaking the South Slav Dream: The Rise and Fall of Yugoslavia*. London: Pluto.

Hutchins, E. 1995. *Cognition in the Wild*. Cambridge, MA: MIT Press.

Hylland Eriksen, T. 2006. *Engaging Anthropology: The Case for a Public Presence*. Oxford: Berg.

Ignatieff, M. 2000. *The Rights Revolution*. Toronto: Anansi.

Ingold, T. (ed.) 1996. *Key Debates in Anthropology, 1988–1993*. London: Routledge.

Jacknis, I. 1996. 'The Ethnographic Object and the Object Of Ethnology in the Early Career of Franz Boas', in G. Stocking (ed.) *Volksgeist as Method and Ethic: Essays on Boasian Ethnography and the German Anthropological Tradition*. Madison: University of Wisconsin Press.

Jezernik, B. 2004. *Wild Europe: The Balkans in the Gaze of Western Travellers*. London: Saqi Books.

Just, R. 1995. 'Cultural Certainties and Private Doubts', in W. James (ed.) *The Pursuit of Certainty: Religious and Cultural Formulations*. London: Routledge.

Kalpaxis, T. 1997. 'The Tyranny of the Ancient Greek Grandeur' [I tyrania tou archaeoellinikou megaleiou], in Society of Modern Greek Culture (ed.), *Art Review: The Crucial Twelve Years*. Athens: Scholi Moraᵃti.

Karakasidou, A. 2002. 'The Burden of the Balkans', *Anthropological Quarterly* 75(3): 575–89.

Kennedy, J.C. 1987. 'Aboriginal Organizations and their Claims: The Case of Newfoundland and Labrador', *Canadian Ethnic Studies* 19(2): 13–25.

_____. 1988. 'The Changing Significance of Labrador Settler Ethnicity', *Canadian Ethnic Studies* 20(3): 94–111.

Keynes, J.M. 1964 [1936]. *The General Theory of Employment, Interest, and Money*. New York: Harcourt, Brace and World.

Kiernan, J. 1997. 'David in the Path of Goliath', in P. McAllister (ed.) *Culture and the Commonplace: Anthropological Essays in Honour of David Hammond-Tooke*. Johannesburg: Wits University Press.

Kirchhoff, P. 1931. 'Die Verwandtschaftsorganization der Urwaldstämme Südamerikas', *Zeitschrift für Ethnologie* 63: 85–193.

Kolakowski, L. 1978. *Main Currents of Marxism*, vol. 1. Oxford: Oxford University Press.

Kotsakis, K. 1998. 'The Past is Ours: Images of Greek Macedonia', in L. Meskell (ed.) *Archaeology Under Fire: Nationalism, Politics and Heritage in the Eastern Mediterranean and Middle East*. London: Routledge.

Krause, F. 1952. 'Chronik des Museums 1926–1945', *Jahrbuch des Museums für Völkerkunde zu Leipzig* 10: 1–47.

Kros, C. 1996. 'Economic, Political and Intellectual Origins of Bantu Education, 1926–1951'. Ph.D. dissertation. Johannesburg: University of the Witwatersrand.

Kruik, S. and M. Veenis. 2005. 'Professor of the Dark Side: An Interview with Bonno Thoden van Velzen', *Etnofoor* 18(2): 87–104.

Kuklick, H. 1991. *The Savage Within. The Social History of British Anthropology, 1885–1945*. Cambridge: Cambridge University Press.

Kulchyski, P. 1993. 'Anthropology in the Service of the State: Diamond Jenness and Canadian Indian Policy', *Journal of Canadian Studies* 28(2): 21–50.

Kuper, A. 1970. *Kalahari Village Politics: An African Democracy*. Cambridge: Cambridge University Press.

_____. 1973. *Anthropologists and Anthropology: The British School, 1922–1972*. London: Allen Lane.

_____. 1976. *Changing Jamaica*. London: Routledge and Kegan Paul.

_____. 1979a. 'Regional Comparison in African Anthropology', *African Affairs* 78: 103–13.

_____. 1979b. 'Determinants of Form in Seven Tswana Kinship Terminologies', *Ethnology* 17: 239–86.

_____. 1979c. 'A Structural Approach to Dreams', *Man* 14: 645–62.

_____. 1980a. 'Review of E. Gellner (ed.) *Soviet and Western Anthropology*', *New Society* 922: 142.

_____. 1980b. 'Symbolic Dimensions of the Southern Bantu Homestead', *Africa* 50(1): 8–23.

_____. 1982. *Wives for Cattle: Bridewealth and Marriage in Southern Africa*. London: Routledge and Kegan Paul.

_____. 1983a. 'The Structure of Dream Sequences', *Culture, Medicine and Psychiatry* 7: 1–25.

_____. 1983b. *Anthropologists and Anthropology: The British School*, 2nd edn. London: Routledge.

_____. 1987. *South Africa and the Anthropologist*. London: Routledge and Kegan Paul.

_____. 1988. *The Invention of Primitive Society: Transformations of an Illusion*. London: Routledge.

_____. 1992a. *Conceptualising Society*. London: Routledge.

––––––. 1992b. 'Postmodernism, Cambridge and the Great Kalahari Debate', *Social Anthropology* 1(1A): 57–71.

––––––. 1994a. *The Chosen Primate: Human Nature and Cultural Diversity.* Cambridge, MA: Harvard University Press.

––––––. 1994b. 'Culture, Identity and the Project of a Cosmopolitan Anthropology', *Man* 29(3): 537–54.

––––––. 1996. *Anthropology and Anthropologists. The Modern British School*, 3rd edn. London: Routledge.

––––––. 1999a. *Among the Anthropologists: History and Context in Anthropology.* London: Athlone.

––––––. 1999b. *Culture: The Anthropologists' Account.* Cambridge, MA: Harvard University Press.

––––––. 1999c. 'A Conversation With Charles Stafford – About Culture and Anthropology', in A. Kuper, *Among The Anthropologists: History and Context in Anthropology.* London: Athlone.

––––––. 2001a. 'Fraternity and Exogamy: The House of Rothschild', *Social Anthropology* 9(3): 273–87.

––––––. 2002a. 'Incest, Cousin Marriage, and the Origin of the Human Sciences in Nineteenth Century England', *Past and Present* 174(1): 158–83.

––––––. 2002b 'The Return of the Native', paper given at the Max Planck Institute for Social Anthropology, Halle, Germany.

––––––. 2003. 'The Return of the Native', *Current Anthropology* 44: 389–402.

––––––. 2005. *The Reinvention of Primitive Society: Transformations of a Myth.* London: Routledge.

––––––. 2006. 'Discussion', *Social Anthropology* 14: 21–22.

––––––. 2007a. 'Growing Up with Stan', in D. Downes, P. Rock, C. Chinkin and C. Gearty (eds.) *Crime, Social Control and Human Rights: From Moral Panics to States of Denial, Essays in Honour of Stanley Cohen.* London: Willan Publishing.

––––––. 2008. 'Changing the Subject', *Journal of the Royal Anthropological Institute* 14(4): 717–35.

Kuper, A. and J. Kuper (eds). 1985. *The Social Science Encyclopaedia.* London: Routledge.

Kuper, H. 1947. *The Uniform of Colour: A Study of White-Black Relationships in Swaziland.* Johannesburg: Witwatersrand University Press.

––––––. 1984. 'Function, History, Biography: Reflections of Fifty Years in the British Anthropological Tradition', in G.W. Stocking (ed.) *Functionalism Historicized: Essays on British Social Anthropology.* Madison: University of Wisconsin Press.

Kyriakidou-Nestoros, A. 1978. *I Theoria tis Laografias.* Athens: Scholi Moraïti.

Latour, B. 1993. *We Have Never Been Modern,* trans. C. Porter. Cambridge, MA: Harvard University Press.

Lazar, J. 1993. 'Verwoerd versus the Visionaries: the South African Bureau of Racial Affairs and Apartheid, 1948–1961', in P. Bonner, D. Posel and P. Delius (eds). *Apartheid's Genesis, 1935–1962.* Johannesburg: Ravan Press and Witwatersrand University Press, pp. 362–92.

Leach, E. 1954. *Political Systems of Highland Burma.* London: G. Bell and Sons.

––––––. 1984. 'Glimpses of the Unmentionable in the History of British Social Anthropology', *Annual Review of Anthropology* 13: 1–22.

Lee, R. 1979. *The !Kung San: Men, Women and Work in a Foraging Society.* Cambridge: Cambridge University Press.

———. 1984. *The Dobe !Kung.* New York: Holt, Rinehart and Winston.

Lee, R. and J. Solway. 1990. 'Foragers, Genuine or Spurious?' *Current Anthropology* 31(2): 109–46.

Le Roux, W. and A. White (eds). 2004. *Voices of the San: Living in Southern Africa Today.* Cape Town: Kwela Books.

Lévinas, E. (1996) *Basic Philosophical Writings.* A. Peperzak, S. Critchley and R. Bernasconi (eds). Bloomington: Indiana University Press.

Lévi-Strauss, C. 1969. *The Elementary Structures of Kinship.* Boston: Beacon Press.

———. 1984. *Paroles Données.* Paris: Plon.

———. 1988. *The Jealous Potter*, trans. B. Chorier. Chicago: University of Chicago Press.

Lewis, H.S. 1975. 'Review of A. Kuper, *Anthropologists and Anthropology*', *ASA Review of Books* 1: 23–26.

Liakos, A. 2001. 'The Construction Of National Time: The Making Of The Modern Greek Historical Imagination', *Mediterranean Historical Review* 16(1): 27–42.

Linimair, P. 1994. *Wiener Völkerkunde im Nationalsozialismus. Ansätze zu einer NS-Wissenschaft.* Frankfurt am Main: Peter Lang.

Locke, J. 1975[1690]. *An Essay Concerning Human Understanding.* P.H. Nidditch (ed.) Oxford: Clarendon Press.

Lutz, C. and L. Abu-Lughod (eds). 1990. *Language and the Politics of Emotion.* Cambridge: Cambridge University Press.

Lynch, M.P. 1998. *Truth in Context: An Essay on Pluralism and Objectivity.* Cambridge, MA: MIT Press.

McAllister, P. (ed.) 1997. *Culture and the Commonplace: Anthropological Essays in Honour of David Hammond-Tooke.* Johannesburg: Witwatersrand University Press.

McLeod, W.H. 1989. *Who is a Sikh? The Problem of Sikh Identity.* Oxford: Clarendon Press.

MacMillan, H. 2000. 'From Race to Ethnic Identity: South Central Africa, Social Anthropology and the Shadow of the Holocaust', *Social Dynamics* 26(2): 87–115.

Malik, K. 2003. 'Why do We Still Believe in Race?' unpublished lecture given at Cheltenham Festival. Retrieved 31 September 2008 from http://www.kenanmalik.com/lectures/race_cheltenham.html

Malinowski, B. 1922. *Argonauts of the Western Pacific.* London: Routledge.

———. 1936. 'Native Education and Culture Contact', *International Review of Missions* 25: 480–515.

———. 1944. *A Scientific Theory of Culture and Other Essays.* Chapel Hill: University of North Carolina Press.

———. 1945. *The Dynamics of Culture Change: An Inquiry into Race Relations in Africa.* P. Kaberry (ed.) New Haven, CT: Yale University Press.

Marais, J.S. 1939. *The Cape Coloured People, 1652–1937.* London: Longmans, Green and Co.

Marcus, G.E. and M. Fisher. 1986. *Anthropology as Cultural Critique: An Experimental Moment in the Human Sciences.* Chicago: University of Chicago Press.

Marglin, S.A. 1990. 'Losing Touch: The Cultural Conditions of Worker Accommodation and Resistance', in F.A. Marglin and S.A. Marglin (eds), *Dominating Knowledge: from Development to Dialogue*. Oxford: Clarendon Press.

———. 1996. 'Farmers, Seedsmen, and Scientists: Systems of Agriculture and Systems of Knowledge', in F.A. Marglin and S.A. Marglin (eds), *Decolonizing Knowledge*, Oxford: Clarendon Press.

———. 2007. *The Dismal Science*. Cambridge, MA: Harvard University Press.

Markus, H. and S. Kitayama. 1998. 'The Cultural Psychology of Personality', *Journal of Cross-cultural Psychology* 29(1): 63–87.

———. 2003. 'Models of Agency: Sociocultural Diversity in the Construction of Action', in V. Murphy-Berman & J. Berman (Eds.) *The 49th Annual Nebraska symposium on motivation: Cross-cultural differences in perspectives on self*. Lincoln: University of Nebraska Press, pp. 1–57.

Markus, H., P. Mullally and S. Kitayama. 1997. 'Selfways: Diversity in Modes of Cultural Participation', in U. Neisser and D. Jopling (eds), *The Conceptual Self in Context*, New York: Cambridge University Press.

Martins, H. 1974. 'Time and Theory in Sociology', in J. Rex (ed.) *Approaches to Sociology*. London: Routledge and Kegan Paul.

Mauss, M. 1950. 'Essai sur le don' in *Sociologie et Anthropologie*. Paris: Presses Universitaires de France.

Mawasha, A. 2006. 'Turfloop: Where an Idea was Expressed, Hijacked and Redeemed', in M. Nkomo, D. Swartz and B. Maja (eds), *Within the Realm of Possibility: From Disadvantage to Development at the University of Fort Hare and the University of the North*. Pretoria: Human Sciences Research Council Press.

Maylam, P. and I. Edwards (eds). 1996. *The People's City: African Life in Twentieth Century Durban*. Pietermaritzburg: University of Natal Press.

Mbeki, T. 2000. 'Address at the Unveiling of the Coat of Arms, Kwaggafontein, 27 April 2000'. Retrieved 2 October 2006 from http://www.dfa.gov.za/docs/speeches/2000/mbek0427.htm.

Merleau-Ponty, M. 1964. *Signs*, trans. R. MacCleary. Evanston, IL: Northwestern University Press.

Merry, S.E. 1981. *Urban Danger*. Philadelphia, PA: Temple University Press.

Meskell, L. (ed.) 1998. *Archaeology Under Fire: Nationalism, Politics and Heritage in the Eastern Mediterranean and Middle East*. London: Routledge.

Michel, U. 1991. 'Wilhelm Emil Mühlmann (1904–1988). Ein deutscher Professor. Amnesie und Amnestie: Zum Verhältnis von Ethnologie und Politik im Nationalsozialismus', in *Jahrbuch für Soziologiegeschichte*: 69–118.

———. 2000. 'Ethnopolitische Reorganizationsforschung am Institut für Deutsche Ostarbeit in Krakau', in B. Streck (ed.), *Ethnologie und Nationalsozialismus*. Gehren: Escher.

Mintz, S. 1994. 'Enduring Substances, Trying Theories: The Caribbean Region As *Oikoumenê*', *Journal of the Royal Anthropological Institute* 2: 289–311.

Mirabeau, Marquis de, and F. Francois. 1973[1763]. *Precursors of Adam Smith*. R.L. Meek (ed.) London: Dent.

Mischek, U. 2002. *Leben und Werk Günter Wagner (1908–1952)*. Gehren: Escher.

Mitchell, J.C. 1956. *The Kalela Dance*. Rhodes Livingstone Institute Papers, 27. Manchester: Manchester University Press.

Modood T. 2005. *Multicultural Politics: Racism, Ethnicity And Muslims In Britain.* Edinburgh: Edinburgh University Press.

Moodie, D. 1975. *The Rise of Afrikanerdom: Power, Apartheid, and the Afrikaner Civil Religion.* Berkeley: University of California Press.

Mosen, M. 1991. *Der Koloniale Traum. Angewandte Ethnologie im Nationalsozialismus.* Bonn: Holos.

Muldrew, Craig. 1993. 'Interpreting The Market: The Ethics Of Credit And Community Relations In Early Modern England.' *Social History* 18(2): 163–183.

Murray, B. 1997. *Wits – The 'Open' Years: A History of the University of the Witwatersrand, Johannesburg, 1939–1959.* Johannesburg: Witwatersrand University Press.

Muršič, R. 2000. 'The Yugoslav Dark Side of Humanity: A View from a Slovene Blind Spot', in J.M. Halpern and D.A. Kideckel (eds), *Neighbors at War: Anthropological Perspectives on Yugoslav Ethnicity, Culture, and History.* University Park: Pennsylvania State University Press.

Musil, R. 1995[1978]. *The Man Without Qualities.* London: Picador.

Nankov, N. 2002. 'Revisiting Ruritania and Vulgaria: Three Invitations for a Dialog', *Slavic and East European Journal* 46(2): 363–68.

Needham, R. 1978. *Primordial Characters.* Charlottesville: University Press of Virginia.

———. 1981. *Circumstantial Deliveries.* Berkeley: University of California Press.

North, D. 2005. *Understanding the Process of Economic Change.* Princeton, NJ: Princeton University Press.

Office for Standards in Education. 1999. *Raising the Attainment of Minority Ethnic Pupils.* London: Ofsted

O'Meara, D. 1982. *Volkskapitalisme.* Johannesburg: Ravan.

———. 1997. *Forty Lost Years.* Athens: Ohio University Press.

Ortner, S. 1984. 'Theory in Anthropology since the Sixties', *Comparative Studies in Society and History*, 26(1): 126–66.

———. 2006. *Anthropology and Social Theory: Culture, Power, and the Acting Subject.* Durham, NC: Duke University Press.

Paine, R (ed.) 1971. *Patrons and Brokers in the Eastern Arctic.* St. John's: ISER.

———. 1977. *The White Arctic: Anthropological Essays on Tutelage and Ethnicity.* St. John's: ISER.

Parsons, T. 1966. *Societies: Evolutionary and Comparative Perspectives.* Englewood Cliffs, NJ: Prentice-Hall.

Parsons, T. and N. Smelser. 1956. *Economy and Society.* New York: Free Press.

Passaro, J. 1996. *The Unequal Homeless: Men on the Streets, Women in Their Place.* New York: Routledge.

Penny, G.P. 2002. *Objects of Culture: Ethnology and Ethnographic Museums in Imperial Germany.* Chapel Hill: University of North Carolina Press.

Penny, G.P. and M. Bunzl (eds). 2003. *Wordly Provincialism. German Anthropology in the Age of Empire.* Ann Arbor: University of Michigan Press.

Peters, K. 1910. 'Die Kolonien in 100 Jahren', in A. Brehmer (ed.) *Die Welt in hundert Jahren.* Berlin: Verlagsanstalt Buntdruck.

Pettigrew, J. 1992. 'Martyrdom and Guerilla Organization in Punjab', *Journal of Commonwealth and Comparative Politics* 30(3): 387–406.

Phillips, M. and T. Phillips. 1998. *Windrush: The Irresistible Rise of Multi-racial*

Britain. London: Harper Collins.

Pina-Cabral, J. de. 1992. 'The Gods Of The Gentiles Are Demons: The Problem Of Pagan Survivals In European Culture', in K. Hastrup (ed.) *Other Histories*. London: Routledge.

——. 1997. 'The Threshold Diffused: Margins, Hegemonies and Contradictions in Contemporary Anthropology', in P. McAllister (ed.) *Culture and the Commonplace: Anthropological Essays in Honour of David Hammond-Tooke*. Johannesburg: Witwatersrand University Press.

——. 2004. 'Os Albinos Não Morrem: Crença e Etnicidade no Moçambique Pós-Colonial', in F. Gil, P. Livet and J. de Pina-Cabral (eds), *O Processo da Crença*. Lisbon: Gradiva.

——. 2005a. 'The Future of Social Anthropology', *Social Anthropology* 13(2): 119–28.

——. 2005b. 'Identités imbriquées: divagations sur l'identité, l'émotion et la moralité', *Recherches en Anthropologie au Portugal* 10: 37–56.

——. 2006. 'Anthropology Challenged: Notes for a Debate' *Journal of the Royal Anthropological Institute* 12(3): 663–73.

——. 2007a. 'A Pessoa e o Dilemma Brasileiro', *Novos Estudos Cebrap* 78: 95–111.

——. 2007b. 'The All-Or-Nothing Syndrome and the Human Condition', paper presented at the Wenner-Gren Foundation/Institute of Social Sciences international symposium 'An Epistemology For Anthropology', University of Lisbon.

Pina-Cabral, J. de and J. Bestard Camps. 2003. 'Os limites do interesse', in J. de Pina-Cabral (ed.) *O Homem Na Família*. Lisbon: Imprensa de Ciências Sociais.

Plaice, E. 1990. *The Native Game: Settler Perceptions of Indian/Settler Relations in Central Labrador*. St John's: ISER.

——. 1996. 'Touching Base: Land, Lives and Militarisation in Central Labrador', Ph.D. dissertation. Manchester: University of Manchester.

——. 1998. 'The Moral and Legal Salience of Claiming Land: Lessons for South Africa from the Canadian Experience', in M. Barry (ed.) *Proceedings of the International Conference on Land Tenure in the Developing World*. Cape Town: University of Cape Town.

Polanyi, K. 1944. *The Great Transformation*. New York: Farrar and Reinhart.

——. 1968. *Primitive, Archaic, and Modern Economies*. G. Dalton (ed.) Garden City, NY: Anchor Books.

Poulter, S. 1998. *Ethnicity, Law, and Human Rights: The English Experience*. Oxford: Clarendon Press.

Prica, I. 2005. 'Autori, Zastupnici, Presuditelji – Hrvatska Etnologija U Paralelizmima Postsocijalistiãkog Konteksta' [Authors, representatives, adjudicators: Croatian ethnology in parallel with the postsocialist context], in L. Gavriloviç (ed.) *Zbornik radova Etnografskog instituta SANU 21*, Belgrade: Serbian Academy of Sciences and Arts.

Proctor, R.N. 1999. *The Nazi War on Cancer*. Princeton, NJ: Princeton University Press.

Pullé, S. 1974. *Police-Immigrant Relations in Ealing*. London: Runnymead Trust for Ealing Borough Council.

Quesnay, F. 1972[1758–1759]. *Tableau Économique*. Trans. and ed. M. Kucynski and R. L. Meek. London: Macmillan.

Quine, W.R. 1969. *Ontological Relativity and Other Essays*. New York: Columbia University Press.

Radcliffe-Brown, A.R. 1952. *Structure and Function in Primitive Society*. London: Cohen and West.

Ramos, A.R. 1998. *Indigenism: Ethnic Politics in Brazil*. Madison: University of Wisconsin Press.

Ranger, T. 1971. 'The "New Historiography" in Dar Es Salaam: An Answer', *African Affairs* 70: 50–61.

Rapport, N. and J. Overing. 2000. *Social and Cultural Anthropology: The Key Concepts*. London: Routledge.

Ricardo, D. 1951a[1815]. *The Works and Correspondence of David Ricardo*, Vol. 4. P. Sraffa (ed.) Cambridge: Cambridge University Press.

———. 1951b[1817]. *On the Principles of Political Economy and Taxation*, P. Sraffa (ed.) Cambridge: Cambridge University Press.

Richards, A. and A. Kuper (eds). 1971. *Councils in Action*. Cambridge: Cambridge University Press.

Riese, B. 1995. 'Während des Dritten Reichs (1933–1945) in Deutschland und Österreich Verfolgte und von Dort Ausgewanderte Ethnologen', in T. Hauschild (ed.) *Lebenslust und Fremdenfurcht. Ethnologie im Dritten Reich*, Frankfurt am Main: Suhrkamp.

Rihtman-Auguštin, D. 1999. 'A Croatian Controversy: Mediterranean-Danube-Balkans.' *Narodna umjetnost* 36(1): 103–19.

———. 2004. *Ethnology, Myth and Politics: Anthropologizing Croatian Ethnology*. J. Čapo-Žmegać (ed.) Aldershot: Ashgate.

Ristović, M. 1995. 'The Birth of "Southeastern Europe" and the Death of "the Balkans"', *Thetis. Mannheimer Beiträge zur Klassischen Archäologie und Geschichte Griechenlands und Zyperns*, 2(169–76).

Robbins, J. 2007. 'Continuity Thinking and the Problem of Christian Culture: Belief, Time, and the Anthropology of Christianity', *Current Anthropology* 48(1): 5–38.

Robins, S. 2001. 'Whose "Culture", whose "Survival"? The ≠Khomani San Land Claim and the Cultural Politics of "Community" and "Development" in the Kalahari', in A. Barnard and J. Kenrick (eds), *Africa's Indigenous Peoples: 'First Peoples' or 'Marginalized Minorities'?* Edinburgh: Centre of African Studies.

Rose, H.A. 1911–1919. *A Glossary of the Tribes and Castes of the Punjab and North-West Frontier Province*, 4 vols. Lahore: Government Publications.

Rosenberg, R. 2001. 'Die Semantik der, Szientifizierung": Die Paradigmen der Sozialgeschichte und des linguistischen Strukturalismus als Modernisierungsangebote an die deutsche Literaturwissenschaft', in G. Bollenbeck and C. Cnobloch (eds), *Semantischer Umbau und Geisteswissenschaften nach 1933 und 1945*. Heidelberg: C. Winter.

Rousseau, J.J. 1913[1762]. *The Social Contract*. Trans G.D.H. Cole. London: Dent.

Ruttan, V. 2003. *Social Science Knowledge and Economic Development*. Ann Arbor: University of Michigan Press.

Sahlins, M. 1968. *Tribesmen*. Englewood Cliffs, NJ: Prentice Hall.

———. 1976. *Culture and Practical Reason*. Chicago: University of Chicago Press.

———. 1994. 'Goodbye to Tristes Tropes: Ethnography in the Context of Modern World History', in R. Borofsky (ed.) *Assessing Cultural Anthropology*. New York: McGraw-Hill.

Said, E. 1978. *Orientalism*. New York: Vintage.

Salat, J. 1983. *Reasoning as Enterprise: The Anthropology of S.F. Nadel*. Göttingen: Edition Herodot.

Sanjek, R. and S. Gregory (eds). 1994. *Race*. New Brunswick, NJ: Rutgers University Press.

Saugestad, S. 2001. *The Inconvenient Indigenous: Remote Area Development in Botswana, Donor Assistance, and the First People of the Kalahari*. Uppsala: Nordiska Afrikainstitutet.

———. 2006. 'Notes on the Outcome of the Ruling in the Central Kalahari Game Reserve case, Botswana', *Before Farming* 4: art.10.

Saunders, C. 1988. *The Making of the South African Past: Major Historians on Race and Class*. Cape Town: David Philip.

Schäffler, H. 2006. *Begehrte Köpfe. Christoph Fürer-Haimendorfs Feldforschung im Nagaland (Nordostindien) der 30er Jahre*. Vienna: Böhlau.

Schapera, I. 1977. *Kinship Terminology in Jane Austen's Novels*. RAI Occasional Paper 33. London: Royal Anthropological Institute.

Schmidt, B. 1996. *Creating Order: Culture as Politics in 19th and 20th Century South Africa*. Nijmegen: University of Nijmegen Third World Centre.

Schneider, D. 1984. *A Critique of the Study of Kinship*. Ann Arbor: University of Michigan Press.

Schoeman, P.J. 1951. *Jagters van die Woestynland*. Cape Town: Nasionale Boekhandel.

———. 1957. *Hunters of the Desert Land*. Cape Town: Howard Timmins.

Schumpeter, J. 1954. *History of Economic Analysis*. New York: Oxford University Press.

Schuster, M. 2006. 'Museum und Institut. Zu Genealogie und Vernetzung der Frankfurter Ethnologie 1904–1965', in K. Kohl and E. Platte (eds), *Gestalter und Gestalten. 100 Jahre Ethnologie in Frankfurt am Main*. Frankfurt: Athenaeum.

Sewell, T. 1996. *Black Masculinities and Schooling: how Black Boys Survive Modern Education*. Staffordshire: Trentham Books Ltd.

Sharp, J. 1980. 'Two Separate Developments: Anthropology in South Africa', *Royal Anthropological Institute News* 36: 4–5.

———. 1981. 'The Roots and Development of Volkekunde in South Africa', *Journal of Southern African Studies* 8(1): 16–36.

———. 2006. 'The End of Culture? Some Directions for Anthropology at the University of Pretoria', *Anthropology Southern Africa* 29(1/2): 17–23.

Shore, C. 2000. *Building Europe*. London: Routledge.

Sider, G. 2003 *Between History and Tomorrow: Making and Breaking Everyday Life in Rural Newfoundland*. Peterborough, Ontario: Broadview Press.

———. 2006. 'The Construction and Denial of Indigenous Identities: Recognition, Misrecognition, and the Question of "Natives" in Nation-states and Anthropology. An Essay Review'. Mimeo, The Graduate Center, City University of New York.

Silverman, S. 2005. 'The United States', in F. Barth et al. *One Discipline, Four Ways: British, German, French, and American Anthropology*. Chicago: Chicago University Press.

———. 2007. 'Eric R. Wolf: Das politische Leben eines Anthropologen', in A. Gingrich, T. Fillitz and L. Musner (eds), *Kulturen und Kriege. Transnationale Perspektiven der Politischen Anthropologie*. Freiburg:

Rombach.

Simmel, G. 1997. *Simmel on Culture*. D. Frisby and M. Featherstone (eds). London: Sage.

Singh, R. 1986. *Some Economic Aspects of the Punjab Problem*. Discussion Papers Series No. 1. Coventry: Punjab Research Group.

Sivanandan A. 2006. *Britain's Shame: From Multiculturalism to Nativism*. London: Institute of Race Relations.

Skopetea, E. 1988. *To Protypo Vasilio kai I Megali Idea: Opseis tou Ethnikou Provlimatos stin Ellada (1830–1880)* [The model kingdom and the great idea: aspects of the national problem in Greece (1830–1880)]. Athens: Polytypo.

———. 1992. *I Dysi tis Anatolis: Eikones apo to Telos tis Othomanikis Aftokratorias* [The west of the east: pictures from the end of the Ottoman Empire]. Athens: Gnossi.

Smith, A. 1976a[1759]. *The Theory of Moral Sentiments*. Indianapolis: Liberty Classics.

———. 1976b[1776]. *The Wealth of Nations*. Chicago: University of Chicago Press.

Solow, Robert M. 1997. *Learning From 'Learning By Doing'*. Stanford, CA: Stanford University Press.

Solway, J. 2006. 'Introduction', in J. Solway (ed.) *The Politics of Egalitarianism: Theory and Practice*. New York: Berghahn.

Srejović, D. 1981. *Lepenski Vir: Menschenbilder einer frühen europäischen Kultur*. Mainz am Rhein: Verlag Philipp von Zabern.

Stewart, C. 1998. 'Who Owns the Rotunda? Church vs. State in Greece', *Anthropology Today* 14(5): 3–9.

Stocking, G. 1968. *Race, Culture and Evolution. Essays in the History of Anthropology*. Chicago: University of Chicago Press.

Strathern, M. 1992a. *After Nature: English Kinship in The Late Twentieth Century*. Cambridge: Cambridge University Press.

———. 1992b. 'Parts and Wholes: Refiguring Relationships in a Post-plural World' in A. Kuper (ed.) *Conceptualizing Society*. London: Routledge.

———. 1999. *Property, Substance and Effect. Anthropological Essays on Persons and Things*. London: Athlone.

Strathern, M. (ed.) 2000. *Audit Cultures. Anthropological Studies in Accountability, Ethics and the Academy*. London: Routledge.

Streck, B. (ed.) 2000. *Ethnologie und Nationalsozialismus*. Gehren: Escher.

Tasić, N., D. Srejović and B. Stojanović. 1990. *Vinča: Centar neolitske kulture u Podunavlju* [Vinča: A neolithic culture centre in Podunavlje]. Belgrade: Center for Archeological Research.

Taylor, R. 2001. 'About Aboriginality: Questions for the Uninitiated', in I. Keen and T. Yamada (eds), *Identity and Gender in Hunting and Gathering Societies*. Osaka: National Museum of Ethnology.

Thrasher, F. 1963[1927]: *The Gang. A Study of 1313 Gangs in Chicago*. Chicago: University of Chicago Press.

Thurnwald, R. 1950. *Beiträge zur Gesellungs- und Völkerwissenschaft. Prof. Dr. Richard Thurnwald zum achtzigsten Geburtstag gewidmet*. Berlin: Mann.

Titley, B. 1986. *A Narrow Vision: Duncan Campbell Scott and the Administration of Indian Affairs in Canada*. Vancouver: University of British Columbia Press.

Todorova, M. 1994. 'The Balkans: From Discovery to Invention.' *Slavic Review* 53(2): 453–82.

———. 1997. *Imagining the Balkans*. New York: Oxford University Press.

Topali, P. 2005. 'Ekei iroida, edo Filippineza: Gynaikeia Metanastfsi Kai Ergasia Ston Logo Ton MME' [A heroine there, a Filipino woman here: female migration and work in media discourse], *Syghrona Themata* [Current issues] 88: 72–83.

Toren, C. 1999. *Mind, Materiality and History: Explorations in Fijian Ethnography*. London. Routledge.

———. 2002. 'Anthropology as the whole science of what it is to be human'. In R. Fox and B. King (eds) *Anthropology Beyond Culture*. London: Berg, pp. 105–124.

Toulmin, S. 1990. *Cosmopolis: The Hidden Agenda of Modernity*. Chicago: University of Chicago Press.

———. 2001. *Return to Reason*. Cambridge, MA: Harvard University Press.

Turgot, A.R.J. 1898[1770]. *Reflections on the Formation and the Distribution of Riches*. New York: Macmillan and Co.

Turner, V. 1957. *Schism and Continuity in an African Society*. Manchester: Manchester University Press.

Van der Port, M. 1998. *Gypsies, Wars and Other Instances of the Wild: Civilization and Its Discontents in a Serbian Town*. Amsterdam: University of Amsterdam Press.

———. 1999. ' "It Takes a Serb to Know a Serb": Discovering the Roots of Obstinate Otherness in Serbia', *Critique of Anthropology* 19(1): 7–30.

Van der Waal K. and V. Ward 2006. 'Shifting Paradigms in the New South Africa: Anthropology After the Merger of Two Disciplinary Associations', *Anthropology Today* 22(1): 17–20.

Van Velsen, J. 1964. *The Politics of Kinship: A Study in Social Manipulation Among The Lakeside Tonga of Malawi*. Manchester: Manchester University Press.

Van Warmelo, N.J. 1935. *Preliminary Survey of the Bantu Tribes of South Africa* Pretoria: Government Printer.

Veblen, T. 1914. *The Instinct of Workmanship, and the State of the Industrial arts*. New York: Macmillan.

Vengroff, R. 1971. 'Review of A. Kuper, *Kalahari Village Politics*', *African Studies Review* 14(2): 313–15.

Viveiros de Castro, E. 2002a. 'O Nativo Relativo', *Mana* 8(1): 113–148.

———. 2002b. *A Inconstância da Alma Selvagem e Outros Ensaios de Antropologia*. São Paulo: Cosac and Naify.

———. 2007. 'Filliação Intensiva e Aliança Demoníaca', *Novos Estudos Cebrap* 7: 91–126.

Viveiros de Castro, E., F. Gordon and F. Araújo. 2008. *The Turn Of The Native*. Cambridge: Prickly Paradigm Press.

Wachtel, A. 2003. 'Writers and Society in Eastern Europe, 1989–2000: The End of the Golden Age', *East European Politics and Societies* 17(4): 583–621.

Wagner, G. 1940. 'The Political Organization of the Bantu of Kavirondo', in M. Fortes and E.E. Evans-Pritchard (eds), *African Political Systems*. London: Oxford University Press.

Wagner, R. 1981. *The Invention of Culture*, rev. edn. Chicago: University of Chicago Press.

Wallman S. 1982. *Living in South London: Perspectives on Battersea 1871–1981*. London: Gower.

Walshe, P. 1987. *The Rise of African Nationalism in South Africa*. Johannesburg: Ad Donker.

Weaver, S. 1983. *The Making of Canadian Indian Policy: The Hidden Agenda 1968–1970*, 2nd edn. Toronto: University of Toronto Press.

Weber, M. 1958[1904–1905]. *The Protestant Ethic and the Spirit of Capitalism*. Trans. T. Parsons. New York: Charles Scribner's Sons.

———. 1978[1956]. *Economy And Society*. (ed.) Guenther Roth and Claus Wittich. Trans. Ephraim Fischoff et al. Berkeley: University Of California Press.

Whyte, W.F. 1943. *Street Corner Society*. Chicago: Chicago University Press.

Willmott P. and M. Young. 1957. *Family and Kinship in East London*. London: Routledge and Kegan Paul.

Wilmsen, E. 1989. *Land Filled with Flies: A Political Economy of the Kalahari*. Chicago: University of Chicago Press.

Wilmsen, E. and J. Denbow. 1990. 'Paradigmatic History of San-speaking Peoples and Current Attempts at Revision', *Current Anthropology* 31(5): 489–524.

Wilson, M. and L. Thompson. 1969. 'Preface', in M. Wilson and L. Thompson (eds), *The Oxford History of South Africa, Vol. I: South Africa to 1870*. Oxford: Clarendon Press.

Wilson, R. 2005. 'Judging History: The Historical Record of the International Criminal Tribunal for the Former Yugoslavia', *Human Rights Quarterly* 27: 908–42.

Wylie, D. 1983. 'Review of A. Kuper, *Wives for Cattle*', *Journal of Interdisciplinary History* 14(1): 196–197.

Yaluri, E. 2001. *The Acropolis: Global Fame, Local Claim*. Oxford: Berg.

Zips, W. 2006 Contribution to 'Kalahari Revisionism, Vienna and the 'Indigenous Peoples' Debate, *Social Anthropology*, 14(1): 27–29.

Živković, M. 2001. 'Nešto izmedu: Simbolićka Geografija Srbije' [Something in-between: the symbolic geography of Serbia]. *Filozofija i društvo* 18: 73–110.

Žižek, S. 2000. 'Da Capo Senza Fine', in J. Butler, E. Laclau and S. Žižek (eds), *Contingency, Hegemony, Universality*, London: Verso.

Notes on Contributors

Alan Barnard is Professor of the Anthropology of Southern Africa at the University of Edinburgh. He has done field research in Botswana, Namibia and South Africa and has special interests in kinship, language, settlement and the comparative ethnography of San and Khoekhoe. His publications include *Hunters and Herders of Southern Africa* (1992), *History and Theory in Anthropology* (2000) and *Anthropology and the Bushman* (2007).

Gerd Baumann works at the University of Amsterdam. Among his books are: *National Integration and Local Integrity in the Sudan* (1986), *Contesting Culture: Discourses of Identity in Multi-ethnic London* (1996), and *The Multicultural Riddle: Re-thinking National, Ethnic and Religious Identities* (1999). With Andre Gingrich, he recently co-edited: *Grammars of Identity/Alterity: A Structural Approach* (2005). Currently he is working, with Marie Gillespie, on an international research project about the BBC World Service.

Aleksandar Bošković is Senior Research Fellow at the Institute of Social Sciences in Belgrade (Serbia), and Visiting Professor in the Programme in Anthropology at the Faculty of Social Sciences, University of Ljubljana (Slovenia). His recent books include: *Myth, Politics, Ideology* (2006), and *Other People's Anthropologies: Ethnographic Practice on the Margins* (2008). His research interests are history and theory of anthropology, contemporary theory, myth, ethnicity, nationalism and gender.

Gillian Evans is RCUK Research Fellow at the Centre for Research on Socio-Cultural Change (CRESC) at the University of Manchester and an Associate of the Centre for Child-focused Anthropological Research (CFAR) at Brunel University. Her research interests, focusing on the white working classes in Britain, include education, learning, social class, multiculturalism, childhood, urban regeneration, phenomenology and personhood. She is author of *Educational Failure and Working Class White Children in Britain* (2006).

Dimitra Gefou-Madianou is Professor of Social Anthropology at Panteion University, Athens. Her research interests are focused on Europe, Greece, the Balkans (Albania) and the Mediterranean, and include issues of ethnicity, alcohol and gender, identity formation, migration, culture and ethnography, and anthropology and psychoanalysis. Her publications include: *Alcohol,*

Gender and Culture (ed., 1993); *Trends in Anthropological Theory and Ethnography* (ed., 1998); 'Cultural Polyphony and Identity Formation', *American Ethnologist* (1999); *Culture and Ethnography* (1999); *Self and Other: Conceptualizations, Identities, and Practices in Greece and Cyprus* (2003), and 'Anthropology, Psychoanalysis', *A Posteriori* (2006).

Andre Gingrich is Professor of Social Anthropology at the University of Vienna, and Director of the Research Center for Social Anthropology at the Austrian Academy of Sciences. In addition to his ethnographic field work in Arab Muslim societies and in Europe, his interests also include the methodology and history of Anthropology. He is co-editor of *Neo-Nationalism in Europe and Beyond* (2006) and co-author of *One Discipline, Four Ways* (2005)

Stephen Gudeman is Professor of Anthropology at the University of Minnesota. He has undertaken field studies in Colombia, Cuba, Guatemala and Panama. He focuses on social life, folk languages of economy, and their use in relation to formal models.

Deborah James is Professor of Anthropology at the London School of Economics. Her research interests, focused on South Africa, include migration, ethnomusicology, ethnicity, property relations and the politics of land reform. She is author of *Songs of the Women Migrants: Performance and Identity in South Africa* (1999) and *Gaining Ground?'Rights' and 'Property' in South African Land Reform* (2006).

Isak Niehaus is Lecturer in Social Anthropology at Brunel University, London. He has done extensive research on the topics of witchcraft beliefs and accusations, local level politics, masculinity and the HIV pandemic in rural South Africa. He is the author of *Witchcraft, Power and Politics: Exploring the Occult in the South African Lowveld* (2001).

João de Pina-Cabral is Research Coordinator at the Institute of Social Sciences of the University of Lisbon. He was founding president of the Portuguese Association of Anthropology (1989–1991), President of the European Association of Social Anthropologists (2003–2005); in addition he is an Honorary Member of the Royal Anthropological Institute and Membro Correspondiente of the Real Academia de Ciencias Morales y Politicas (Madrid). He has carried out field work and published extensively on the Alto Minho (Portugal), Macau (China) and Bahia (Brazil).

Evie Plaice is Associate Professor of Anthropology, jointly appointed to the Faculty of Arts and the Faculty of Education, at the University of New Brunswick, Canada. Her interests include land restitution and ethnopolitics, and she has conducted research in both South Africa and Canada. She is author of *The Native Game: Indian-Settler Relations in Central Labrador* (1990).

John Sharp is Professor of Social Anthropology at the University of Pretoria. His research interests include identity politics in contemporary South Africa, de-industrialization and the white working class in Pretoria, and the history of anthropology in South Africa. Among his recent publications are chapters in E. Wilmsen and P. McAllister (eds), *The Politics of Difference* (1996) and J. Benthall (ed.) *The Best of 'Anthropology Today'* (2002), as well as articles in *Development Southern Africa* (2006) and *Anthropology Southern Africa* (2006).

Christina Toren is Professor of Social Anthropology at the University of St Andrews. Her field work areas are Fiji and the Pacific, and Melanesia, and her theoretical interests include exchange processes; spatio-temporality as a dimension of human being; sociality, kinship and ideas of the person; the analysis of ritual; epistemology; and ontogeny as a historical process. Her books include *Making Sense of Hierarchy: Cognition as Social Process in Fiji* (1990) and *Mind, Materiality and History: Explorations in Fijian Ethnography* (1999).

Index